G000241988

sistas on a vibe

IJEOMA INYAMA

The X Press

Published in United Kingdom by
The X Press, 1997
6 Hoxton Square, London N1 6NU
Tel: 0171 729 1199
Fax: 0171 729 1771

Printed by Caledonian International Book Manufacturing Ltd, Glasgow, UK.

Distributed in UK by Turnaround Distribution, Unit 3, Olympia Trading Estate, Coburg
Road, London N22 6TZ
Tel: 0181 829 3000
Fax: 0181 881 5088

ISBN 1-874509-52-2

For my sister
Mgbafor Nenna Inyama
(1963-1986)

Sistas on a vibe

RONNIE SMART HAD NEVER BEEN a good
traveller. She just couldn't relax while in motion.
Reading made her head spin, listening to the personal stereo
gave her a headache, and eating made her feel sick. The only
way she could make it through a journey was (in Ronnie's
own words) to "chat the backside off someone", and
provided they weren't completely dull she could just about
make it to her destination. Fortunately for Ronnie, she
found herself sitting next to someone reasonably interesting
on the early-evening Paris to Waterloo Eurostar train.
Otherwise it could have been three hours of hell.

The person in question happened to be Lynval Gibbons
who, as Marvellous Lee, had been touted as Britain's answer
to Stevie Wonder in the sixties. But after three top-ten hits
he'd faded into obscurity. As he explained to Ronnie, the
numerous comebacks — including a disastrous Gary
Glitter-style ballad in the mid-seventies — had come to
nothing. He now spent his time travelling around Europe
doing session work wherever he could find it.

So Ronnie told Lynval — Marvellous — that she was
involved in the music business, and that she wanted to start

1

her own club and record label, "maybe go on to market my own club gear". She told him that she'd studied fashion design and, although she hadn't graduated, she'd been very close to setting up her own Ronnie Smart label but had been let down at the last minute. Still, Ronnie was optimistic: "After all, if Soul II Soul can do it, so can I."

And then Marvellous asked her, "So, what took you to Paris?"

Ronnie smiled at him, trying to get away from the fact that this balding middle-aged black man in an M & S woolly cardigan had once been such an idol. "I had to get out of London for a while, y'know what I'm saying? Things were happening, but not as fast as I wanted them to happen. It was like there was all these roads, man, and I was going nice and easy, I knew where I was heading, no need for an A-Z, y'know what I'm saying? And then — bang! — I hit the Hanger Lane gyratory system and it's ram, you know what I'm saying?"

"Yeah, I get the drift," Marvellous Lee said, although coming from Wolverhampton he had no idea what the Hanger Lane gyratory system was.

"So, anyway, I was with my girl Nancy — we've been friends from time, right? Anyway, we met this crowd in a club, New Year's Eve just gone. French, right? Not the club, the people. But their English was wicked, y'know what I'm saying? Anyway, they was going on about how Paris was kicking, man, kicking! And they had contacts, y'know what I'm saying? They shared this house in Paris, right? And one of them gives me a business card with an address and that, and tells me any time I want to go across the channel I could reach by them. Anyway, I didn't think too much of it cos you know how some people speech, innit? But my girl Nancy, she had a thing going with one of the guys, Thierry, and he wanted her to spend the weekend with him, get to know Paris by night from his bed kind of t'ing. But she goes to me, 'I don't want to reach there by myself in case the guy turns out to be some crusty business. Come with me.' So the two of us went, man. I mean we're talking gone, y'know what I'm saying?"

Marvellous Lee nodded. When he'd first seen her waiting on the platform at Gare du Nord he'd prayed he might end up in the same carriage as this tall, slender black woman, with such clear skin and almond shaped eyes. Although her bulky suede jacket concealed her top half, her black woollen bell-bottoms showed off her long legs. Her hair was fashioned into shoulder-length twists pulled back into a ponytail and, on closer inspection, he could see they weren't extensions. He couldn't believe his luck when, not only were they in the same carriage, but she sat down next to him and introduced herself.

Now Ronnie was explaining how Nancy and Thierry had spent the entire weekend in bed while she had gone clubbing with the others. By the Sunday, both of them had enjoyed a kicking two days for very different reasons. But it was only Nancy who'd returned to London as planned. Ronnie had been made an offer she couldn't refuse. A chance to deejay.

"I never go anywhere without my vinyls," she said now, patting the rectangular black box by her feet. She told Marvellous how she'd spent the following week in Paris, checking out the night-life, playing out in clubs. She had only meant to stay on for a couple of extra days, but the scene had been so happening she'd lost track of time. The crowd she'd hooked up with were into the hip-hop, trip-hop, funky, swing, rare groove scene, and produced an underground magazine called *Le Retro Metro* that was doing things in a big way.

Ronnie had loved the change of routine: getting up no earlier than midday, dropping into a café or a bistro for breakfast, then strolling through the Latin quarter and Montmartre or along the banks of the Seine. Then it would be back to her friends' rambling, spacious home, where it was open house for anyone and everyone who was in on the scene. They'd hang out smoking spliffs till midnight, when it was time to hit the clubs. Then it would be a mixture of dancing and deejaying till dawn, finally catching the first metro home.

"Yeah, I could handle Paris," Ronnie sighed.

"So what brings you back to London?" Marvellous Lee asked.

"Family business. My sister's getting engaged tonight," Ronnie replied.

But that wasn't the only reason, Marvellous Lee could tell. But he was too polite to probe further. Instead he asked, "Has she got a bloke's name as well?"

Ronnie laughed. "No, she's called Paula. I've got another sister too — her name's Dawn. They're both younger than me. No brothers."

"So how come you got stuck with 'Ronnie'?"

"I didn't 'get stuck', I chose it. It's better than my real name."

"Which is … ?"

She screwed up her nose. "Veronica. Anyway, Ronnie's a cool name: think of Ronnie Laws, Ronnie Bird, Ronnie Jordan …" She hummed the intro to Jordan's 'The Jackal'.

"They're all guys," Marvellous pointed out.

A steward trundled along with a trolley laden with drinks and snacks. Marvellous bought a turkey sandwich and a can of Coke. Ronnie didn't buy anything.

"D'you get along with your sisters?" Marvellous asked as he opened his can.

"We all do our own thing cos we're so different. Dawn's a honey, the baby of the family. We get on fine. She takes people as she finds them and doesn't judge you."

"And Paula?"

"Oh my days!" Ronnie grimaced. "We have some times, you know what I'm saying? We've had some bust-ups."

In fact they were always falling out. Ronnie was sure

4

Paula didn't want her to be at the engagement. They had rowed just before she'd left for Paris. Ronnie couldn't remember the exact details, but Paula had gone on about "responsibilities" and stuff. Ronnie had said some things that she shouldn't have (but didn't particularly regret); no doubt Paula would still be holding a grudge, being the uptight, dry buppie she was. Now she was getting engaged to another uptight, dry buppie. Good luck to them. Still, Ronnie was into peace and love, so she'd bought her sister an engagement present.

The train pulled in at Waterloo just after eight. Marvellous Lee offered Ronnie his card before they disembarked, which she accepted and shoved into her pocket. She had a policy of keeping business cards; some might even call her a collector, as she had well over two hundred of them. Mr Lee wouldn't have minded doing some other kind of business with her, but she'd made it clear that she wasn't interested. All she'd wanted was the chat.

After saying goodbye to Marvellous Lee and promising to call him (she refused to give him her number), she went looking for a taxi. She didn't have a suitcase, just a rucksack and her box of vinyls, but she didn't want the hassle of dragging herself on to the tube.

She had to wait almost ten minutes in the taxi rank, but it gave her time to adjust her ear to the London accents and get used to posters and notices written in English instead of French.

When she finally got a taxi she told the cabbie to take her to Ladbroke Grove. As the cab pulled out of the station, Ronnie wondered what kind of reception she was going to get at home. Life in the Grove never seemed to change. It was always buzzing with an eclectic mix of rastas, trendies, students, winos, would-be musicians, up-and-coming musicians and established musicians. This heady concoction gave Ronnie a high almost as potent as prime sensimilla. Born and bred in Harlesden, Ronnie had discovered the neighbouring area of Ladbroke Grove in her early teens and had been hooked ever since. It had only been a matter of time before she moved there.

Now she was standing outside the four-storey Edwardian house, divided into an assortment of flats and studios, one of which she'd bought with Cameron.

She wasn't sure if he was still her husband.

She struggled up the steps with her record case in one hand and her door key in the other. She wondered for a second if he'd carried out his threat to change the locks. But no, her key fitted — maybe things weren't as bad as she feared. But of course this was just the communal door; maybe he'd changed the locks on their flat.

There were three flights of stairs to climb and Ronnie took her time, a million thoughts going through her head, all stemming from the same memory: that phone call.

Cameron hadn't exactly been pleased with her decision to go to Paris for a weekend — especially with her "rampant, loose slapper of a friend", as he called Nancy. Moreover, their choice of hosts worried him. He had never met this French crowd — he'd been working on New Year's Eve. But Ronnie had stressed her need for chill time. Besides, she'd added, her entrepreneurial skills weren't being appreciated in London; maybe in Paris she could get a kick-start. But when she had called him on the Sunday night to say she was extending her stay they'd had a heated row — or, rather, Cameron had done all the shouting while Ronnie, perhaps unwisely, had told him to take a chill pill. His last words had been: "If you can't accept your responsibilities, I can't accept you!"

And now she found herself at their door. She took a deep breath and tried the lock. Her key worked. She was in!

She'd barely had time to put her case down when a pretty, six-year-old girl dressed in pyjamas careered down the hall.

"Mummy, Mummy!"

Ronnie scooped up the girl in her arms and kissed her. "Where's Daddy, sweets?"

"Working. Granny Taylor's looking after me."

Ronnie groaned inwardly. Not many people got under her skin, but Cameron's mother was an exception. Right on cue, Mrs Taylor, a slightly framed light-skinned woman, appeared in the hallway. "I told my boy he should have changed that lock."

"He can't. I live here, y'know what I'm saying?" Ronnie gently lowered Jhelisa to the floor and took off her rucksack and her jacket. "So, you're looking after my pickney, nice one."

Mrs Taylor glared at her and then at the rucksack. She let out a long, slow, abusive kiss from her teeth. If only her son had found himself a nice St Lucian or any other small-island girl, instead of this piece of Jamaican trash, with her hair all locksed up and always talking rubbish. "I'm looking after this child till her daddy return, so you can swan off back to wherever it was you swan off to."

Ronnie ignored the remark, took a giggling Jhelisa by the hand, and strolled into the living room with her rucksack. Mrs Taylor followed them. Ronnie threw her jacket on to a chair and glanced around at the familiar surroundings: the green sofa from IKEA that she'd spilt coffee over, the black wooden table with a cigarette burn on it that she'd been accused of doing but couldn't remember if she had. On the television was a small framed photograph, taken at their wedding seven years ago. Ronnie was wearing a long, white, flared halter-neck dress, and Cameron was in a chocolate-brown velvet suit. Since that day they had split up and reconciled several times, but the fact that the photo remained in place was a good sign, a very good sign.

Jhelisa had a thousand questions, such as "Where's Paris?" and "Where's France?". Mrs Taylor had questions too, but she didn't ask any of hers. It wouldn't have been pleasant for the little girl to hear them.

"I've got something for you, sweets," Ronnie said, taking out a package from her backpack.

Jhelisa squealed as she ripped it open. "Look, Granny! It's Mickey Mouse!" She laughed as she waved the large cuddly toy in the air.

"It's nice that your mummy remembered you," Mrs Taylor snorted.

"I got it from EuroDisney, and I'm going to take you there one day."

"And Daddy?"

Ronnie ignored Mrs Taylor's cutting glare. "Of course!"

Jhelisa jumped around the room, squealing and laughing. She had Cameron's gap-toothed grin, but the rest of her was all Smart. She had the distinctive almond-shaped eyes of her mother and aunties. A legacy from her grandfather, Evan.

Ronnie checked her watch. It was almost nine. "I'm just going to freshen up."

She walked down the hall and into the bedroom. It had white walls and black furniture — Ronnie's idea; she loved stark contrasts. Above the bed on the wall was a large framed black and white photograph of Cameron, taken during his modelling days. He hated having his own image on the wall, thinking it vain, but Ronnie had insisted, so the picture had stayed. He was gorgeous, with his fine, chiselled cheekbones and amber-coloured eyes (which couldn't be shown to their best advantage in the photo, but in the flesh were truly amazing). His modelling fees had helped them put down a hefty deposit on this place.

Ronnie took a quick shower in the bedroom's en suite bathroom. Afterwards she selected a pair of blood-red suede trousers and a matching waistcoat from her wardrobe. She left her hair as it was.

When she went back into the living room, Mrs Taylor had Jhelisa on her knee and was reading her a story.

"If Cam's working, d'you know if he'll be going to my

sister's engagement do after?"

Merle Taylor winced. She hated the shortening of her son's name. "You're the one with a ring on your finger, you should know ..." Her voice trailed off in disgust when she took in Ronnie's appearance.

Ronnie sighed, grabbed her suede jacket from the chair and put it on. "Mummy's got to go now, Jel," she said.

Jhelisa jumped off Mrs Taylor's knee and ran across the room. "Oh, don't go again, Mummy," she protested, wrapping herself around her mother's legs.

Ronnie hugged and kissed her as she edged out of the living room. "I'll be back soon, don't worry."

"What about that?" Mrs Taylor was frowning at the rucksack lying on the floor.

"What about it?"

Ronnie heard her mother-in-law kiss her teeth loudly before she slammed the front door behind her.

Even though she was spending the night in one of London's best hotels, Paula Smart was highly irritated. She had personally made the arrangements for the engagement party with the hotel's events manager six months before. That had been an event in itself.

The man was a cretin. When she'd sat in his office to make the booking back in July, he'd almost fallen off his chair when she told him she wanted a jazz band. "Not a reggae band?" he'd said. "You know, I saw Bob Marley at the old Rainbow in Finsbury Park back in seventy-nine ..."

Paula had sat back in her chair and given him one of her looks. "Like I'm supposed to be impressed? Can we get down to business, please?" And she'd taken great satisfaction in seeing him turn a bright crimson.

That aside, he was an incompetent, and Paula was now well vexed. She had asked for the tables to be placed around the banqueting suite, not across it. Of course she'd made them move them into the arrangement she had originally requested. And as for the floor — like hell it had just been varnished! Of course, she'd made them re-do that too. Okay, she had made herself unpopular — but you get what you pay for, and when that happens to be close to three thousand pounds you expect a lot more than a mangy hole. Worse still, she hadn't had any support from her fiancé, Germaine. He'd left all the dirty work to her.

She studied her reflection in the full-length mirror next to the bathroom, where Germaine was showering noisily. Paula was always pristine and chic in her appearance, never a chipped nail nor a hair out of place, but tonight she had surpassed herself. She was proud of her toned, slim figure (a product of the three-times-a-week sessions she maintained at the in-house gym at work), and what she wore showed it off to maximum effect: a full-length, body-hugging, emerald-green velvet dress with a halter neck, that she'd spotted in Harrods when she'd bought her wedding dress. She'd gone back later and bought it secretly, paying with her American Express Gold Card. She had wanted to surprise everyone when she showed it off. On her feet were a pair of dark-green velvet court shoes she'd bought in the sale at Karen Millen.

Dawn had piled her hair into an elegant chignon with soft tendrils falling down either side of her face. Paula's younger sister's talents were wasted working in a tacky little back-street dive that some joker has seen fit to call a hairdresser's. Paula had given up trying to persuade her to move on to an exclusive hair salon (even once going as far as making an enquiry at her own Mayfair haunt) because Dawn wouldn't even entertain the idea. She said she was happy where she was. But then, that was her sister: twenty-four years old, with a life leading to Nowhere Close, London NW10.

Paula dabbed some loose powder from her nose with a tissue. She had done her make-up herself. It was subtle except for the lipstick, a dangerous and ruby red. Paula had the same lips as her elder sister. People often took them for twins or — worse — mistook her for Ronnie and vice-versa.

The thought of her elder sister made Paula wince. It wound her up that Ronnie had rung their mum the night before to say she was coming. It was just what Paula didn't need: her sister making a big entrance on her special night; her sister, who had no shame in abandoning her six-year-old daughter while she partied in Paris for a week with a bunch of drug-crazed French people she'd met in a dodgy nightclub on New Year's Eve. Ronnie was supposed to be gone for just the weekend; even Nancy, that slusher friend she'd gone with, had come back as planned. But not Ronnie. No, she'd partied on. And with whose money? Their mum's? Cameron's? For sure it wasn't her own; Ronnie never had any.

That had been the cause of their row last Friday night. Germaine had been at work in a meeting, so Paula was alone when Ronnie had come round begging for dollars for the Paris trip. "Only a hundred or so," she'd said. Of course, Paula had refused. So Ronnie had gone off on one: "Oh my stars, Paula! You can shell out three grand for an engagement but not borrow me a piddling three hundred!"

Paula had replied, "I can afford to lend you the money, that's not the problem. It's the principle, Ronnie. You're always borrowing money but never paying it back, and I'm fed up. I've lost count of the amount of cash I've lent you." Then she'd decided to give her sister some advice. "You know, there are places you can go — regularly, like five days a week or so — and they give you some tasks to do, and you do them. Then at the end of each month they give you some money. They're called 'jobs', Ronnie. Why don't you go and get one?"

And so had followed a slanging match. Paula had pointed out that, at thirty years old, Ronnie should be acting like the adult with responsibilities that she was instead of

11

some carefree teenager (which she definitely wasn't).
Ronnie had called her a "wound-up — no — uptight dry
buppie", and some other names Paula would rather she
hadn't, so she had kicked her out. On Germaine's return
she'd filled him in on what had happened. His reply had
been to forget it. *Forget it?* After the things Ronnie had said
to her that was the last thing Paula intended to do. Not that
she was one to hold a grudge, but she wasn't like Ronnie
(thank God), who had a memory span of five seconds flat
when it came to arguments. Paula would bet her life on her
sister turning up tonight and acting like their fight had
never happened.

She strolled over to the large bay window. The room
overlooked Tower Bridge, giving her a view of London that
tourists see only on postcards: the lights of the bridge with
the river rippling below it and, beyond, the illuminated
Houses of Parliament and Big Ben. All of this was a far cry
from the London she'd grown up in. You wouldn't find
Harlesden on a picture postcard, that was for sure.

Not that Paula lived in Harlesden now. Unlike Ronnie,
who'd moved to the Grove the first chance she got, three
years ago Paula had moved north to Belsize Park,
sandwiched between trendy Camden and affluent
Hampstead. And she loved it. She shared a two-bedroomed
first-floor flat with Germaine. They were the only black
couple in the block and their neighbours — especially the
left-wing journalist daughter of a leading Tory MP — had
gone out of their way to show how non-racist they were.
They'd received endless invitations to dinner parties,
including one where the left-wing journalist had denounced
her father's racist immigration diatribes before going on to
proclaim the virility of the great black dick. Neither Paula
nor Germaine had been surprised. They came across that
type of person almost every day, in the course of their work
for the very reputable chartered accountancy firm, Stennard
& Blake.

Paula's face softened and she smiled to herself as she recalled the first time she'd seen Germaine. It was towards the end of her first week at the firm, and she'd been having lunch in the canteen with some other trainees. Then, across the room and through a sea of white faces, she'd noticed him and found herself immediately attracted. It wasn't simply that he was one of the very few other black people working there, but also because he was so good-looking and, as she later found out, newly-qualified.

The following week she'd approached him by the lifts and introduced herself. He'd been a bit taken aback by her straightforwardness, but seemed to relax when she made it clear that she wasn't making a move on him. A week later they had gone on their first date, a month later they were sleeping together, and now, after six years, they were getting engaged.

And what an engagement it was going to be! A reception in the banqueting suite, a live jazz band, and nouvelle cuisine. With the circles they mixed in, having a quiet party at their flat or a meal in a restaurant wouldn't have been right. They had to make the right impression.

Paula was concerned about their families mingling with their stuffed-shirt colleagues, but it couldn't be avoided.

Suddenly she had a vision of Ronnie turning up in an outrageous outfit and offering a spliff to one of the senior partners, and wanted to scream. Then the bathroom door opened and Germaine stepped out, clad only in a towel wrapped round his waist.

"Whoa! Darling, you look the business!"

Paula faced him with a frown, her mind still on Ronnie. "I don't know why I bothered. If she turns up, everything'll be ruined!"

"Who?"

"My sister, who else?" she snapped.

Germaine rolled his eyes. "Don't get all het up."

"What, you mean you aren't even a little concerned?"

He pondered for a second or two. "Yes, I'm worried that Rebel Ronnie might turn up and wreck the night with her antics ... but at the same time, she might not come."

"She will. We invited Cameron, so she's bound to waltz in on his arm like she didn't walk out on him and their daughter for a whole week."

"How d'you know for sure it'll happen that way?"

Paula began to pace the room. "Because I know my sister, Germaine. The gal renk! My mum spoke to Cameron. He was talking like he wanted a divorce. Divorce, my arse! You just watch. She'll chat him up and he'll go for it and then it'll be like nothing ever happened. That's how it is with Ronnie. She always gets away with murder."

Germaine carefully took out his suit from the wardrobe. It was a beige Armani that Paula had persuaded him to buy in the January sales. He laid it down on the bed. "What about Dawn?" he asked.

"What about her?"

"Well, what does she think about Ronnie?"

Paula waved her hand dismissively. "She wouldn't run Ronnie down for what she did. She reckons she must've had her reasons. Yeah, right: selfishness, irresponsibility, immorality, amorality ..."

"Give it a rest, Paula."

Paula slumped into one of the two luxurious armchairs but, remembering her dress, quickly straightened up so it wouldn't crease. She watched Germaine sulkily as he inspected his shoes. "You just don't understand what I'm going through," she moaned. "I wanted everything to be perfect."

"And it will be, darling. I mean, just look at this room. It's the business: cable TV, real shagpile, and a king-size bed." He pointed to the window. "And have you checked out the view?"

"It's night-time."

"Yeah, but the city's lit up. It's lit up for you and me."

"Germaine!" Paula groaned.

"But it is." He strode across to her. "You look stunning, man. Stunning." He gently pulled her up from the chair and held her hands. "Look at your ring."

Paula gazed at the engagement ring on her finger. It was a diamond surrounded by sapphires.

Germaine kissed her hands. "Now, in half an hour we're going to walk into that hall—"

"It's a banqueting suite," Paula corrected.

"Whatever. Anyway, we're going to walk in there and everyone's going to know how much we love each other."

She let her eyes travel down his well-toned body, glad she'd persuaded him to increase his training regime from three weekly sessions to five, and suddenly she didn't care if her dress got creased. Germaine usually liked to take his time, but sometimes Paula longed for a change. "How about showing me some of that love now?"

Germaine shook his head slowly. "Not in half an hour."

Paula whipped the towel from his waist and Germaine stepped backwards. He knew she wasn't really into a short-and-sweet, and there would be complaints afterwards. "Look, we've got all the time in the world for this after the reception — all night, in fact, that's why we booked the room ..."

He made a grab for the towel but she waved it above her head. "Oh, c'mon, Germaine. You're so passive sometimes." She laughed as she yanked his manhood.

Then the phone rang. Germaine scooted past Paula and reached across the bed to answer it. She flung the towel at him and it landed in a ball on his arse.

"Hello. Yeah. Oh, right ..."

Paula frowned at him. "Who is it?"

He cupped the phone. "Reception."

Paula stamped her foot. "Oh, not another problem! Well you can sort it, because—"

"No. Kim's down there." He held the phone out to her.

15

"She wants to speak to you."

Paula took the phone. "Kim? You're early."

"Hi, Paula. Listen, I've got a bit of a problem. Can I come up?"

Actually, Kim had two problems. One was called Marlon and the other was called Monique. They were her two-year-old twins, and shortly after Paula put the phone down they were sat in their double buggy in the hotel room.

"You see, I was just about ready to drop them off when Conrad rang to say he had a dance to go to and couldn't babysit, the rahtid bollocks ..."

Paula stared in disbelief at the squirming toddlers. "Couldn't you have found someone else?"

"Paula, it's Saturday night," Germaine reasoned.

"Yeah, I tried everyone," Kim sighed.

"But, Kim, the invite expressly said 'no kids'," Paula reminded her. And for a good reason too: Paula wasn't big on kids. She got on fine with Jhelisa, but she was an exception. Her niece was well behaved, perfectly mannered, bright, rarely had tantrums, a delight to be around, despite having Ronnie's genes in her.

Kim looked pained. "Yeah, but Paula, I really didn't want to miss your engagement. We go back a long way."

Paula looked at her friend with disdain. Kim Oliver had started at Stennard & Blake six months after her, in the January intake. She'd been notable for three reasons: she was black, overweight, and she spoke with a broad Midlands accent. The two women couldn't have been more different: Paula, confident and stunning, always dressed to kill; Kim, self-conscious and rather plain, always dressed to cover up her body. However, they'd found themselves on training sessions together and, although they were opposites, had fast become friends. Now they regularly lunched together, along with Germaine. Paula marvelled at the way Kim always had a sunny smile, even though she was forever having problems with her so-called boyfriend, a poor excuse for a man named Conrad Biddle, whom she'd had the misfortune to meet in a nightclub not long after moving down from Birmingham. As Paula had told her at the time, his name alone should have told her something about him.

But Kim had stuck with Conrad through thick and thin; she'd let him move in with her even though he spent her money and messed around with other women. When finally she had fallen pregnant she told Paula he'd changed. And he had: he'd gotten worse.

For most of her pregnancy Conrad had been M.I.A. — Missing in Action — but Kim had still taken him back. Then, when the twins were eighteen months old, he'd walked out on her one last time. To this day there had been no reconciliation.

All Paula could do right now was feel sorry for her.

"Listen, if it's too much trouble I'll stay up here with the kids while you two go down and—"

"Kim, are you mad? You're here now ..."

Paula's voice trailed off as she watched Germaine unclip the straps of the buggy and haul Marlon out and on to his shoulder.

"Hello, big man," Germaine said.

"Watch he doesn't dribble over your suit," Paula warned.

Germaine ignored her and cuddled the boy.

"He's good with kids," Kim observed.

"You haven't told me how I look." Paula quickly changed the subject. Germaine would have had her breeding from time if he'd had his way.

Kim gasped as though seeing Paula for the first time. "You look beautiful!"

Paula took in Kim's plain maroon blouse and black stretch pants. Her thighs looked huge...

There was a large black shoulder-bag attached to one of the buggy's handles.

"You can change in the bathroom if you want," Paula said.

"I *am* changed." Kim followed Paula's gaze to the bag. "That's got the kids' stuff in it."

DAWN SMART DRUMMED HER FINGERS ON the table. What she wouldn't give to hear some ragga or drum an' bass, even some mellow soul — anything but Alexander's Ragtime Band up on the stage. She had no idea what Paula and Germaine had paid for hiring this place, but it must have been megabucks. For a start it was huge, with plenty of room for people to dance — only, no one was dancing. Then there were the huge chandeliers hanging from the ceiling, three in all; and each table had two bottles of wine, one red and one white, and not the cheap stuff either, judging by the fancy labels on them. There were twenty tables, each seating six or seven people. Dawn had counted. Twice. Yeah, she thought to herself, this must have cost Paula and Germaine a packet.

Dawn wondered why they had to be so extra. They could have had a quiet party at their flat, with decent food like rice and peas, jerk chicken, ackee and saltfish. So far all this place had served up was some tired, crusty salad. Pure renkness! After all, it was the end of January and cold and raining outside. People needed hot food.

As if someone had read her thoughts a group of waiters and waitresses filed out of the kitchen at the back of the hall, carrying trays of something hot and steaming.

As a waiter neared her table Dawn saw what it was. Someone had gone outside, fetched a whole heap of rain, heated it up on a stove and called it soup. Yeah, man —

Paula and Germaine must have money to burn.

But Dawn knew the score. Her sister and her fiancé had an image to keep up. The girl from Harlesden and the boy from South Tottenham wanted to be accepted by the Hooray Henry crowd. Even though there were not that many of their colleagues here, they made their presence felt. Dawn couldn't understand how Paula could work with these people. Not that they were horrible or anything, but you just couldn't be yourself. Dawn never had that problem working at the salon.

She glanced at Tony, her boyfriend of nearly eight years, who was seated next to her. He was shifting uncomfortably in his chair, and kept fingering his collar as though his shirt was strangling him. Poor Tony, he wasn't used to stiff suits and fancy hotels. He was down-to-earth, like Dawn. That was one of the reasons she loved him. He was also her best friend.

She glanced down to the other end of the hall and the head table. Her mother was chatting away to the Valentines, Germaine's parents — probably cussing down the food. But Dawn knew that her mother was probably impressed with the do, even if she didn't know what to say to Paula's work colleagues either. Her mother always stressed the importance of status. Germaine came from a good, solid, middle-class Jamaican background and, as a high-flying accountant, he didn't just have a good job, he had an excellent job. He was a fine catch.

Dawn knew that her mother didn't hold the same opinion of Tony. For a start, he was one of "those Marshall boys".

The Marshalls were well known in the NW10 area: the eldest, Lee, was doing time in Pentonville for burglary; the next one, Claude, had done time for drugs possession; and Duane had stood trial at Snaresbrook on an assault charge but had been acquitted. Everyone, especially the local nick and Dawn's mother, reckoned it would only be a matter of time before the youngest, Anthony, headed in the same direction. But Dawn knew better, they were wrong about Tony. They didn't know him like she did.

It didn't help that Tony was unemployed. He was a trained mechanic, but had been made redundant by the main dealer garage for whom he'd worked for five years. That was almost six months ago now, and he was still jobless. Dawn's mum thought the countless interviews he told her about were just talk. Even when Tony showed her the rejection letters she didn't believe he was trying hard enough. With her sisters' men being so well employed (Ronnie's husband Cameron was a computer engineer), Tony looked even worse.

Finally, he was blamed for keeping Dawn from reaching her full potential. She'd left school with eight GCSEs and had started to do A level courses in English, History and Geography at the local tech, but had dropped out after the first term and decided to do a hairdressing course instead. Her mum had been livid; Ronnie and Paula had both gone on to further education, and she'd expected Dawn to do the same. To make matters worse, the decision to quit studying had coincided with a strengthening of her relationship with Tony, their having had an on-off affair at school. So everyone put two and two together and came up with five.

No one believed Dawn when she told them Tony had wanted her to continue with her A levels and go to university. No one believed that working in a hairdresser's in Harlesden suited her just fine. And she didn't want to live in Ladbroke Grove or Belsize Park anyway. At the moment she lived at home with her mum, and Tony lived a few streets away with his mum. And if they ever inched further up the council waiting list and got a place of their own it would be local. Dawn didn't need a ring on her finger to know that Tony loved her. They were fine as they were.

She looked at her watch. It was almost quarter to nine. She hoped Paula and Germaine would make their entrance soon; boredom was threatening. She had been here since eight.

Tony had picked her up. He'd offered to drive her mother but she'd given the excuse of not wanting to arrive so early and booked a cab to drop her later. (Both Dawn and Tony knew the real reason: she was avoiding being around him.) As soon as they had reached the hotel they had gone up to Paula and Germaine's suite. Tony and Germaine had chatted about swingbeat and football — the only two things they had in common — during the twenty minutes it took for Dawn to style her sister's hair. That had been a headache and a half, as Paula had spent most of the time cussing Ronnie.

Dawn often felt like piggy-in-the-middle with her sisters, although less now both of them had left home. Tonight Paula had wanted Dawn to admit how bad it was that Ronnie had deserted her husband and daughter by staying on in Paris. Well, Dawn did think it was a bit out of order, but she hadn't said anything to Paula. She had no intention of getting caught up in World War Three. In the end, her sister had been going on so much that Dawn had become irritated and couldn't wait to get away. Tony too, as he'd just about run out of things to say on the subjects of swingbeat and football.

They had entered the banqueting suite and exchanged small talk with Dawn's mother, who was seated at the head table, before finding a table of their own. When they'd heard the upper-crust accents of the white couple already there, they'd felt as if they had walked out of the frying pan and into the fire.

"God, he's gorgeous," the blonde woman had just whispered in Dawn's ear, obviously attempting to comment out of earshot from her boyfriend, husband, or whoever the freckle-faced guy sat beside her was.

She followed the woman's lustful gaze. Cameron Taylor had just entered the hall. As usual he looked great — and, moreover, comfortable — in his suit and tie.

"He's delicious."

Dawn gave the blonde a pitying smile. The poor girl was craven, but she had no chance. Cameron only had eyes for one woman.

But she wasn't here. Dawn watched as Cameron went across and shook hands with Germaine's parents and kissed his mother-in-law on the cheek. There was a brief exchange, and then Cameron scoured the large room with his eyes. Dawn waved him over, noting the look of relief when he spotted her.

"You know him?" the blonde exclaimed.

"Yeah, he's my brother-in-law." Dawn wanted to add "so put your tongue away", but resisted the temptation.

The blonde wasn't the only one impressed by Cameron. Several women watched as he ambled towards Dawn's table, but he didn't seem to notice. Dawn could see why women fancied him, but personally he did nothing for her. Her Tony wasn't as tall or as handsome, but she adored his baby-face looks and cheesy grin.

When he reached, Cameron shook hands with Tony and kissed Dawn on the cheek. Then came an awkward moment as Dawn and Tony racked their brains to remember the names of the couple sharing their table.

Luckily, the white guy held out his hand. "Hi, I'm Roger Harcourt, and this is my partner Susanne Hurry."

Cameron shook Roger's hand and, as Susanne had inclined her head seductively, he pecked her on the cheek.

"She seems to be in a hurry for something," Tony muttered as Cameron sat down next to him. Dawn bit back a laugh.

"Haven't we met before?" Susanne purred as she watched Cameron pour himself a glass of wine.

"I don't think so." Cameron glanced round the table and saw that every other glass was still full, so he set the wine back down.

"You look familiar. Doesn't he, Roger?"

Roger shrugged his shoulders and Cameron gave Dawn and Tony a quick here-we-go-again look.

About eight years previously, Cameron had been very familiar. He'd gained a lot of publicity starring in a commercial for a leading brand of men's shower gel. Women all over the country had fantasised about being in the shower with him. The ad had been groundbreaking for it's risqué nature, but also because the handsome model they had used was black.

"Oh, I know," Roger said, snapping his fingers thinking he'd solved the mystery. "You work at the gym, don't you?"

"Don't be silly, darling! How would I recognise him? I've never been to your gym!" Susanne sighed, then she studied Cameron's face again. "Oh, well. It'll bug me all evening, but I'm determined to remember."

Dawn decided to move on to something more important. She leaned across Tony and asked Cameron where Ronnie was.

"Your mum asked me the same question. I don't have a clue," Cameron said.

"But she is coming?" Dawn asked.

Cameron glanced down at the wedding band on his finger. "You know, I don't give a shit whether she does or not."

Dawn and Tony exchanged looks.

"So, what *do* you do for a living — as you don't work at the gym?" Roger asked after a moment's uneasy silence.

"I work with computers. Installing systems."

"Really?" Roger looked impressed.

"I've just come from work, in fact. Our firm's installing a system in an office complex near here. Been working round the clock to get it done on schedule."

"What kind of systems?" Roger wanted to know.

Dawn rose to excuse herself from the table. Tony gave her a pleading look. "I'll only be a minute," she assured him in a low voice.

"I don't feel right in here, man. I don't belong," he whispered back.

"What, and I do?"

Tony sighed. She looked chic and stylish in her black short-sleeved mini-dress and knee-length suede boots. She belonged. "And your mum's been looking 'pon me bad all night. That don't help."

"She's vexed because of Ronnie."

"Sure she is," he said sarcastically.

Dawn sighed. "D'you want to leave, Tony?"

"Yes. But I ain't going to, because it'll make you look bad."

"I don't want to stay if you're all tense up. I don't want the hassle; I could really do without—" She broke off suddenly, realising that Susanne was looking at them with interest.

Tony gave her the most reassuring smile he could muster. "Look, I'm sorry, Dawn. Don't mind me."

She gave him a doubtful look. "I'm just going to the ladies'. I won't be long."

Tony watched her head towards the door, her curvy figure and slinky walk causing him to cross his legs.

"So, what do you do for a living, Tony?"

Susanne was gazing at him intently, as if she could read his mind. Tony was suddenly extra grateful for his black skin. If he'd been any lighter his face would have turned bright red.

"I'm unemployed."

"Oh," she replied flatly, and Tony laughed to himself as she then desperately tried to get involved in the computer dialogue going on between Roger and Cameron. He couldn't care less that she was embarrassed. He was too busy thinking of ways to be alone with Dawn after this dry evening was through.

Dawn eventually found the toilets on the second floor.

Two young, smartly dressed white women walked out and smiled politely at her as she was about to go in. Dawn couldn't remember if she'd seen them in the banqueting suite or not. Inside, she was surprised to find Paula's friend Kim Oliver and her children. Kim was standing in front of the sink, dabbing at the front of her blouse with a wet tissue. Her little girl was propped up on the top next to her, playing with a tub of face powder. Her boy was jumping up and down beneath the automatic hand drier, trying to make it work.

"Hi, Dawn! You look lovely."

"Thanks, so do you." Dawn thought the maroon blouse complimented Kim's reddish skin tones. "What happened to your top?"

"This wild pickney here spilt powder all over me as I was trying to freshen up." Kim indicated Monique with a nod of her head. "Never let a two-year-old near loose powder," she added, snatching the said item from her daughter's hands.

There was powder all over the sink. Otherwise the toilet was spotlessly clean.

"So, Paula and Germaine backed down on the 'no kids' rule?" Dawn said, stroking Monique's cheek.

"They didn't have much choice in my case."

"How come?"

So Kim explained the reasons while Dawn used the toilet. By the time she came out of the cubicle Kim had cleaned up the mess around the sink and dabbed the powder off her blouse, but now had a sizeable wet patch above her left breast.

"Why don't you use the drier?" Dawn suggested, washing her hands.

Kim clicked her fingers in agreement, and with Marlon gripping on to her ankles she adjusted the nozzle of the drier and began to blast the wet patch.

"You just reach?" Dawn asked her.

"A while ago. I think I'm on your table. Who else is there?"

"Me, Tony, Cameron and Ronnie — if she shows her face — and some guy called Roger Wargreaves with his woman Susanne."

"Harcourt," Kim corrected. "So, everyone's a couple except me ..." she sighed.

Dawn gave her a sympathetic smile as she shook her hands dry. However, from what she'd heard about Conrad, Kim was better off single. "D'you know this Roger guy then?"

Kim nodded. "He's Paula's line manager. That Susanne he's with is a real slapper. She screwed one of his colleagues at the Christmas party."

Dawn raised her eyebrows, but she wasn't really surprised.

"I'm glad you're here. I don't get to see you very often," Kim said.

Dawn smiled at her. The feeling was mutual. Strictly speaking, Kim was her sister's friend, but she'd impressed Dawn on the few occasions they'd met. Kim was down to earth, warm and friendly. It was a constant source of surprise to Dawn that she was friends with her uptight snob of a sister. "Hold on. If you've been here from time, where've you been? I could've done with having you at the table earlier." Dawn was thinking of the dry conversation with Roger and Susanne.

"I've been with Paula and Germaine. I wanted to warn them about these two little devils."

"I'm sure it's not a problem," Dawn lied, knowing Paula's aversion to kids. "Did you get to see what Paula's wearing? When I was up there doing her hair she had it stashed away, wouldn't let me see."

"Yes, well I've seen what's she's wearing, but she's sworn me to secrecy. But I can tell you she looks criss."

"I guess I won't have long to wait. They should be down

any minute." Dawn patted down the sides of her hair, which Verna, the owner of the salon where she worked, had recently cut. The short crop framed her face and brought attention to her cat-like eyes.

"We don't want to miss that," Kim said as she scooped up Marlon. "Could you grab madam for me?"

"With pleasure."

Unlike Paula, Dawn adored kids. She rested Monique against her hip as she carried her towards the door, glancing at the pushchair folded up and propped against the wall. "Don't forget the buggy."

As they reached the middle of the stairs a loud burst of applause broke out from the banqueting suite. It was difficult hurrying down the last few steps with two toddlers and a buggy, but they managed to arrive in time to see Paula and Germaine make their entrance from the other side of the room.

Everybody was on their feet. Dawn had to stop in the doorway to take stock of how beautiful her sister looked in her long green dress.

"Quick, let's make a move while everyone's still standing," Kim suggested. So they edged round the backs of the tables, and were able to reach their own just before Paula and Germaine took their places at the head table and everyone seated themselves again.

Monique was happy to cling on to Dawn while Kim, still holding Marlon and the buggy, said her hellos to the others at the table. Tony reached across and tickled Monique, making her squeal with delight. Then he squeezed Dawn's hand, making her smile. Still smiling, she looked over to the head table to check out Paula's outfit again, but caught instead a frosty glance from her mother.

Her smile froze. She knew her mother thought she was wasting her life on Tony and was praying for the day when they broke up, but as far as Dawn was concerned that day was not on the horizon. Especially now. Because, although

28

she hadn't consulted a doctor or done a test, Dawn knew she was carrying his child.

Ronnie turned up half-way through the dessert course. Heads turned and stared as she strode confidently towards the head table with a long, neatly wrapped box under her arm. She smiled broadly at everyone seated there. Only the Valentines returned the gesture.

Then she squeezed her sister's bare shoulder. "My girl Paula, you look kicking!"

Paula looked like she wanted to kick her sister. "I thought you weren't going to show up."

Ronnie knew she meant "hoped", not "thought". But she also knew that her sister wouldn't want a scene right here in front of everyone. Paula was knocking herself out to keep her cool.

Ronnie turned to Germaine, who was seated beside her sister. "My guy G, looking the business!" She gave him a peck on the cheek.

He smiled warmly. "Cheers, Ronnie. It's good to see you."

Paula gave him a sharp look, then rolled her eyes as Ronnie wrapped her arms around their mother's neck.

"Mum, you look like a star!"

"Veronica ..." Shirley Smart always addressed her firstborn by her full name. "Is where you was all this time?"

Ronnie wasn't sure if her mum was referring to the week away or just this evening. She plumped for the latter. "The traffic was mentally blocked up, boy — big, heavy roadworks business, y'know what I'm saying?" She released her mum's neck. "Where's Cam?"

"Over there."

Ronnie looked to where her mother was pointing. Cameron was engrossed in conversation with Paula's friend Kim Oliver. Ronnie wondered momentarily if he'd seen her walk in, then he glanced in her direction. She smiled at him — a warm, friendly, forgive-me smile — but his response was a stark, glowering glare.

"Perhaps you'd better join him," Paula remarked acidly. "It's a while since you've been together."

"You been away, Ronnie?" Mrs Valentine chirped.

"Yeah — Paris. I was working out there ... well, it was like a working holiday."

"What were you doing?" asked Mr Valentine, a plumper version of his son.

"I'm in the music business, so I was doing clubs and stuff, getting some new contacts."

"Really? What kind of music?" Mr Valentine was an ardent soca fan.

Ronnie was about to launch into a description of trip-hop and acid jazz, but the evil eye Paula was giving her was too offputting. "Oh, a real mix," she said. "Look, I'm going to park my backside. I'll chat to you later, Mr V."

Paula winced as her elder sister gave them all a wink. Then Ronnie leaned close to her and said, "Now, I know we had words before I went away. But, listen — I want to give you and my guy G your present." She put the parcel on the table in front of her.

Paula stared at it. "Cameron's already given us your gift," she said.

Ronnie gave her a blank look.

"A bottle of champagne," Paula reminded her drily.

"Hmm. Open it anyway, P."

"We're saving the wrapped presents till afterwards—"

"Oh go on," Ronnie urged.

Paula sighed and slowly unwrapped the box. She opened it, and pulled out a cylindrical vase in emerald green. Everyone around her gasped in awe.

"I know it's your favourite colour."

Paula felt momentarily deflated. "Yeah. Thanks."

"It matches your dress." Ronnie smiled, and Paula thought she would die of shame when, under everyone's gaze, Ronnie bogled all the way to her table in perfect rhythm to the old-time jazz beat of the band.

"Hey, guys, what's occurin'?" Ronnie said as she embraced Dawn with one arm and squeezed Tony's shoulder with the other. "This place arid or what?" she added in a low voice.

Dawn and Tony laughed. But, deep down, Dawn was concerned. Had Cameron meant what he'd said earlier — about not caring whether Ronnie turned up or not? She gave him a quick glance. The stony expression on his face said he had.

"You look safe and criss, Ronnie," Tony said — and it was rare for him to pay a compliment to any woman other than Dawn.

She pecked him on the cheek. "Them chubster cheeks of yours deserve a kiss."

Then Roger Harcourt and Susanne introduced themselves. Ronnie shook their hands and Roger started to introduce Cameron, but Ronnie cut him short.

"Oh, I know him already. He's my husband."

Susanne's face dropped, but brightened a little when she saw Cameron's jaw twitch in annoyance.

Ronnie spied an empty chair between Kim and Roger and assumed it was for her. She wondered if her husband had arranged the seating so he wouldn't have to sit next to her.

"I'm in your place, Ronnie. Sorry." Kim rose hastily, a twin on each hip.

"Maybe you are, maybe you're not," Ronnie quipped, brushing against Cameron's back as she went to sit down in the seat Kim had just vacated. Kim moved to the empty chair next to Roger.

"How are you, girl?" Ronnie asked. "I ain't seen you since last November." She remembered how narked Paula had been that evening to find that Germaine had invited her, Cameron and Jhelisa to celebrate getting a promotion. They'd met in some restaurant; it was Moldovian or

31

Mongolian, something beginning with an M, and the food had been terrible. Jhelisa had been sick the next day. Dawn and Tony had been spared that dry evening; she'd had flu and he wouldn't go without her.

"I'm okay," Kim replied. "These two are keeping me occupied. But we're all coping very well without a certain person."

Ronnie gave her a sympathetic smile. She was obviously referring to that boyfriend of hers. A real monster. If Ronnie hadn't known better she would have sworn that, thirty odd years ago, Dr Frankenstein had created an Afro-Caribbean version of his original and called it Conrad Biddle. But then she remembered her own domestic situation.

She squeezed Cameron's lap, but he brushed it off.

"Cameron, I know you're angry with me ..."

"Yeah, and I'm out of prescription for those chill pills you're always recommending."

His voice was low and shaky from trying to control his anger. But it wasn't only Ronnie he was angry at. He was angry at himself. During her one-week disappearing act he'd sworn it was all over between them, and he'd been planning what he'd say to her when and if she ever turned up. He was going to tell her to go, leave him the hell alone. He was going to tell her that he wanted sole custody of Jhelisa. People — his family and his friends — had been saying from time that he was crazy to stick with Ronnie, that she was a fair-weather friend, a user. After her latest act, his mother had threatened never to speak to him again if he took her back.

However, while he'd been sharing parenthood experiences with Kim she had entered the banqueting suite, and from the moment he'd seen her stroll first to the head table and then to his, he'd found himself faltering from his resolve. Her husky voice, her crazy hair, seductive eyes ... hell, just about everything about her was beginning to work its way back into his system. It had been easy to say that he wanted her out of his life over the phone, but when she was inches away from him ...

"Cameron ..."

Her hand was on his lap again. He couldn't look at her as he prised her fingers off.

She was about to try again when somebody across the hall demanded that Germaine make a speech. Soon the chorus began, growing louder and louder until Paula's fiancé rose from his chair.

He cleared his throat three or four times and then, in a well spoken accent, said, "I always dreamt of finding a woman who was beautiful, intelligent, exciting, loyal and faithful ..."

Paula gave him a broad smile. Ronnie exchanged bemused glances with Dawn.

"... and Paula is all of those things to me. I feel like I'm the luckiest man alive."

Everyone in the hall clapped and cheered as Germaine finished his speech and led Paula on to the dance floor. The band had switched to a romantic ballad — Dinah Washington's "Mad About the Boy" — and the now officially engaged couple began to sway cheek to cheek. This was the cue for other couples to take to the floor, and gradually the middle of the hall began to fill up.

Dawn was tired of being sat down for so long. "C'mon, Tony, let's dance."

"Nah, man, I can't wind to this."

Dawn tugged his sleeve until he relented and allowed himself to be led to the dance floor, and then immediately reaped the benefits of the slow dance as Dawn pressed her body tight against his.

Ronnie watched as Roger and Susanne followed Dawn and Tony to the floor. As Kim was still at the table she couldn't have a private conversation with Cameron, so she grabbed his hand and said, "Please, Cameron."

Realising that he couldn't ignore her for ever, he rose

slowly to his feet. Kim sighed as she bounced the twins on her lap and tried not to think about feeling and looking out of place.

"See? I told you she'd worm her way back in," Paula said to Germaine as she watched Ronnie wrap her arms around Cameron on the dance floor.

Germaine kept his position, cheek to cheek with Paula.

"And if she thinks that tacky little vase has won me over—"

"Don't go on, Paula."

She pulled away from him slightly. "I'm not going on! I'm just pointing out that Ronnie's got away with it again. I mean, the way she stays with her 'I was making contacts'! The only contacts she's got are the ones she wears in her eyes!"

"Yeah, well, this is *our* night, Paula. We shouldn't be bothering about anyone but us," Germaine reminded her.

"Yeah, but she bothers me. I bet she's just wound him round her little finger. Just look how they stay! Like bloody lovesick lovebirds."

Across the floor Cameron and Ronnie were swaying gently to the ballad. "I swear to God, Cam, I didn't realise I'd given you the wrong number."

"What — the same wrong number you told Nancy to give me?"

"Nancy only ever had Thierry's mobile number, and that got teefed from his car just after we reached. But I never phoned these people. She did, on the guy's mobile. The first time I even looked at the card that lot gave me was when I gave it to you before I left. Then, out there, they told me the code you've got to use if you're dialling from the UK, but obviously it was wrong. It was a whole heap of confusion."

"Yeah, right. So were you confused about our number as well? Is that why you only called twice?"

"I know, I know. I should have called more, but I got so caught up. The time just flew."

"You knew I had that job to do. You knew I'd be doing lots of overtime and Jhelisa would need someone to be with her — that someone being her mother."

"Yeah, but—"

"No buts about it, Ronnie." Cameron paused. "Between me, your mum and my mum, miracles were performed. I damn near broke my neck dropping her to school and getting myself to work on time. Our mothers took turns in picking her up from school, and I'd rush round at nine or ten or however late it was to bring her back home. And you forgot all about tonight, didn't you? The arrangements we'd made from time. My mum was only supposed to babysit this evening; she had things to do during the day, y'know?" He paused again. "You want to know what else? I didn't even bother waiting for you when I left work tonight. I knew you wouldn't be there. And I was right."

"Hey, hang on! I'm sure your mum let you know I was on my way as soon as I left the yard tonight, probably cussing me left, right and centre. Okay, I didn't meet you at work. I'll be honest with you, that did slip my mind, plus I was running late ..."

"Yeah, but why should it be my mum who rings to say you're on your way? I appreciated the phone call you made yesterday to your mother to say you were coming back."

"I phoned—"

"And left a message on the answering machine, because you rang me while I was at work. I wonder if that was intentional."

"I didn't know where you were working."

"But you didn't ring me later, did you? No, you just rang Shirley. And what about this evening? Couldn't you have asked my mum for the number of the place I was working at?"

"I didn't think of that."

"How convenient."

They were silent for a few moments, then Ronnie added

softly, "I also knew you'd have blasted me if I'd phoned."

Cameron glowered at her. "Don't you think you deserve it?"

Ronnie looked down at the floor.

A few feet away Tony and Dawn were locked together. Tony ran his hands the length of Dawn's back. He knew every curve of her body — though he didn't get to see it as often as he'd like. With both of them living at home it was hard getting time alone. Shirley made him feel as welcome as a cardiac arrest, and his mum's place was too small and always full of the nieces and nephews his brothers and their baby-mothers couldn't look after. Dawn's breasts were crushed against him. He loved her breasts. They were full and round, unlike Ronnie's — which it had to be said were as flat as a board — and Paula's — not much bigger, tangerines compared to Dawn's grapefruits.

Dawn interrupted his thoughts. "Tony, is my dress cut too low?"

"No, babe ..."

"Then why are you staring at my chest?"

He gave her a lustful smile and she realised.

He kissed the side of her neck. "I wish there was somewhere we could go ..." Then a thought occured to him. "What about Paula and Germaine? They got a suite here, innit?"

"We can't do that!"

He pressed his groin against her. "We must," he insisted. "Tell her you want to fix up your hair and you can't use your tongs in the ladies'."

"But they paid for the room—"

"And you spent all that time making Paula's head look nice, listening to her speeching ..."

Dawn pondered for a second. He had a point. "But we can't use their bed, Tony ..."

"We can do it standing up! Go on, Dawn, ask her for the key," he pleaded.

Dawn saw the desperation on his face. She also couldn't deny her own desire for him. "All right."

Tony sighed with relief as she broke away from him to make her way over to where Paula and Germaine were dancing. He thanked his lucky stars that he was wearing loose trousers as he imagined himself pressing Dawn against the wall of the suite, hitching her dress up ...

"Tony?"

Dawn's voice brought him back to earth. Then he noticed Paula beside her. He gave Dawn a quizzical look.

"Paula wants me to fix up her hair as well," she said resignedly.

"Don't look so upset, Tony. I won't keep her long." Paula patted him on the shoulder before leading Dawn away.

The ballad had finished by the time Tony had made the uncomfortable walk back to the table. Roger and Susanne were already seated and Ronnie and Cameron were making their way over as he sat down.

Arguing.

"Just tell me one thing — where d'you leave your things?"

"What d'you mean?"

"Where are they? Your backpack with your toothbrush, your clothes ... all the stuff you took with you."

Ronnie didn't know what he was getting at. "At home."

"I'm that easy, huh? Without hesitation you've got your feet back under the table."

"Nah, it's not like that. I wanted to see Jhelisa. I had to leave my stuff, I couldn't drag it all the way here, y'know what I'm saying?"

"No, course you couldn't. Just like you couldn't drag yourself away from your new friends in Paris, just like you couldn't remember that you had responsibilities. Just like you couldn't pick up the phone more than twice during the whole time you were gone—" He broke off suddenly, not trusting his control.

"Cameron, there wasn't a day went by when I didn't think of you and Jhelisa. I got carried away, like with these crazy ideas going round in my head."

"Yeah, and Jhelisa missed you too." They'd reached the table now, and Cameron walked straight past. Ronnie made to go after him but he motioned her away with a wave of his hand. "I'm going to the toilet."

Ronnie stood there for a second. Everyone at the table had heard, but they were trying to act like they hadn't.

A waitress appeared and replaced the empty bottles of wine with full ones. "Can I get you anything else?" She addressed the whole table.

Ronnie slumped down in her chair. She could do with a good spliff. But instead she asked, "You got any mineral water?"

"D'you want me to fix up your head or not?" Dawn asked, tapping a comb in her hand. "The tongs are plugged in, hot and ready to be used." She thought of Tony and wanted to add "just like me".

Paula ignored her sister and continued to pace up and down. "You should've heard her, Dawn! How she could sit at that table and chat about how she did this and that in Paris? She don't tell no one she lef' her pickney and her man to do it, eenh?"

Dawn wondered what Paula's stuffed-shirt friends would make of her change in accent and dialect. "Paula, if we don't go down soon people are going to start wonderin'."

"I don't want to see the renk bitch!" Paula yelled.

Dawn threw the comb onto the bed.

"Don't take it out on me, man! I ain't done a t'ing. You drag me up here saying your hair needs doing and all you want is someone to shout at. That someone ain't me. It's Ronnie."

Paula slumped down on the bed. "I'm sorry, Dawn, but she really gets to me. She doesn't work; she spends all her time clubbing till all hours and has the cheek to call that work. I mean, she says she's involved in the music industry. How? Just by going into a club? Going to a blues almost every night of the week?"

Dawn strolled over and began to straighten up Paula's chignon. "You're being a bit extra. She's not always like that."

"No, you're right — she does it in phases. Three months of the year she's the model mother, model wife, doesn't go out; then she goes through a phase of hers and it's back to clubbing. She's a clubaholic. She should join Clubaholics Anonymous. 'I'm Ronnie Taylor Smart. It's been six hours since I've been to a rave ...' "

Dawn laughed in spite of herself.

Paula winced as her sister prodded her neck with the comb. "I tell you one thing, I could do without her being a bridesmaid."

"No you can't. She's your sister."

"Yeah, that's what Mum keeps saying. But I told you the names she called me when we had that row before she swanned off."

"Yeah — uptight, dry buppie," Dawn recited. If she had a pound for every time Paula had recounted that argument she and Tony would be living in a palace by now.

"How dare she! And you can see how she makes sure the attention's on her. Strolling in half-way through like that with her 'nuff-traffic-on-the-road excuse! Imagine what she'd be like at my wedding! I've a half a mind to ask Kim to take her place."

"I'm surprised you've not asked her anyway."

"Only if she could get down from a size eighteen to a twelve in seven months. I can't see that happening, can you?"

Dawn dropped the comb. "Paula! You've got some front!

You telling me you didn't ask Kim to be a bridesmaid because of her weight?"

"Oh, c'mon, Dawn. I've got a video and photographs to think of."

"I don't believe you!" Dawn climbed off the bed. "She's your best friend! I hope she doesn't know what you think of her."

"Of course not. I told her I'd love her to be bridesmaid, but I have to have my sisters."

"Yeah, well, one of your sisters will be a few sizes bigger herself by then."

Paula turned and frowned at her. Then her face dropped. "Don't tell me Ronnie's pregnant!"

"No. I am ... Well, I might be."

Paula's jaw dropped even lower. "Oh, Dawn!"

"What?"

"What — it's good news then?"

"Yeah, I reckon it is," Dawn snapped.

"It was planned then?"

"No. I changed pills to a lower dosage because my periods were so bad ..."

Paula sighed.

Dawn read her thoughts.

"I know, I know. Me and Tony don't have a place together and he's unemployed; but really, this is one mistake I don't mind making — if I *have* made it. And, Paula, for now this is strictly between you and me. Don't breathe a word. Not even Tony knows." She straightened her dress and headed for the door.

"I thought you wanted to use the tongs."

"No, it don't need tonging. You coming?"

Paula reached across and unplugged the tongs. She looked at Dawn standing by the door and hoped to God she wasn't pregnant. Her life was rough enough already.

Then she rose from the bed and wondered with concern what Ronnie was up to.

"I'm sorry, but moves like that should be confined to the bedroom," Ronnie said to Kim.

They were sitting at the table watching Susanne wind her body against Cameron, even though the band were playing "Zippedy Doo Dah" — not exactly a smoochers song.

As soon as Cameron had returned from the toilets Susanne had thrown herself at him, saying how much she wanted to dance with him … if Ronnie didn't mind. Of course, Ronnie had told her to help herself. But now everyone had noticed the couple. Tony had even stopped chasing the twins around the floor to look at them. Roger had been chatting to some guy at another table, but now he was looking at his girlfriend and Cameron as well, his lips sealed in a thin, straight line.

Ronnie wasn't normally the possessive type, but tonight she was feeling more vulnerable than usual. Cameron hadn't held her like that when they'd danced earlier. And it didn't help that Kim had happened to mention that Susanne was known for her elastic, stretch-for-any-man mentality when it came to sex.

Finally the band stopped playing and Cameron and Susanne returned to the table and sat down. Susanne leaned across to Ronnie and said, "You know, it was as we were dancing I remembered where I'd seen your husband." She giggled.

"Oh yeah?"

"It was the amber eyes, just like a tiger's." She giggled again, then lowered her voice to a husky drawl. " 'Tiger shower gel — brings out the animal in your man.' Only I didn't recognise him with all his clothes on." She devoured Cameron with her eyes. "I'd have recognised you naked …"

Paula and Dawn walked back into the hall just in time to see Ronnie drench Paula's boss's girlfriend's hair, face and dress with half a bottle of red wine. Dawn saw Paula tense up, and put her hands on her shoulders as if to restrain her.

PAULA PUSHED HER TROLLEY OUT of the supermarket, vowing never to shop there on a Saturday again. It was a madhouse. First she'd driven round the car park for almost ten minutes trying to find a space. Just as she'd been backing into one, a Hooray Henry had fronted his Land Rover into the coveted area. Paula had sworn and cursed him under her breath. She had been tempted to let down his tyres, but the car park had security cameras. She'd located the offender by the pedigree pet foods, and had driven her trolley at him and rammed his foot. An accident, of course, and she'd apologised profusely. Then she'd discovered the store was out of the dark chocolate truffles she'd been intending to scoff on her own tonight, because Germaine was going round to Conrad's place to watch a boxing match. And finally she'd queued for ages at a checkout only to have the till break down when it was her turn.

Now she had arrived back at the car park to find that she had been boxed in by a Volvo estate. She dropped her bags, leaned against her car door, and swore.

Just when she thought things couldn't get any worse she heard a familiar voice. "Auntie Paula!" She turned to see her niece skipping towards her, with Ronnie not far behind, and groaned inwardly. Not that she wasn't pleased to see Jhelisa — she adored her niece — but Ronnie she could have done without.

"Yo, P! What's occurin'?" Ronnie greeted her.

Paula glowered at her sister but managed a smile and a hug for her niece. "Ronnie, I've had the misfortune of being your sister long enough for you to know that my name's Paula. 'Pee' is something you do in a toilet. But then you'd know all about pissing on something, wouldn't you?"

"Oh, c'mon, Paula, you've not been round Mum's for Sunday lunch since that night just to avoid me, and you don't answer my phone calls. How long is this going to go on? A grudge ain't like a bottle of wine — it don't mature with age, y'know what I'm saying?"

"Nice choice of words, Ronnie."

Exactly three weeks had passed since the engagement party. Three weeks since the moment when Paula had thought her reputation, if not her job prospects, was in tatters. The engagement do, intended as a night to remember, had succeeded in that but for all the wrong reasons. After Ronnie had thrown the wine over her rival, Susanne had hurled insults at her, and if it hadn't been for Roger restraining her she would surely have gone for Ronnie. Paula was at least grateful for that. If there had been a brawl ...

"As I keep saying, it was an accident, Paula. The bottle just slipped from my hands."

"And defied the laws of gravity to project itself at a right angle and spray itself up and down Susanne's dress, hair and face."

"Listen — right? — the bottle took on wings and flew. So, okay, maybe I was the pilot, but that bitch had her co-pilot's licence, man. She asked for it."

Paula glared at her. "I don't believe you, Ronnie. That was my boss's girlfriend you attacked. Her dress was ruined. *I* was nearly ruined. I could have lost my job! All my colleagues were there ..."

"I said I'd pay for the dress to be replaced, didn't I? And you ain't lost your job."

Paula had to admit that she was probably guilty of making too much out of what had happened that night. Roger had been embarrassed but not angry. In fact he had apologised to Ronnie before leading a still screeching Susanne out of the banqueting suite. At work the next day, he'd apologised to Paula about his girlfriend's behaviour. As for her colleagues, most of them reckoned that Ronnie deserved a medal for her actions. "Imagine if it had been Germaine," they had said.

Ronnie continued. "See, the thing is, you're my sister, and that Susanne, who is definitely not your sister, was causing me grief. But did I get any support from you?"

"Oh, sorry! It's all right for you to hijack, sabotage and decimate one of the most important nights of my life, of course! Yeah, Ronnie, I support you one hundred per cent."

It annoyed the hell out of Paula that everyone had been on Ronnie's side. That included Tony, Kim, even her mother, who defended Ronnie's actions with the same old line: "Imagine if it had been Germaine ..." Germaine himself had said that Paula should have seen the way Susanne had been rubbing herself up on Cameron. Typically, Dawn had refused to commit herself one way or the other, but Paula knew she was in agreement with Ronnie's actions. If Paula was completely honest with herself and not blinded by her discord with Ronnie, maybe she would be in agreement too. But she could never do that. Her big sister had done what Paula had always feared she'd do: upstage her. That was what was so unforgivable.

"Auntie Paula, why are you and Mummy fighting?"

Paula exchanged a guilty glance with Ronnie and then tugged one of her niece's pigtails. "We're just having a discussion."

"Just like Mummy and Daddy!"

Now it was Ronnie's turn to look guilty. She decided to change the subject. "What are you doing here anyway?"

"I've just had lunch with Denzel Washington ... What's

45

it look like?" Paula kicked one of the shopping bags on the ground.

Ronnie took in Paula's sandwiched car. "So, what's occurin'? You got a problem?"

Paula let Jhelisa wrap herself around her legs. "I can't get out. Some f—" She checked herself, remembering the six-year-old staring up at her. "I'm boxed in."

Ronnie walked round to the front of the car. "Nice car. Company job?"

"Only managers get cars."

"I thought you were a manager ..."

Paula cut her a deadly stare.

Ronnie patted her daughter on the head. "Auntie Paula's got a BMW. Ooh!"

"Ooh!" Jhelisa copied.

Paula rolled her eyes even though she was secretly chuffed they thought her car was a big deal. "So, what you doing here? Bit far to come shopping, isn't it?"

"I'm working."

Paula snorted. "Where?"

"The market. I'm doing a stall with Nancy. She parks her van here and we sort it out with the car park attendant later, y'know what I'm saying?" Ronnie winked.

Paula shook her head. "Who's he got the hots for — you or Nancy?"

"Hey, we don't pay with flesh! It's the green stuff, P, *argent, dinero*. I was just coming to get some more gear. We're doing wicked business today." Ronnie stood between the two cars and measured the gap. "You could get that out easy."

"I've got about a centimetre of space either side; it's not possible. "

"Sure it is. And why worry about scratching it? It's only a car, y'know what I'm saying?" Ronnie held out her hand. "Give me the keys. I'll do it."

"No way!"

"Paula ..."

"No, Ronnie."

"So what you going to do then?"

Paula tutted.

Ronnie, never one for harbouring grudges, didn't want to miss the opportunity to make her peace with her sister. "Tell you what. Why don't you help me and Jhelisa get the rest of the gear and come and see the stall?"

"Oh, I don't think so." Paula shuddered. She couldn't stand markets, especially second-hand markets where you didn't know where things had been and you could catch all kinds of germs. She couldn't stand Nancy Keenan either; the woman was a walking spliff joint as far as she was concerned.

"You still vexed with me over the engagement?"

Paula gave a heavy sigh.

"Listen, the market's wicked — there's a real buzz ..."

"I really don't—"

"You'd rather stay here waiting for Mr or Ms Volvo to come out and move?"

Jhelisa tugged her sleeve. "Please come, Auntie, please!"

So five minutes later Paula found herself reluctantly following her sister and niece to the market, weighed down with bin liners full of the crap Ronnie saw fit to call merchandise. The weather wasn't bad for mid-February. Although there was a cold snap in the air it was bright and sunny, which meant good business for the market stalls in Camden. As they weaved in and out of the crowds, Paula took special care not to touch anything.

"Can't you feel the vibes?" Ronnie asked as they neared the stall.

"No, but I can feel the fleas."

Ronnie and Nancy had a pitch close to the supermarket. Over the last ten years they had become regulars, but today was their first Saturday this year. Early in the morning they had piled up Nancy's Metro van with their collection of sixties and seventies fashion. At the market they had spread the clothes and shoes across two large paste boards. Jhelisa had loved helping them set up and then taking money from customers. Ronnie had taught her how to distinguish which clothes were from what era, and now Jhelisa was an expert.

"Hey, Paula, how's it going?" Nancy asked with a frosty smile, making no effort to hide her dislike for Ronnie's sister. Nancy was a tall, very slim, light-skinned black woman, around the same age as Ronnie. Her taste in clothes was too outrageous for most people. Today she was wearing a long afghan coat and blue suede DM boots. Her eccentric style and her unusual, oriental features — a legacy of her family's Chinese ancestry — ensured that heads always turned when she was around.

"Fine. How's life at the council?" Paula asked with an equally frosty smile as she dumped the bin liners on the ground.

"Dry as ever. But it's a job, eh?"

Paula found it hard to believe that Nancy could hold down the post of environmental health officer. Especially since she'd once confessed to rolling up a spliff before she even ate breakfast.

"Watch this," Ronnie said, as a prospective customer approached the stall.

Paula looked on in amazement as Ronnie convinced the young woman, who turned out to be an American art student, into buying a pair of six-inch pastel blue platforms which were at least one size too small.

"How could anyone buy a pair of dutty shoes that have been worn by who knows who else? That's disgusting!" Paula said when the customer had walked away.

"Yeah, but look at this — we've made a packet and it ain't even lunchtime." Ronnie counted out the cash.

"It's your mouth, Ronnie. You could talk a nun into buying a suspender belt," Nancy joked.

Ronnie smiled. Apart from making money it was good to

see the familiar faces at the market, especially Ola, the funki-dred who ran a nearby record stall. Everyone had wanted to know where Ronnie had been and what she'd been up to, and nobody had judged her for her stay in Paris.

Nancy nudged her before addressing Paula. "Heard your engagement went well. Ronnie's told me all about it. She said the wine went down really well." She stifled a giggle.

Paula shot her sister a dirty look and Ronnie attempted to look contrite. "So, you know all about the slusher, then?" Paula asked Nancy.

"Yeah!" Nancy was laughing openly now.

"Yeah." Paula smiled. "You know, when everyone was going on about this woman at my engagement party who was, as they say, a slusher — in fact, rather like eggs on a battery farm; you know, getting laid very often and very easily …" She paused to join in with Nancy's laughter, then added, "Yeah, it's funny, because I thought to myself, 'Hang on a minute, I didn't invite Nancy …' "

Nancy immediately stopped laughing. "Excuse me?"

"Well, I presumed they were describing you."

"But stop! Who d'you think you is?" Nancy snarled.

Ronnie stood between them. "Hold it! Hold it!"

"Ronnie, I'm going," Paula insisted. "I've seen the stall, now I'm gone."

"Be gone," Nancy said harshly. "You think you're so … Oh my God!"

"What is it?" Ronnie asked.

"It's Michael."

Ronnie and Paula followed Nancy's gaze to the tall figure winding his way through the crowds towards Ola's record stall. It was ages since Ronnie had seen Michael Quinones. He had run the stall with Ola years ago, and also deejayed, putting on blues parties and warehouse parties. His talent for mixes, and for knowing what the crowd wanted, had made him legendary. Then, about a year ago,

49

he'd left for New York, where his father lived, with the intention of making it there.

"God, he's gorgeous," Nancy sighed.

"You on the lookout?"

"If you was going out with Ty, wouldn't you be?" She patted her short, dyed-blonde hair.

"What happened to the French guy?" Paula asked drily.

"Like that revolution they had, he's history," Nancy replied dismissively. "How do I look?"

Ronnie replied, "Delectable, sweetheart," and Paula almost choked. The way her sister's friend looked, she was surprised no one had reported her as being a U.F.O. — Unidentified Fashion Object.

Nancy called out to Michael and waved. He saw them and waved back. He stopped by Ola's and chatted to him for a few moments, then strolled across to their stall. When he reached them he kissed and hugged Ronnie and Nancy. Paula held Jhelisa tightly so he wouldn't have a chance to touch her. She didn't trust Ronnie's friends — but, more than that, this guy was making her feel uneasy, something that rarely happened.

"Ronnie and Nancy Reagan! Long time no see. What's occurin'?"

"Could ask you the same question," Ronnie replied.

"Been in the States, checking out the scenario, y'know. Got some breaks, didn't get others. But life's generally good for me out there."

Ronnie smiled at him, the guy who often signed autographs as Lenny Kravitz. His dreads had grown and were now way past his shoulders, but he still had the same lazy smile. He was wearing sunglasses which hid the soft brown eyes that women went crazy over. Before she'd met Cameron, Ronnie had had a little thing going with him. It had never got serious, perhaps because they were too alike, too laid-back; as Ronnie had said at the time, "Two laid-backs don't make an upright." But even after they'd split up he'd been a regular fixture in her life, and she'd missed him since he'd left for the States.

"So, what you doing back?" Nancy asked him.

"I'm just over to see family, my mum and that."

"Hey, did you know Ronnie's been deejaying in Paris?" Nancy said.

"For real?"

Ronnie smiled again. "Did more partying than the deejay stuff. The scene's good out there, especially in the suburbs."

"Yeah, yeah, I heard that's where it's really happening. So how long were you out there for?"

"Just over a week."

Michael smiled at Jhelisa. "Did your mum take you to EuroDisney?"

Jhelisa shook her head and Michael raised his eyebrows.

"I went there on my own."

His mouth twitched a little. "So, you still with Cameron?"

"Yeah, course."

Suddenly it was awkward. Then Paula cleared her throat and gently let go of Jhelisa's hand.

"I've really got to go."

"Oh, Michael, I ain't done the intro job. This is my sister Paula."

Michael removed his sunglasses and held out his hand. Paula shook it gingerly, all the time aware that his big brown eyes were leisurely appraising her from head to toe. She felt as though he was stripping her naked and quickly looked away.

"There's a blues going down tonight, up Clapham. You going?" Nancy asked him.

"Yeah, should be a session," Michael replied, tapping his fingers on the paste board. "What about you?" He was looking at Paula.

"It's not my scene." She avoided his gaze, which annoyed her. She didn't like it when people made her feel

51

awkward.

"How d'you know if you've never tried it?"

"I just know."

Michael shrugged his shoulders.

Paula kissed Jhelisa goodbye and nodded at the others, then disappeared into the crowd.

"You got more than one sister, right?" Michael asked Ronnie.

"Yeah." Nancy sighed and lit a cigarette. "That's the uptight one. Dawn's a honeybun."

"I've met Dawn, then. But not her — Paula?"

"Renkness personified," Nancy insisted.

Ronnie frowned at Michael. "You a savings account?"

"What?"

"Well what's with the interest?"

Michael laughed. "None. I'm just curious."

Ronnie put her arm around his shoulder. "I know you ... But let me tell you something — you know when you dial a number and you can't get through? Well Paula's the same. Engaged."

Michael gave her a lazy grin. "That don't mean a thing."

"Don't tell me you like her!" Nancy exclaimed.

"Why, what's it to you?" Michael teased. He knew Nancy had the hots for him, but he also knew her reputation as a man-eater.

"Nothing," Nancy pouted. "I always had you down as someone with good taste, that's all."

"Hey, don't diss my sis!" Ronnie warned.

"She dissed me — big time, man."

Then the intro to a much-forgotten old sixties track blasted out from Ola's stall.

"Hey, I know that tune," Ronnie said, tapping her feet.

"That's whatsisname — Marvellous Lee. 'My One and Only'," Michael said. "Still kicks it, man. Check out the beat."

"I'm into it, man, I'm into it." Ronnie was digging

around in her pocket for money. "I met him not long back, on the Eurostar."

"For real?" Michael asked. "He's still around?"

"Sort of, but to be honest I'd say he was struggling." Ronnie found what she was looking for — a twenty-pound note. "I hope I can cut a deal with Ola. That tune is rarer than rare."

"Hey, listen, my guy's hung up on me. Put your money away, I'll do the deal." Nancy winked.

It was an attempt to make Michael jealous, but he wasn't affected. He was thinking about Paula. She did something for him, which came as a surprise. His women were normally funky dressers and into the music business, tripping on the underground scene. But Ronnie's sister definitely took the overground; the tameness of her clothes had said it all — a smart raincoat and low-heeled loafers. But he liked the way she'd carried herself, like she was better than everyone else. He got a kick out of her being uptight. Maybe he could be the one to loosen her binds. That would be a challenge he'd enjoy. And it had been a long time since he'd had one of those in his love-life. Probably not since Ronnie. It was ironic that the two were sisters.

"Where's your mind at?" Ronnie was clicking her fingers in his face.

"Nowhere."

Nancy, standing by Ola's stall, let out a coquettish laugh, then turned round and grinned at Ronnie.

"I've been robbed, man — fleeced like a sheep!" Ola yelled as he handed the record over to Nancy. "You owe me one, Ronnie. It just so happens I've got a birthday coming up. So you can be sure you'll be spinning them Technics for free. Hey, no — start with tonight, man."

"Ronnie ain't going," Nancy said petulantly.

"Stop going on about it, Nance."

"Don't become so dry-dry then. One night ain't going to hurt."

Ronnie wanted to go out — desperately. In the three weeks she'd been back she hadn't gone out at all. The situation was still too delicate back home. She hadn't seen any of her friends because she didn't want to rock the boat with Cameron, a boat which was just about managing to stay afloat. She hadn't even asked Nancy to come round because she knew that Cameron thought her best friend was bad news and a bad influence. In fact, today was the first time she'd seen Nancy since her return, and Cameron hadn't exactly been wild when she'd mentioned doing the stall today.

The last three weeks had been turbulent to say the least. After hurling the wine over Susanne, Ronnie and Cameron had left the hotel. They had argued all the way home in her car, she accusing him of flirting to make her jealous, he claiming her behaviour was proof of her irresponsibility. Since then he had slept on the sofa. So she had no idea how she could now get round him to do a deejay spot.

Right now they were just about talking — at least, that was when they saw each other. Cameron spent as much time at work as he could. Ronnie knew this was simply to avoid her — Paula wasn't the only one who could keep a grudge. Ronnie had done everything she could think of to thaw out the freeze. Apart from not going out or seeing her friends she had cooked meals that were edible, taken Jhelisa to and from school, and looked after her during the half-term break. She'd kept the flat clean and tidy-ish ... She was living like a nun. She couldn't live like that for ever.

Maybe it was time to test the waters.

Tony pulled up outside Shirley Smart's house in his twelve-year-old Ford Escort. Dawn, sitting in the passenger seat, could barely stand the tension. They had taken her mum shopping in the local supermarket, and throughout the trip Shirley had hardly said a word to Tony. Not that she normally did — but over the last week or so she had been worse than usual. Dawn wondered if somehow she knew about her pregnancy.

Tony got out and held the back door open for Shirley. She nodded a thank you but said nothing. Then Tony started to unload the car — Dawn took a bag and Shirley took another; the rest were left for him — and they walked up the path towards the front door.

Shirley's was a small three-bedroomed terraced house like all the others in the street, but it was her pride and joy. Five years ago, at Paula's suggestion, she had bought it from the council at a great discount, having lived there for twenty-five years as a tenant. Since then she'd become a fully-paid-up member of the DIY club and had had double glazing put in, the bathroom fully re-tiled and the kitchen fitted, among other improvements.

Shirley stopped to inspect the outdoor plants which guarded each side of the front doorstep.

"It was good of Tony to drive us to the shops," Dawn said as she rummaged in her pocket for her key.

Shirley snorted. "In that old jalopy t'ing?"

"Mum, that car's taken him to Manchester and back."

"I heard it was hook up to a recovery vehicle."

"Only for the last twenty miles."

Dawn opened the door and they walked down the hall and into the kitchen. Shirley dropped her bag on the floor and hurried out, almost crashing into Tony as he wandered in with the rest of the shopping. They heard her thundering upstairs.

"Your mum can't even stand to breathe the same air as me," Tony said.

Dawn brushed his cheek. "Don't let it stress you."

He put his arms around her and nuzzled her neck. "D'you remember the time your mum was in here cooking the dinner and we were on the sofa in the lounge?"

"Tony, stop!" Dawn put her fingers to his lips and he

kissed them.

Dawn was now very keen to tell him about the baby — she'd had confirmation from the doctor a week ago — but every time she had tried there had been some kind of interruption.

"What are you staring at?"

"You." She smiled at him. She wanted to place his hand on her stomach.

"Oh, Dawn," he sighed, kissing her softly. They wrapped their arms around each other and kissed more deeply, staying like that until they heard the flushing of the toilet upstairs.

Shirley Smart regarded them suspiciously when she walked back into the kitchen. "I'd thought you'd gone," she said to Tony, and Dawn rolled her eyes.

Tony hovered in the middle of the room. He felt awkward in this house, unwelcome. He never knew what to do with himself. "I've got to go. I said I'd work on Duane's car."

Shirley wondered if it would be used in their next bank raid, but stopped herself from saying so.

"Have something to drink first," Dawn insisted as she put some cartons of juice away in the fridge.

"No, I've got to go." Tony stepped out of the way as Shirley attempted to charge through him to get to the cupboards behind. "I'll pick you up later tonight."

Dawn had to bend down to put the juice away. When she stood up she suddenly felt dizzy and gripped the fridge door. Shirley didn't notice but Tony rushed towards her.

"You okay?" He rubbed her back.

"What's going on?" Shirley was facing them now.

"Nothing," Dawn said as Tony helped her to the table. "You know how it is when you get up suddenly. I'm all right, stop fussing." She sat down and massaged her forehead.

"Maybe we shouldn't go out tonight," Tony suggested.

"Yes we should!" They had booked a meal at a local Indian restaurant. Dawn's idea. She wanted somewhere nice and intimate to tell him her news.

"Yeah, but—"

"No buts, Tony. I'm fine, so we're going, okay?"

Tony shrugged his shoulders, then kissed her on the head. "Laters then," he said, then he nodded at her mum. She gave him a brief nod in return.

When the door had shut behind him Shirley asked, "Are you pregnant?"

Dawn was so stunned by the question that she couldn't find any words.

"Lord Jesus!" Shirley cried and slammed the cupboard doors shut. "Does he know?"

Dawn sighed as she shook her head. She'd wanted to tell Tony before her mother. "How did you know?"

"I'm your mother, Dawn. Anyway, that isn't the point. What are you going to do?"

Dawn stared at her. "What kind of question is that? I'm having it!"

Shirley sat down opposite her youngest daughter and gave the deepest sigh she could muster. "Girl, what are you doing with your life?"

"What? What's wrong with my life?"

"I've watched you change from someone with promise to this. You're wasting it on him. You might as well consider yourself a single mother, cause he ain't going to help you."

"You don't know what you're talking about!"

"He's got no job, he's got no place of his own—"

"He's looking for a job and we'll get a place of our own."

Shirley stared at her. "Did you get pregnant so you'd get a place of your own? Because that don't work no more."

"No I did not!" Dawn stood up and walked over to the window. "This is an accident, but it ain't a disaster. Tony'll make a good father."

"Dawn, you're so young. You're a pickney yourself."

"Mum, I'm twenty-four. I'm no teenager. Ronnie was around my age when she had Jhelisa. And as I remember it, you kept telling her not to have an abortion."

"That was because I thought that becoming a mother would make Ronnie act more mature — which I know hasn't been the case ... but anyway, I haven't told you to have an abortion."

"Yeah, but you've asked me what I'm going to do. To me that's the same thing." Dawn leaned against the sideboard. "You were eighteen when you had Ronnie. By twenty-four you had three kids to bring up on your own."

"That was different. Your father was a hard-working man who was taken away from me young. Don't even favour him to your man — if I could even call him that. He's not man enough to be a father, I know that."

Dawn battled to keep her anger in check. "That's the trouble, Mum. You know nothing about Tony. You just think you know. He ain't no high-flyer like Germaine, he ain't good-looking like Cameron, but he is so good to me ... He loves me bad, and to me that's more important than earning a whole heap of money. Why can't you just accept that?"

When Shirley stood up and began to unpack the bags in tight-lipped silence, Dawn knew she'd been wasting her breath. So, as she helped her mother unpack, she focused instead on ways of telling Tony he was going to be a father.

"You all right, sweets?"

Tony and Dawn were in Freddie's, a smoky club in Stoke Newington where the drum an' bass and ragga beats made the floor shake. It was packed solid with girls in gold or silver bikini tops and batty riders, their hair styled and brightly coloured. Dawn's red mini-dress and knee-high lace-up boots seemed tame in comparison.

"Yeah, just fine," she snapped. "You done good, inviting your brothers to our intimate, romantic meal."

"Dawn, really and truly, I didn't invite them. They invited themselves. Anyway, Duane paid for the meal."

"Yeah, as payment for working on his car! But that ain't the point. I wanted us to have some time alone together."

"Yeah, that's what I'm always working on."

"I don't mean for sex, Tony, I mean for talking ..." But he hadn't heard her. He was giving a clenched-fist greeting to a guy he knew.

Dawn had been extremely vexed when Tony had turned up with his brothers Claude and Duane in the back of the car. At the restaurant she'd hardly eaten a thing even though she'd been starving herself all day. Then his brothers had wanted to go raving and, despite Duane's car being newly fixed and running, Tony had somehow ended up driving them all, Dawn tagging along in the hope of finding some way of getting him alone to tell him about the baby.

Of course, Claude and Duane had disappeared almost as soon as they had arrived at Freddie's. That had vexed Dawn as well. They were happy enough to ride in the car with Tony, but once in the club he might as well have been a stranger. Tony couldn't see how they were using him; he was their unpaid chauffeur and car mechanic.

But that wasn't all that was worrying Dawn. Normally she loved being in places like this, especially when the deejay played such killer tunes, but tonight her head was throbbing and she felt dizzy and stifled.

Suddenly the floor seemed to rush towards her and she grabbed Tony's arm. He held her steady.

"I need some fresh air," she gasped.

She leaned against him as he pushed his way to the exit. A bouncer, twice the size of Tony, grunted, "You step outside these doors and you'll have to pay again to re-enter."

"Wait here while I look for Claude and Duane," Tony said before disappearing back inside.

Dawn went over to a hatch and handed two tickets to a

girl in charge of the coats. She put hers on and slung Tony's over her arm, then stood in the doorway where she could feel the cold night air on her face. A police car sped by, sirens screaming, the noise hurting her ears. It was two o'clock in the morning, and nobody was entering or leaving the club. A couple of drunks staggered by, but otherwise the street was empty.

"Y'all right, sister?"

Dawn jumped a little. It was the bouncer, all twenty stone of him. She nodded, and the giant moved a little closer.

"Your man gone and left you ..."

Dawn groaned inwardly. "He'll be back."

"He shouldn't be leaving a gorgeous princess like yourself out here on your own."

The two young women who took money on the door stopped their conversation, suddenly interested in what was going on.

"Like I said, he'll be back in a minute."

"What would you say if I said he wasn't man enough for you?"

Dawn sniffed and replied in a cool voice, "I'd say you don't know what a man is."

The two cashiers laughed.

The bouncer didn't. "G'wan from the step!" He gave her a shove, but Dawn stood her ground. He shoved her again, pushing her on to the pavement.

"Hey, what's going on!"

Everyone turned to look at Tony, who was flanked in the doorway by his brothers. He was dwarfed by them, each of them standing head and shoulders above him.

"You touch my girl? You touch her?"

The bouncer laughed. He thought he'd got what he wanted: a fight.

But Dawn wasn't about to let him get his way. "C'mon, Tony, let's go," she said, holding out her hand to him.

"No. I want to know what's been going on." Tony's voice was shaking with anger. Suddenly two other bouncers appeared from nowhere.

"Nothing — let's go!" Dawn insisted.

Tony and his brothers were squaring up to the bouncers. Dawn felt her legs go weak. She couldn't give a damn if his brothers brawled — they did it often enough — but she couldn't bear Tony getting involved.

She glared at him. "Tony, if we don't go now, I'm having nothing to do with you ever again." Then she started to walk away.

She could hear his brothers saying, "It's cool, bro, it's cool," then footsteps running up behind her.

"What d'you think you're doing? Shaming me up, man!"

Tony had her by the arm. She shook free. His brothers were strolling a couple of metres behind them. She flung his coat at him and he caught it. Just.

"I want to go home."

"My brothers—"

"If they get in your car I'm walking."

"I can't leave them!"

"Fine. I'm walking."

"All the way to Harlesden at this time of night? I don't think so …"

She was walking fast.

"You shamed me up back there. I was standing up for you."

"I can take care of myself, Tony. I don't need you to get your face pulverised to protect me."

"That wharf dog couldn't have mashed me up."

"Tony, whether he could or couldn't ain't the point. I don't want to go out somewhere and have the night finish up in a fight. Every time we socialise with your brothers that's what happens. It weren't me that shamed you up back there. It was them, egging you on to fight."

Tony paused. "What can I say to them?"

"Say what you like. I'm going home. With or without you."

She continued to walk, but could hear Tony bargaining with his brothers. Then she heard the kiss of teeth and something about letting a woman run your business, and Tony was back at her side.

"I didn't like having to diss my brothers, Dawn."

"Am I supposed to feel honoured that you did it for me?"

He shook his head in disgust. "I can't believe how moody you are, man."

They were outside a kebab shop. "I'm hungry. D'you want one?" Tony asked grumpily.

Dawn shook her head. The mere thought of a kebab made her stomach churn. Tony shrugged his shoulders and went inside. He was the only customer. Dawn looked down the street for his brothers, but they had disappeared.

Tony had once said, "If you mess with one Marshall, get ready to take on all four." That was their unofficial family motto. At the time, Dawn had tried to think of a suitable motto for herself and her sisters. All she had been able to come up with was "Three Smart sisters making a few mistakes along the way", and Tony had asked her if he was her mistake, which had started a heated argument.

Tony emerged from the kebab shop and they walked in silence to his car, parked in a side street, while he crammed in mouthfuls of the greasy food. Once inside the car, he tried the ignition. As usual, nothing happened.

"I hope we don't have to push-start it," he muttered.

"Tony, I'm pregnant."

He stared at her. This wasn't the response he'd expected. His eyebrows were raised so high they almost touched his hairline.

"But ..." he managed to say. He opened the car door and threw out the kebab.

"What'd you do that for?"

Tony shook his head slowly. "You can't expect me to eat after telling me something like that."

Dawn studied his face. He looked petrified. "I want to have it," she said softly, almost to herself.

"Hey, hey — I want this baby bad ..." He grabbed her by the neck and pulled her close to him. "I want this baby bad, Dawn. Like I want you."

As the news slowly sunk in, Tony could hardly contain his excitement. He was going to be a father! He was already an uncle several times over, but this time he was going to be the one with all the cigars.

They stayed locked in the embrace for several seconds, until Tony said, "That explains your moodiness, you fainting ... But how long have you known?"

"I got confirmation from the doctors a week ago."

"A week ago!" Tony pulled away from her. "So how come it's taken you so long to tell me?"

Dawn was defensive. "I'm telling you now."

"What about your mum? I bet you told her ..."

"Don't get all vex. My mum knew without me saying a word."

"She ain't happy about it, is she?"

Dawn shrugged her shoulders. It would be too painful to repeat the things her mother had said earlier that day.

"She's going to be less happy when we tell her we're getting married ..."

Dawn frowned at him. "What?"

"Of course. Our baby's going to have my name — or both of our names ..."

"Tony, me being pregnant don't add up to us getting married."

"You saying you don't want to marry me?"

Dawn wound down the window. Although it was a cold night she needed some air. "Tony, it's enough for me to be pregnant. Let's work through that before going on to another equally serious matter like marriage. Okay?"

Tony gritted his teeth and nodded. He tried the ignition again and this time the car spluttered into life.

They had turned out of the side street and were driving along the main road when a police car whizzed past them in the opposite direction, sirens wailing. Neither Tony nor Dawn paid any attention.

Ronnie lay in bed staring up at the ceiling. For the first time since the night of Paula's engagement Cameron lay beside her, snoring gently. The freeze had finally thawed.

For the millionth time she glanced across at the clock. It was eight fifteen. She jumped as the telephone rang. Cameron stirred as she stretched across him to answer it.

As soon as she said hello, the caller hung up.

She shook Cameron until he stretched, yawned and finally opened his eyes. "Cam, your mum's just rung."

He groaned.

"I'll bet she'll say she dialled the number by accident."

His mother had carried out her threat to stop speaking to him if he got back with Ronnie. Her tactic of late had been to ring and hang up. Of course she denied it whenever Cameron confronted her.

He glanced across at Ronnie. Neither of them wore clothes in bed. Her skin looked like dark silk. He shifted so that his hands were at her shoulders, and began to massage them. "You know, you're really tense here."

"Am I?" Ronnie tried to relax a little.

"Yeah, you've got a lot of tension. Don't let her get to you."

"Who?"

"My mum, of course."

"I won't."

"Hey, I was thinking we could go to the park with Jhelisa before heading down to your mum's. What d'you reckon?"

"Hmm, yeah," Ronnie replied distractedly.

"You look wrecked."

"I didn't get much sleep last night."

He chuckled. "It was great, wasn't it?"

"Yeah …"

But Ronnie's lack of sleep had been due to something entirely different.

Nancy had driven her and Jhelisa home from the market. While Jhelisa had nodded off in her arms, they'd discussed ways of getting out that night to the blues in Clapham. By the time they were at her front door Ronnie's ears had been ringing with Nancy's women's rights rhetoric, and she was all fired up for a confrontation with Cameron if he made a fuss about her going out.

What she hadn't reckoned on was a luscious meal of coconut rice and barbecued chicken ready to be served. Or a bottle of white wine chilling in the fridge. Or a blackcurrant cheesecake defrosting in the microwave. Or the smile on Cameron's face when he said it was "time to talk". The three of them had devoured the food and Jhelisa had had an early bedtime. Surprisingly, she didn't complain. It was as though she could sense that her parents needed time out.

Cameron had put on some mellow jazz — John Coltrane and Miles Davis, amongst others — and he and Ronnie had lounged in the front room with the remains of the white wine while they talked. This was one of what Ronnie had early on in their relationship called their "peace sessions". They didn't shout, they didn't yell, they just talked.

It was all stuff that had been said during previous peace sessions: Cameron didn't want to split up and neither did Ronnie. They had to find some way of living together in harmony. Which basically meant that she had to give up twenty-four-hour raving and he had to accept that she would never be a twenty-four-hour housewife and mother. He'd told her how much he wanted her. Three weeks without conjugal relations had been torturous for them both.

The mellow jazz had got to them in a big way, and at around nine o'clock the peace session had ended to make way for the love session. It had been about this time that Nancy had rung. Ronnie had answered the call.

"What's the deal?" Nancy had hissed.

Ronnie had looked across at her husband, who was in the process of unbuttoning his shirt to reveal his perfect torso. "Sorry, no deal," she'd said, and hung up.

It was only later, much later, when the doubts had started to creep in and the old familiar craving had taken over. From the moment when Cameron had dropped off to sleep with Ronnie lying in his arms, she had watched the time go by like it was some kind of countdown. Every hour, minute and second had represented what she would have been doing if she'd gone out with Nancy, Michael, Ola and the rest of the crew. She'd thought of what music would be playing, what clothes people would be wearing, even what drinks people would be knocking back, until it had become like some kind of unspeakable torture.

Lying there, her bed had felt like a prison to Ronnie — and for somebody that worshipped the great god Sleep that was saying something.

Cameron interrupted her thoughts. "You happy, Ronnie?"

He was staring down into her face. Before she could reply their daughter came bounding into the room and jumped on to their bed. She was delighted to see her parents together again, and demonstrated this by jumping up and down on top of them.

Ronnie thought about Cameron's question, and the answer frightened her. It was one that she would keep to herself. For now.

Paula padded into the bedroom in a navy Adidas track suit. She had just returned from a session at the gym, and was vexed that Germaine hadn't been in a fit state to come with her. He had been fast asleep when she'd got up to get ready at nine-thirty.

"You got in late last night," she remarked sourly.

Germaine was sitting on the bed wearing only a pair of boxer shorts. He had just taken a shower, and the scent of his perfume filled the room. "You know what it's like when I get together with the boys."

"Yeah, spending the night watching two grown men mash each other up is so interesting."

Paula stripped to her underwear, folded her track suit neatly, then walked past the bed without looking at him, heading for the wardrobe. As she bobbed her head in time to the rhythm of a swingbeat tune playing on the radio, Germaine took in her finely toned and muscled body. He knew men who would kill to be in the position he was in now, and that had once been a source of pride for him. He sighed as he watched her open the wardrobe and browse through her clothes. Each item of clothing was either hanging up or stacked neatly on a shelf with garments of a similar shade. That was her idea. She'd been trying to get him to do the same for years, but he still preferred to open his side and watch all his clothes tumble out. That drove her mad.

"But you had a good time?" she was asking as she rubbed her chest distractedly.

"It was the business."

"I can't believe that!" she scorned. "Who was there?"

"Matthew."

"What — yardie Matthew?"

"He ain't no yardie. God, you're as bad as the *Sun*. Just because he wears a Kangol and has a couple of gold teet' …"

"Yeah, whatever. Who else?"

"That was it."

"Oh yeah, I forgot: Conrad hasn't got many spars, has he?" She was holding up a dark blue jacket that you could take out a second mortgage on. It had been custom made by a famous designer whose name escaped him. "So how come he's got a satellite dish? I mean, he lives in a bedsit, right?"

"We didn't watch it round his place."

"What d'you mean?" Paula carried the jacket over to the bed and laid it down like it was a newborn baby.

"We were round Kim's."

Paula stared at him.

"You lie! He had all his friends round Kim's place? Was he babysitting the kids or something? Please tell me he was."

"He reckoned he was, but when we got there Kim didn't know anything about it."

"Unbelievable! I bet she ended up playing hostess and all."

Germaine didn't answer. He seemed ashamed.

Paula shook her head. "That girl's too soft for her own good. Her ex comes tramping about the place, using up her electricity and her food and drink like he still lives there. And even when he did live there he never paid rent. And she lets him! Jesus!"

She toyed with the ring on her left hand; it hadn't moved from her finger since their engagement night. "You tried anything like that on me ... Lord have mercy 'pon your soul!"

She caught her reflection in the full-length mirror and her hands wandered down to her backside. "You know, I reckon I could do with toning," she said.

Germaine shook his head. "Paula, I've never seen a more perfect body."

She turned to face him. "Is that why we haven't made love since the night we got engaged?"

Germaine looked at her for a second, stunned. "It's been that long?"

"Yes." Paula couldn't keep the bitterness out of her voice. "I'm beginning to think my perfect body turns you off."

"Paula, that just isn't true," Germaine insisted.

"I know we've both been busy at work, and of course there's been the wedding arrangements, but last night I was sat down watching Denzel in *Mo Better Blues*, munching on my chocolates, and I missed you not being there." The smell of his perfume had hit her now.

Germaine was tired — it had been a long night. But he didn't dare tell Paula that; she would think he was making excuses, and that would lead to a row. That prospect seemed more tiring than sex. So he smiled at her.

"What about now?" Paula cooed huskily. "We don't have to be at my mum's till two. It gives us an hour or so."

He watched as she peeled off her underwear and sauntered towards him. She had a body to die for.

He would be crazy to want anyone else.

Dawn stretched and yawned in her bed, looking at the sunlight shining through the blinds. She glanced at the clock ticking away on her bedside table — it was almost midday.

Tony had dropped her off at around three that morning. Their world had changed since she had fallen pregnant; their relationship had moved on to a different level. That made Dawn feel good — really good. She just wished her mother could have heard the wonderful things Tony had said about her carrying his child.

Her bedroom was above the kitchen, and she could hear the radio blasting away. It sounded like a gospel tune. Dawn could imagine her mum downstairs, tapping her feet in time to the music while slicing onions or preparing the vegetables. Shirley's Sunday lunches were legendary. There were always two types of meat, usually pork and chicken, and Dawn's favourite — sweet potatoes, or sometimes yam. But the meal was never without rice and peas and an assortment of vegetables. And last, but definitely not least, was Shirley's legendary gravy made from the meat juices and a secret ingredient that seemed to change every time she made it.

Dawn thought her mother was almost as proud of her lunches as she was of her house. Even if she didn't appreciate all her guests — such as the men Ronnie had been involved with before she'd met Cameron and, of course, her Tony — Shirley prided herself on the fact that nobody left her house hungry.

Dawn began to stretch her legs, feeling guilty for not being downstairs helping her mum. She threw back the covers, swung out of bed and pulled on her heavy red dressing gown. So far there were no signs of morning sickness — for which she was truly grateful.

By the time Dawn made it into the kitchen her mother was sowing in a chicken the size of Wembley Stadium, and the gospel had been interrupted by the local news bulletin.

"Afternoon," Shirley said drily.

Dawn smiled apologetically. "D'you want some help?"

Shirley nodded at the mountain of sweet potatoes on the sideboard. "You could start peelin' them for me."

Dawn strolled across and picked up a knife (the potato peeler was broken and both she and her mother had been meaning to replace it). As she began to peel the sweet potatoes she was thinking of ways to bring up the subject of Tony. She wanted to try and convince her mum that he was a worthy man, certainly deserving of her. But before she opened her mouth to say anything her heart stood still. The radio announcer was reporting a brutal beating outside Freddie's Nightclub in Stoke Newington. The victim, Travis Barnes, a twenty-eight-year-old father of two and bouncer at the club, was in a "critical" state in the Whittington Hospital. Police were looking for two men seen fleeing the scene, and were urging witnesses to come forward.

Shirley clicked her tongue and chastised the young black people of today: "I hope that Tony don't take you to places like that ..." but Dawn didn't hear her. Her head was elsewhere.

Dawn cornered Tony in the hallway. "Your brothers did it, didn't they? They did in that bouncer!"

"Hey, look, I just got here and I'm starved."

"I'm surprised you can even *think* of eating. I know I can't."

"Think of the baby ..."

Dawn wanted to scream. She didn't want her baby to have near-murderers for uncles. "They went and mash up that guy almost to death!"

Tony put his fingers to her lips. Her mother, her sisters and their men were in the kitchen waiting to pounce on the food. "Shh. Keep your voice down. My brothers had nothing to do with no beating."

"Well how come you're so late? Where've you been? With your butcher brothers getting rid of the blood-stained clothes? Come to think of it, what did you do after you dropped me off? Did you go back and help them mash up the guy?"

"Dawn, don't be so extra. I ain't been nowhere but in my bed." He put his hands on her shoulders. "Honest."

Dawn vaguely remembered police sirens as they had been driving away from the club; if they had been called because of the attack on the bouncer, she was Tony's alibi. But what if they had been dealing with another emergency? "Tony, did you help your brothers do the guy?"

He shook his head in exasperation. "You think I'm capable of that? Almost killing a man?"

"Okay, not you — but your brothers are. Everyone knows Duane assaulted that guy at the blues." She was referring to his brother's acquittal.

"It was self-defence, and you know it. The guy pulled a knife on him — what was he supposed to do? Stand there and let the guy cut him up?"

Dawn's eyes were welling up with tears. "All right. But last night … It was them, wasn't it?"

Just then, Ronnie popped her head round the kitchen door. "Hey, you two love-birds, we're planning on starting without you, y'know what I'm saying?"

Dawn blinked away the tears and composed herself. "You are telling me the truth, aren't you?" she whispered.

Tony held her gaze steadily. "Yeah."

She didn't believe him.

"Okay, let's go and eat."

As he followed her into the kitchen, Tony promised himself that he would never lie to her again. He hated to see her upset.

Shirley believed in generous helpings. She wasn't satisfied until every plate was spilling over with food. Tony, the person she wanted least at the table, normally ate the most. Paula, always watching her perfect figure, ate the least. Jhelisa never liked eating the chicken skin, and always drank her juice faster than she ate her dinner. Ronnie was always so full of chat that her food got cold before she finished it. Cameron liked to swap recipes with Shirley. Dawn and Germaine shared something in common: they barely breathed a word during a meal.

Shirley gazed round the table. This Sunday was the first time since the engagement party that the whole family was eating together. The tension between Ronnie and Paula had simmered down a little, as had the tension between Ronnie and Cameron. Paula and Germaine seemed as solid as ever, but Shirley was bracing herself for news that would spoil her appetite.

Sure enough it came, about half-way through the meal. Tony cleared his throat and declared, "Dawn's having my pickney."

The mother-to-be toyed with her chicken leg.

Ronnie laughed. "Hey, that's wicked! Another Smart mother!"

"Congratulations, you two." Cameron smiled.

"Yeah, that's excellent news," Germaine added. He loved kids, but Paula had told him she wasn't yet ready to have stretch-marks ruining her perfect body. Sometimes he wondered whether "yet" really meant "not ever".

Of course, the baby wasn't news to Paula. She had kept her word and not mentioned her conversation with Dawn the night of her engagement party. Now she feigned surprise and pleasure at the news. But deep inside she was sure that her sister had now definitely taken up permanent residency in Nowhere Close, London NW10 — which happened to be a dead-end street.

Shirley remained silent, even when Jhelisa wanted confirmation that Dawn and Tony's baby would mean another grandchild for her. She merely snorted.

"So, no wedding then?" Paula was up to her elbows in soap suds. It was part of the Sunday tradition that the Smart sisters would clear up in the kitchen while their men battled with Shirley and Jhelisa for control of the TV remote: football versus black and white movie.

"What, just because I'm pregnant? That's not very nineties." Dawn dried another dish and handed it to Ronnie.

"Yeah, I mean look at it," Ronnie said. "We're three black women. I've had my child in wedlock, and I'm still wearing the ring — just. Paula's about to do the right thing and is childless. One of us had to fit the stereotype. Well done, Dawn!"

"Yeah, but my man's standing by me."

"A small diversion."

"What are you going to do about getting a place?" Paula asked as she rinsed off some cutlery.

"We're going to see someone at the council and take it from there."

Ronnie and Paula exchanged glances, which didn't go unnoticed by their younger sister. "Well, that's how we plebs do it, okay?"

"Dawn, it was just a question ..." Paula said.

Dawn took her time drying the cutlery. She hadn't meant to snap, but what Tony's brothers had done was getting to her. Bad.

"You know, you could always get on to the council and tell 'em that your mum's threatened to throw you out. Make yourself homeless," Ronnie suggested.

"That ain't entirely a lie."

"What, is mum giving you a hard time?" Paula asked.

"Is Nelson Mandela black?" Dawn handed Ronnie the knives and forks.

"She gave me a hard time when I fell," Ronnie said as she mixed up the cutlery in the drawer. "She thought Cameron was just some fly-by, y'know what I'm saying? But she came round eventually."

"She'll never come round to the idea of me and Tony. I mean, it's been years and she still don't want to know."

"It's because of his family. I mean, his brothers are regulars on *Crimewatch UK*, aren't they?" Paula said.

"That's all hype," Ronnie scoffed. "Right, Dawn?"

"Yeah," Dawn replied quietly.

Then Shirley entered the kitchen and announced, "I just want a glass of water."

"Yeah, and the Pope's Jamaican," Ronnie muttered. Her sisters laughed. Every family Sunday lunch, Shirley would come into the kitchen to carry out her inspection, always under some flimsy excuse.

As usual, Shirley noted that Paula had made an excellent job of washing up, and as always Dawn hadn't dried thoroughly enough and Ronnie had put things back in the wrong place.

That seemed to sum up her girls.

"HOW ARE THE WEDDING PLANS GOING?" Kim was sprinkling a sachet of salt over her chips.

"All in hand," Paula replied as she picked at her Waldorf salad.

The Stennard & Blake canteen was busy. The food was not bad and reasonably priced; even some of the senior accountants ate there — when they weren't having business lunches.

"Remember Claudette Price's wedding — with the North London Inspirational Choir?" Kim asked.

Paula remembered. Claudette Price was head of one of the auditing teams in the Reading office, the only black female to have achieved that feat so far. "Yeah, well, if I had a cousin in one of the top gospel choirs in the country I'd have them sing at my wedding for almost nothing too."

Kim sighed as she began to carve up her meat and potato pie. Paula studied her puffy face and enhanced figure. She had piled on the pounds since she'd had the twins.

Paula knew Germaine loved her toned figure. What would he think if she was as big as Kim? "What happened to your diet?"

"It happened," Kim scoffed.

"Why don't you join the gym?"

Kim scoffed again. "I don't have the time, what with the kids and everything."

"That's a weak excuse, Kim. The gym's got a crèche."

"Paula, crèche or no crèche, I honestly don't have the time."

"Conrad could take care of them when he comes round to watch satellite TV," Paula went on. "I honestly can't believe you let him do that."

"That was ages ago. He hasn't been back since, unless it's to see the kids." Kim crammed a forkful of chips into her mouth.

"How long will that last?"

"This time it's permanent."

"Temporarily permanent."

"Believe me, Paula. That man's out of my life for good. The only thing he ever gave me that was worth anything was the kids. All the other stuff I could have done without. I used to think, well I'm fat and ugly, I'm lucky to have him, but now ..." Her voice trailed off.

"What's brought this on? Or should I ask *who*?"

"It's got nothing to do with men. I've just seen the light."

"I'm glad to hear it."

Paula waved at someone, and Kim turned round to see Germaine striding towards them. He had been to the barbers recently and his hair was more closely cropped than normal. Paula loved guys with the three Cs — cropped hair, clean-shaven and classy — and Germaine was all of those and more.

"Hi, gorgeous," he crooned to Paula when he reached their table. He pecked her on the cheek and smiled warmly at Kim.

"You had lunch?" Paula asked, making room for him beside her.

But Germaine didn't take the hint. "I lunched with some of the guys from audit. We've got a meeting in a few minutes, so I can't stay. I just wanted to see you."

Paula smiled at him. "I didn't hear you leave this morning."

"I went to the gym early," he replied, leaning against the

table.

"I'm glad to see you taking more interest in your body. I've been trying to persuade Kim to do the same."

"I am interested in my body. It's fitness that bores the hell out of me," Kim challenged.

Paula exchanged glances with Germaine. It wasn't like Kim to be snappy. "Is it your time of the month?" Paula asked her.

"No. I just wish you'd stop going on about my weight."

"I'm just expressing an opinion. I don't go on. Do I, Germaine?"

"You are a little obsessed with keeping fit," he said.

"Obsessed? That's rubbish!" Paula realised that the level of her voice had attracted an audience, so she lowered it to a whisper. "I like to take care of myself — that isn't a crime."

Germaine put a hand on her shoulder and squeezed it gently, and Paula felt herself regain her composure. She gave Kim an apologetic glance, and her friend returned it with a forgiving smile.

"You working late tonight?" Germaine asked.

"No. But I'm hooking up with my sisters at the bridal shop, remember? They've got their dress fittings. Why? Did you have something special in mind?"

"A quiet, candlelit dinner for two, something we haven't had in a long while."

Kim sighed. "That's so romantic."

"How long d'you reckon you'll be?"

Paula shrugged her shoulders. "A couple of hours. I should be back by around nine."

"Okay. I'll have everything ready for you." He pecked Paula on the cheek. "I've got to love you and leave you."

"Go on then, you heartbreaker," Paula teased.

Germaine stroked her cheek before making his way out of the canteen. She didn't take her eyes off him until he'd disappeared.

"You've got a good one there, Paula," Kim said.

"I know," Paula replied, smiling.

Delia's Wedding Emporium was situated next to Dalston Kingsland station. It wouldn't normally have been Paula's choice, but since Delia happened to be a cousin of Shirley's she'd felt obliged to go there for the hiring of the bridesmaids' dresses. It was also a form of compensation for deliberately forgetting to invite Delia to the engagement.

Normally Delia closed at six, but tonight she kept the shop open late especially for Paula and her sisters, knowing that it was an awkward journey for them. Ronnie, bringing Jhelisa, had picked up Dawn and they'd left the car at Willesden Junction station to take the North London Line to Dalston. Driving all the way would have been a nightmare at that time of day, even though they would have been going against the traffic. Paula's journey had been easier; there were plenty of buses from the city to Dalston.

While Ronnie, Jhelisa and Dawn went into the changing rooms to try on their dresses, Delia, a young looking forty-something, engaged Paula in small talk over coffee and home-made ginger cake. She reminisced about when she and Shirley had been little, and had played at being big women back home in Jamaica. Then she went on about how time had flown and how it seemed like only yesterday that the three sisters had been playing with her own daughter.

"How is Simone?" Paula asked, although frankly she wasn't that interested — it was years since she'd seen her. Simone in her younger days had been wild, shacking up somewhere in South London with some yardie type who was old enough to be her father. She'd only contacted Delia when she needed money. Then, about two years ago, she'd mysteriously disappeared to stay with some relative in Brooklyn, New York.

"She's still in America. She getting married next year," Delia said with pride.

That's one way of getting your green card, Paula thought. But she didn't press any further.

"Ah! Look at these two!" Delia clasped her hands together.

Ronnie and Jhelisa had emerged from the cubicle in their outfits. Ronnie's dress was in peach satin, short-sleeved and three-quarter length, taken in at the waist and flowing out from the hips like a frilly bell. Jhelisa's was a miniature version of her mother's, but with more frills.

While the little girl was smiling from ear to ear, Ronnie had a sour expression on her face. "No offence Auntie D but, Paula, I think you should have us bridesmaids in black."

Delia was dumbstruck; Paula simply shook her head. They could hear Dawn laughing in her cubicle.

"Is it a wedding or a funeral?" Delia said when she'd recovered from the shock.

"But why not, P?" Ronnie persisted. "Have us in black velvet mini-dresses with black knee-length platform boots."

"Jesus of Nazareth!" Delia exclaimed.

Ronnie ignored her and Dawn's laughter in the background and went on, even louder. "What a contrast to your white wedding dress!"

"My dress is off-white," Paula corrected her.

"Whatever. We'd look wicked!"

"Just like the devil's pickney," Delia scorned as she ushered Jhelisa towards her and started to fuss over her dress.

"Paula, I ain't big on peach and peach ain't big on me, y'know what I'm sayin'?"

If Paula had had her way her big sister wouldn't have been a bridesmaid at all. How could she be sure that Ronnie wouldn't be spliffed up to the eyeballs on the wedding day? But their mum had insisted. It irritated Paula to think that Ronnie had waltzed back from her adventures in France and slotted nicely back into everyone's good books. But that was Ronnie. She'd always gotten away with murder. However,

Paula had drawn the line at Ronnie being matron of honour. That was down to Dawn — the reliable sister.

"Ronnie, the dresses are hired — end of story."

Ronnie scowled at her as she helped herself to a slice of ginger cake. "But don't you remember my wedding?" she said as Delia turned her attentions to her dress. "Well ... not so much the ceremony, that was a registry job, but the reception. That was the business — and not a frilly dress in sight."

Paula rolled her eyes. Ronnie and Cameron (although it was mainly Ronnie's idea) had hired out a small club in the East End, providing three floors of pounding rave music. Most of the guests who weren't family had been decked out in some kind of raving gear. Shirley had walked out almost immediately, swiftly followed by Cameron's mother and most of the other relatives. Paula had just started going out with Germaine at the time, and had feared he would dump her after seeing what a nutter she had for a sister. Luckily he hadn't.

"Dawnie, what you doing in there, darling?" Delia called. "Big up yourself, don't be shy."

Dawn stepped out of the changing room swamped in a peach satin tent. Paula gasped and Ronnie held back a giggle.

"Auntie Dee, I'm going to be six months gone, not a heifer carrying triplets!"

"Yes, well, it's better to be on the safe side."

"But this is a size twenty and I'm only a twelve. I'm sure I'll only go up two sizes at the most."

"Okay, I'll put an eighteen on stand-by."

The phone went and Delia ran over to answer it.

"I think I agree with Ronnie," Dawn said. "A black mini-dress and chunky boots would be better."

"Damn right!" Ronnie said as she opened a can of Pepsi for her daughter.

"Don't start," Paula warned.

"Yeah, but you get to wear a nice slinky white dress straight out of a Grace Kelly or Audrey Hepburn film. Us two get to look like what would happen if ragga fused with ballroom dancing. And what does Germaine think of all this?" Ronnie asked. "Or is he too busy at the gym to know or care?"

Paula rounded on her sister. "What would you know?"

"I know he practically lives there. He's hardly lifted a finger to help you organise things."

"Yeah, like you have. Actually it's me who's encouraged him to go more often. And he does do his fair share."

"Who did all the invitations then?"

"He can't do italic handwriting. Anyway, there ain't nothing wrong with him wanting to keep fit."

"Easy, you two," Dawn intervened.

Ronnie hid a smile. It was amusing when Paula got annoyed, as she'd always start to replace her "isn'ts" with "ain'ts". If her work colleagues could hear her now …

Ronnie gave a husky laugh. "You're better off just having sex. It's cheaper and just as effective!" She nudged Dawn.

"Oh, you're just so nasty!" Paula snapped.

"You act like you're some pure virgin," Ronnie laughed.

"Ronnie, I'll remind you that you have your six-year-old daughter here," Paula said.

"Oh, Jhelisa knows what sex is; it's nothing to be ashamed of and hidden away. Right, sweetheart?"

Jhelisa had just crammed a handful of cake into her mouth and wasn't in a position to speak, so she nodded.

Paula shook her head.

"Oh, speaking of six year-olds," Ronnie continued, "can either of you babysit for me Saturday night?"

"You going out?" Paula asked.

"Yeah. Don't look so shocked. I'm going out with my husband to a friend's birthday party. There ain't nothing wrong with that, is there? Besides, I ain't been out since I got back, and that's almost two months ago."

"Now you're back on the slippery slope," Paula said, a tad nastily.

"Can you do it or not?"

Paula shook her head. "We're going to the cinema. There's an Ingmar Bergman season showing locally."

"*Casablanca* — now there's a kicking movie ..." Ronnie snorted.

"I said Ingmar, not Ingrid."

"Them all from foreign, innit?" Ronnie said, doing an accurate imitation of their mum.

"I'll do it. I might as well get some practice," Dawn said. She knew how much Ronnie was looking forward to her night out; she'd ranted on about it throughout their train journey.

Ronnie hugged her. Then she turned to Jhelisa and said, "Aunty Dawn's looking after you on Saturday. Won't that be nice?"

Jhelisa smiled, revealing Pepsi-coloured teeth.

Just then, Delia finished on the phone. She scooped up an assortment of peach ribbons and dried flowers and approached the sisters. Ronnie's eyes rounded in horror when Delia asked Paula innocently, "Now, d'you want ribbons or flowers in your bridesmaids' hair?"

"If you could have seen Ronnie's face when she clocked the dried-out wreath Auntie D wanted to plonk on her head ... Laugh? I nearly died!"

Tony toyed with a strand of Dawn's hair. "Don't you have to wear one too?"

"No chance! Like Ronnie said, 'Wreaths are for a front door at Christmas or a gravestone at a funeral.' No way my head is either one of those."

Tony laughed, then cooed as Dawn ran her hands across his chest. R. Kelly was playing softly in the background and seductive sticks of incense were burning. Since Jhelisa had fallen asleep a half-hour ago they had been in bed together, careful not to make too much noise as she was only next door in Paula's old bedroom.

"You're going to get me going again," Tony warned as Dawn kissed his neck.

"Then I'd better stop. Mum'll be getting in from bingo soon."

"And you want me gone."

"I don't want you gone but we both know it's best. My mum'd do her nut if she knew what we've been up to."

"How would she know if we was just sitting side by side on the sofa downstairs watching the telly?"

"Tony, trust me, she'd know."

Dawn tried to pull away from him, but he held her fast and kissed her on the lips. "I don't want this to end. How often do we get opportunities like this?"

"I know …"

"We've got to get our own yard. Things can't stay like this, not with our baby and everything."

Dawn loved the way he'd said "our baby".

"You're starting to show already." Tony was studying her stomach with blatant admiration, drawing circles round it with his fingers. "And your tits are getting bigger."

"They're not tits, they're breasts," Dawn cajoled as his hands worked their way towards them. "And they were big enough before I got pregnant."

"You know when you was down at the wedding place, how did you feel when you tried on the dress?"

Dawn frowned at him. She didn't like where this was leading. "Like a big heifer. Why?"

"I wondered if it gave you any ideas."

"Yeah, it did."

Tony's eyes brightened.

"I was glad it was a bridesmaid's dress I was trying on and not a wedding dress."

As soon as the words came out of her mouth Dawn

regretted them. Tony turned his back on her.

"I'm sorry ..." Dawn put her hand on his shoulder but he flinched and shook it off.

"Don't apologise for something you ain't sorry for," he said, sitting up in her narrow bed.

Dawn couldn't think of anything to say that might appease him, so she watched in silence as he picked up the half-finished spliff from the ashtray on her bedside table and lit it up.

"Hey, I know I'm a nothing — no job, no money, no yard of my own ... Your mum thinks I'm some roughneck raggamuffin bwoy, and compared to your sister's men I am. But, Dawn, I don't want to be calling you my girlfriend for ever. I want to start calling you my wife."

Dawn took this in slowly, then tried to choose her words with care. "Tony, I know all that. I hear what you're saying. But right now it's enough for us to worry about our baby. We don't want to add marriage to our troubles."

"Now why would marriage be trouble?"

"We can't afford it, for a start."

"It don't have to cost a lot. Just the fee for the registry office. What else?"

"It changes things."

"A piece of paper don't change nothin' if you don't want it to." Tony took a deep drag of the spliff. Normally he would have shared it with Dawn, but since she'd gotten pregnant a spliff hadn't touched her lips.

"Exactly. It don't change a thing, so why can't we stay as we are? We're happy, aren't we?"

"Yeah — you living with your mum, me living with mine, snatching moments here and there. We ain't together like I want us to be — twenty-four-seven, three-sixty-five."

"Three-sixty-six when it's a leap year."

"Dawn, I'm being serious ..."

"I'm sorry, but you know how that number t'ing winds me up."

Tony took another drag. "Why don't you want to marry me? I mean, you keep saying you're not with me for money or a nice house or my job — which is good, seeing as I ain't got none of those things — so what is it?"

"Like I said, let's concern ourselves with our child and then we can think about marriage."

"You know, normally it's the other way round. People get concerned with marriage first and then pickneys."

"Tony, it's the nineties not the sixties. Things have changed." Dawn sat up in bed and brought the sheets up to her neck. Without Tony's arms around her she was feeling the cold. "Back in the days, kids got taunted for not having fathers. Well, Ronnie told me the other day that Jhelisa was getting taunted not only for having parents who lived together, but for having parents who were married. Can you believe that?"

"Boy, that's sick." Tony shook his head. "Well, I tell you something — I don't care if our kid gets taunted, he's going to have my name."

"We don't have to be married for that. Our child can have both our names, he or she will be called Something Smart-Marshall. Or should it be Marshall-Smart? No, I like the idea of a Smart Marshall ..."

Dawn giggled at her own joke but Tony remained stoic. She sighed and rested her head on his shoulder. "Tony, look, I'm your woman and you're my man. A marriage certificate won't change that."

"Yes it would."

Dawn lifted her head. "How?"

"It would show me that you ain't ashamed of me."

"Tony!"

He raised his hand, motioning for her to keep quiet. "Let me finish. It would show me that you ain't ashamed of me or my family."

Dawn bit her lip. "I'm not."

"Don't lie, Dawn."

She brought her knees up to her chest and rested her chin on them. "Okay, I'll level with you …"

"Please." Tony was facing her now, staring into her eyes.

"Even though you'll get vexed."

"Take the chance." He continued to stare at her even though she was looking at anything but him.

"It never really bothered me before."

"What didn't? My family?"

"Your brothers, to be precise." Dawn sighed. She was starting to get a vicarious high from the spliff he was smoking. "But after that night at the club … Oh, I don't know. You say your brothers weren't involved, but we both know they were. Level with me, Tony, as I'm levelling with you."

"Okay, it was them, but I can't be responsible for what my brothers do."

"Tony, a man is lying half dead in a hospital because of them. And you are partly responsible — you were ready to fight."

"Yeah, but I didn't."

"Whatever. But, you know, what I don't like is your attachment to your brothers. They're bad news. And mud sticks — people seeing you hanging around with them, they'll tar you with the same brush, and that means me and the baby'll get tarred too."

"Is that it? Is that the reason you don't want to marry me? My roughneck brothers? So, if I said to you that I'd stop hanging with them — not that I do anyway — if I said I'd have nothing to do with them, not speak to them, nothing … would you marry me then?"

"Let's just say it'd put a different complexion on things."

"What — rosier?"

"Yeah, maybe."

Tony shook his head and laughed.

"What's the joke?"

"You. You lie." He stubbed his spliff out and swung his

legs over the side of the bed, reaching for his clothes on the floor.

"Tony!"

"You're a liar, Dawn!" he snarled as he started to dress himself. "If it weren't my brothers it'd be something else, some other excuse."

He kissed his teeth loudly.

"That ain't true!"

"It's got to be. Don't you know? Just by being my girlfriend you're tarred. And we're talking about living together, marriage certificate or not. So what's the difference?"

"It ain't that simple, Tony."

"Baby, it's as simple as black and white. You don't want to marry me no matter what. That's the truth. I hope maybe I can change your mind someday; and if so, I hope it happens soon. Because there ain't no way I'm carrying on like this."

"We'll try to get a place sorted out. I mean *really* try."

"Yeah, whatever."

"Tony, please don't go."

He glanced at her. She was still sitting up in bed, but she'd let the sheet drop to her waist. It took all of Tony's self-control not to tear off his clothes and leap back into bed with her. "Your mum'll be back soon, remember? I'd better chip."

"Tony!"

But he was already out of the door, and Dawn didn't go after him.

"What's the matter with you?" Shirley was peering over the TV listings guide at Dawn, who was stretched out on the sofa.

"Nothing."

"So how come your eyes are all puff up and red, eh?"

"I'm tired, that's all. What's on the other channel?"

"Some Sylvester Stallone film that's been on a million times before." Shirley kissed her teeth. "I could do with some cheering up after that lousy bingo night. That Althea Miller favour nonsense with her screeching and ranting just 'cause she pick up some big dirty fifty pound. When I won my four hundred pound did I screech up the place? No. I was dignified. And what's the fool-fool woman gwan spend it on? That drunken useless pile of crap she call a husband! *Tcha!*"

"You know, Mum, I think I'll hit the sack …"

Shirley glanced at her watch. "But it only gone ten-thirty. Ain't your man taking you somewhere?"

Dawn felt her eyes well up again but she fought back the tears. "Nah, not tonight. I'm too tired. Must be looking after Jhelisa that's worn me out."

"You only t'ree month gone. I tell you something, that didn't hold me back. Your father took me dancing — not every week, but often — when I was carrying each one of you. If you're tired it's cause you ain't eating right. Or is it your man-friend can't afford to take you out 'cause him still not got a job, innit?"

Dawn rolled her eyes. "Look, it's no major drama. I'm just tired so I'm going to bed."

She got up slowly just as the pattering of footsteps were heard coming down the stairs. Seconds later Jhelisa burst into the room.

"Granny! Granny!" she squealed as she threw herself on to Shirley.

"And what you's doing up, eh?" Shirley laughed as she squeezed her granddaughter tight.

"I wanted to see you."

"You can see me well and good tomorrow morning, chile, so gwan up to bed with your Auntie Dawn."

Jhelisa looked across at Dawn. "Where's Uncle Tony gone?"

Dawn glowered at her niece. But before she had a chance to say anything Shirley demanded, "What d'you mean by that?"

"Uncle Tony was here and he was sexing Auntie Dawn. I heard them."

At that moment Dawn wished that Ronnie wasn't quite so open about matters sexual with her six-year-old daughter.

"Jhelisa, go on upstairs to bed," Shirley said with a steady voice, although she was fuming inside.

"With Auntie Dawn?"

"No. Auntie Dawn and Grandma need to talk. You gwan by yourself, you's big enough."

Shirley waited until Jhelisa had marched upstairs singing a pop tune before she faced Dawn.

"A who you think you are, girl? You t'ink it all right to bring your roughneck man into my house and sleep with him when you s'posed to be looking after your baby niece? Jesus Christ! The chile say she heard you! Lord a' mercy. An' you was in my bed—"

"We was in my bed."

"Ain't you got no shame?"

"I'm carrying his baby, so obviously I haven't."

"I'm talking about a lickle chile hearing you and your man ..." Shirley broke off, unable to trust herself.

"We weren't noisy. Jhelisa must've heard Tony arrive. She must have just assumed—"

"Assumed! Assumed what?"

"Listen, that's down to Ronnie. She's very open about sex with Jhelisa."

"So if the milkman was to come round tomorrow for his bill, and I answered the door, would she assume me and him were having sex?"

"He don't come round on Sundays," Dawn mumbled.

"Girl, don't come fresh with me! You t'ink just cause you's pregnant I wouldn't lick you?"

Dawn sighed as she rose from the settee. "Look, I'm tired and I want to go to bed."

"I ain't finished with you, girl."

Maybe the fact that she was pregnant made Dawn feel stronger, or maybe it was because she was on the verge of tears and she didn't want her mum to see, but she surprised both herself and Shirley by stomping over to the door anyway.

"Come back here!"

"No, I'm going to bed," she said before closing the door behind her.

"No wonder you's tired!" Shirley yelled as Dawn headed up the stairs. "Well don't think that raggamuffin can come back into this house! He ain't eating none of my chicken tomorrow, d'you hear?"

Jhelisa was crouched by the banisters on the landing.

"Did I get you into trouble, Auntie Dawn?" she asked softly.

Dawn pulled her gently to her feet and kissed her on the forehead. "No, darling. Your Auntie Dawn can do that all by herself."

In her tiny booth in the corner of the crowded dance floor, Ronnie was in her element. She had the crowd going with her mix of seventies classics and eighties funk with a touch of the nineties thrown in for good measure. From his vantage point by the stage, Cameron could see the exhilaration on her face as tune after tune continued to move the crowd.

He should have known when Ronnie had first mentioned it a couple of weeks back that there would be more to Ola's party than a simple night out. His suspicions had been confirmed tonight, when he'd arrived back from dropping off Jhelisa at Shirley's to find Ronnie on her knees rifling through her immense record collection.

"Just a few tunes to spin at the party," she'd said sheepishly.

Cameron had surveyed the room — there were records lying all over the place.

"A few? It looks like a hundred to me." He'd toyed with the car keys and had tried to sound casual in asking, "You wouldn't be planning to do your thang on the Technics by any chance, would you?"

And Ronnie had given him one of her I-can't-help-it smiles. "It's Ola's birthday. You can't expect the man to deejay at his own party."

"So, you always intended to deejay?"

"Oh, Cam, don't start speechin' me. This is the first time I've—*we've* been out in ages."

"I know, and if you drop a few tunes tonight it ain't a problem. I just wish you'd been upfront about it from the beginning."

Ronnie had jumped up and run over to him. "You star!" she'd squealed, hugging him tight.

And all the way down to the tiny club in Shoreditch that Ola had hired for his birthday, Ronnie hadn't stopped talking about what tunes she was going to play and how she was going to hook the crowd. Cameron had used his need for concentration while driving as an excuse for his silence. The truth was that he was scared her enthusiasm for deejaying and all things clubland would drive a wedge between them — maybe this time for good.

When they'd arrived at the club, which was packed with Ola's trendy friends, Ronnie's expression had been orgasmic and Cameron had died a little inside. Now, in her tiny booth, spinning her tunes, Cameron could see that her happiness was complete without him.

He caught her eye and she waved at him happily. He waved back, meeting her smile. He'd not seen her this happy in a long while, so he knew deep down that this was Ronnie's thing.

Maybe he'd been selfish in wanting her to diss the club scene completely.

In the beginning that hadn't been his attitude; in fact, they'd met in a club. It was a trendy place, the place to be at the time — somewhere in the West End where it was notoriously hard to get in. Cameron was a model in those days, and Ronnie, typically, was in between careers, having just dropped out of fashion college. The attraction had been instant and lustful. They had spent nights and days together in bed, when they weren't clubbing or Cameron wasn't working. Then Ronnie had fallen pregnant and everything had changed — at least for Cameron. In the early years of parenthood he'd appreciated her need to have a life of her own. But she'd taken liberties, first staying out all weekend and then some weekdays too. Cameron couldn't remember the number of times they'd argued and split up over her irresponsible behaviour, but each time she promised to change. Things would be okay for a while, until Ronnie got the itch again and had to scratch it. Like her Parisian escapade at the beginning of the year ...

"She's the business, isn't she?"

Cameron turned to find himself facing Michael Quinones. "Michael! How you doin'?"

"Safe. Didn't Ronnie tell you I was back?"

Cameron shook his head, wondering what Ronnie had to hide by not telling him, and then listened while Michael filled him in on what he'd been up to in New York. Then he repeated his compliment regarding Ronnie, adding, "There ain't a lot of female deejays kicking it out there, but Ronnie should be there. Definitely. She's got what it takes. Especially with your support."

Cameron frowned at him. "My support?"

"Listen, man, there ain't a lot of guys out there that would give their women the freedom you do. I mean, she told me how she was in Paris for a while and you took care of your kid ... what's her name?"

"Jhelisa," Cameron answered drily.

"Yeah, right — Jhelisa. I like that name. Anyway, she's got Ola's party all warmed up for me to take over. I'll catch you later."

He was about to move off when Ronnie dropped a familiar but hard-to-place tune and mixed it in with a wicked hip-hop beat. The crowd went wild.

Cameron stood there racking his brains. "I know this tune ..."

" 'My One and Only' by Marvellous Lee," Michael informed him. "I was there when she bought it off Ola's stall. The track is rare now; I wish I'd got in there first, man. But it's kind of like fate, since she met the guy on the train back from France."

Cameron didn't have a clue what he was on about.

"But check out the mix, it's kicking! Like I said, Ronnie's the biz, man. The biz ..." And he patted Cameron on the shoulder before making his way through the throbbing throng towards the deejay booth.

"They liked me didn't they?" Ronnie asked (for the hundredth time) a few minutes later. She was standing next to Cameron by the bar, nodding her head in time to the beats that Michael was dropping at the other end of the small dance floor.

"Yeah, they liked you."

"Did you like me?"

Cameron took a swig of his can of Tennants before answering. "Sure."

"You ain't just saying that cos I'm your missus?" Ronnie giggled as she tickled his chin.

He smiled and shook his head. Ronnie couldn't stand still; she was like a live wire. It had nothing to do with alcohol, as she never touched the stuff. No, Ronnie was on a natural high.

"Ola done well to get this place. It's cool. It's small and intimate. If I had a club, this is how I'd want it to be."

Cameron pretended not to hear, but his heart skipped several beats as two girls in Lycra hotpants and platform trainers leaned across him to compliment Ronnie on her deejay prowess.

"Oh, Cam, I'm made up! I am definitely made up!" she enthused when the girls had wandered off in the direction of the dance floor.

"Great," he replied. But Ronnie was too wrapped up in herself to notice the sarcastic tinge to his voice. "So, what's with this guy you met on the train from Paris?"

She frowned at him. "Who — Marvellous Lee?"

"The singer from the sixties, the guy whose record you played."

Ronnie nodded. "What about him?"

"How come you never told me?"

"Cam, anything to do with Paris or France was a no-no with you. I was even afraid to buy croissants from the bakery."

"You didn't mention Michael Quinones was back either."

"I didn't think you'd be interested."

Just then Ola, who was merry on the way to being drunk, staggered over to them accompanied by Nancy. "Ronnie Smart, you was kicking!" he enthused, planting a sloppy kiss on her cheek.

"D'you reckon?" she laughed.

"You know you were. Eh, Cameron?" Nancy said.

Cameron gave a brief nod.

Ola turned to Nancy. "You could be kicking if you deffed that embryo Ty for a grown man named Ola."

Nancy nudged him in the ribs. "I'm old enough to be your big, big sister!"

Ola threw his head back and laughed as though she'd told a hilarious joke. Then he sobered up a little and said, "Cameron, I wanna make a business-to-business call to your lady," and he took Ronnie by the arm and steered her out of earshot.

Nancy grinned at Cameron.

"What are you on?"

"I dropped an E," Nancy squeaked. "You seen Ty?"

"Who?"

"My bloke. I've lost him."

"That ain't all you've lost. What happened to your head?"

"What?"

"You're mad to take those things."

"It's just recreational."

Cameron swore.

"Hey, Mr Innocent, don't knock it till you've tried it!"

"You've got to be joking."

"Cameron, Prince of Dryness, you ... are ... so ... up ... tight." She punctuated each word with a prod of a finger on his chest. "You should learn to loosen up a little, otherwise it's a waste of your good looks and fit body."

She moved in close and pressed herself against him. In her tight-fitting silver mini-dress she didn't leave much to the imagination. Cameron, however, had no difficulty in resisting her charms.

"Nancy, your best friend — my wife — is standing inches away from us."

"What if she wasn't?" she pouted.

He shook his head in disgust. "I'd still send you packing."

"Spoilsport," she scowled, and headed for a crowd of people she knew, dancing and waving her arms madly.

Cameron closed his eyes. He didn't want to be here.

"Wake up, sleepy!" Ronnie was clicking her fingers in his face. "You'll never guess what."

Cameron shrugged his shoulders.

"Ola knows someone who's got this place, like a designer shop or something ... What's it called again, Ola?"

Ola said something that neither Ronnie nor Cameron caught.

"Well whatever it's called it's on the King's Road, fairly new, doing the business though. Loads of heads hang out there, y'know what I'm sayin'? Anyway, this guy is looking for someone to play in his shop — he wants to get a kind of club feel in the place, y'know what I'm saying? Anyway, the deal is that my guy Ola's going to recommend me to him. How about that?"

Cameron mulled this over for a few seconds and Ronnie's excitement began to deflate. Then finally he asked, "We talking full-time?"

"Just Saturdays," Ola, who was standing behind Ronnie, interjected.

"In fact, just Saturday afternoons," Ronnie corrected.

"What about Jhelisa?"

"Well, if you can't look after her my mum or sisters will. At the very worst I can take her with me." She turned to Ola. "Would the guy mind that?"

"Nah, it's safe man."

"It's only a few hours, Cam."

"Yeah, right," Cameron said sadly.

"Be sure to drop that M.L. track," Ola advised.

"M.L?" Ronnie frowned, then it registered. "Oh, Marvellous Lee ..."

"Damn right."

"Y'know, I met him recently, on a train. I was coming back from Paris and—"

Cameron had heard enough.

"Excuse me."

Ronnie watched him go, ruing the fact that she'd mentioned Paris.

"What's with him?" Ola asked.

Ronnie didn't reply. She hurried after Cameron, catching up with him near the men's toilets. "Cam, wait up!"

"I want to go."

"Okay, I'll wait here for you."

"No, not the toilet — I want to go home."

She glanced at her watch. It was barely one a.m. "But it's early yet, Cam."

"Yeah, but I'm tired. I'm going to go."

Ronnie searched his face but found no room for persuasion.

"You stay, Ronnie. I'll catch a cab; you can take the car when you're ready." He dug into his trouser pocket and brought out the car keys.

"You sure?" she asked, taking them.

"Course."

"You didn't enjoy yourself, did you?"

"I was tired tonight."

She moved in close to him and kissed him softly on the lips. "Well, save a little strength for me for when I reach, okay?"

Cameron nodded. "Go on, enjoy yourself." He started to turn away.

"What about the job, Cam? Is that okay with you? I mean, if it ain't I won't do it."

"No, it's cool. Go for it. I mean, it's only a few hours on a Saturday, right? It's not like you'll be out every night raving, is it?"

He ambled off in the direction of the exit. She had half a mind to follow him, but a group of about six people approached her and started going on about her wicked deejaying, and Ronnie was wrapped.

Ronnie rolled into bed next to Cameron just after six a.m., her clothes lying in a heap where she'd flung them on the floor.

It had been ages since she'd felt this alive — not since Paris. Her ears were tingling and her head was still throbbing from the beat at Ola's party. She smiled to herself, remembering a time not so long ago when she'd been lying in this same bed, clockwatching, itching to be out there in clubland instead of staring up at the ceiling.

She was excited about deejaying in the shop, but knew that Cameron didn't share her enthusiasm. Nancy had commented that it was because he didn't like the idea of his wife working, but that wasn't true. Actually he didn't like the idea of his wife working on the club scene, because that meant plenty of late nights and, of course, plenty of raving. But he had to understand — it was her world, it always had been and always would be. There was no way she could be content without it.

She looked across at her husband. He was naked under the sheets, lying with his back to her. She remembered how it was back in the old days — sex and clubbing — and realised how much she missed those times.

She traced a finger down his spine. His skin was so smooth ...

He didn't stir, so she blew softly against his neck. Still no movement. Ronnie sighed as she snuggled up next to him. She would join him and get some sleep; then, when they both woke up, she'd get some action.

Cameron waited until he could hear her gentle snores before he dared to turn round and look at her. He hadn't slept at all, waiting for her to return. Now he wondered grimly if this was the first of a new wave of sleepless nights. If that was the case he wasn't going to let the wave wash over him this time. He would fight it all the way.

If you happened to be a trendy, up-to-the-minute kind of person you would have been to Freedom. Situated in the trendy King's Road, near the Town Hall where many a celebrity had tied the knot, it sold mainly club gear, but you didn't necessarily have to be in a club to wear it. Some devotees did their weekly shopping in the supermarket wearing Freedom rubber catsuits. But the truth was that the place was really pricey and hardly any of the stuff was worth it. It was the name you were paying for.

Everyone who worked there was a clubber. It must have been the only place where you could use a bouncer for a reference. In the staff room at the back of the shop there was a futon, so that if any member of staff had been out clubbing the night before they could go straight from the club to the shop and kip until opening time. There were times when it couldn't even be guaranteed that the futon would be free. Nico, the fake-Italian, failed-fashion-designer-but-excellent-businessman who owned Freedom, had even had a shower installed to appease his funky workforce.

But it had been money well spent. The shop had been open a month and was doing a roaring trade — especially on Saturdays.

"What are we doing here?" Paula asked Dawn as a shop assistant strolled past them with an armful of leather thongs, her hair twisted into short red locks. To their left, by the doorway, another assistant with knee-length hair extensions was arranging ten-inch-high platform boots into a display. The shop was crowded, and the sound of seventies funk was thumping away. Paula would have preferred to have been browsing through the rails at Karen Millen or Nicole Farhi.

"We're here to big up our sister on her debut," Dawn reminded her tersely.

Ronnie was at the back of the shop with her much loved Technics, tapping her feet to the funky rhythm that was booming out. When the couple in front of her moved away to check out the leathers hanging on the wall, she got a clear view of her sisters looking decidedly out of place with their tame clothes, both in blue denim jeans (Paula's being Versace, of course). She was chuffed they had come — especially Dawn, as it was hard for her to get time off from the salon on a Saturday.

"Yo! Sisters!" she screeched as she switched tracks to Sister Sledge's "We Are Family".

"Oh God!" Paula groaned as everyone in the shop turned to stare at them. "Does she have to be so extra?"

"Shut up," Dawn hissed, dragging her by the arm in Ronnie's direction.

When they reached she gave both of them a hug.

"Wow, Ronnie, the place is ram!" Dawn said in admiration.

"Yeah, it's kicking. But I'm telling you, I'm bushed, man. I done the stall this morning and left Nancy to continue while I bombed it down here like nobody's business, y'know what I'm saying?"

"So, has Cameron been in?" Paula asked, glancing around her.

"I dunno if he'll reach, because he's taking Jhel to a birthday party."

Paula's eyes fell on a white hotpants suit hanging up on a rail to her right. It was made from stretchy material and had a very low cleavage. Beneath it was a pair of white knee-length lace-up boots.

Ronnie noticed her looking at them and mistook her expression of disgust for admiration.

"That would suit you. I get a twenty-five per cent discount as part of the deal."

"I've seen bikinis with more material," Paula remarked with disdain.

Ronnie laughed. "So? You've got it, flaunt it!" She unhooked the garment and handed it to Paula.

"I think it's criss," Dawn said, feeling the Lycra.

"Try it on then," Ronnie urged.

"You're joking!" Dawn gestured with her hands. "Even if it *is* stretchy I'm going to be out here in a few weeks' time. What's the point?"

"You know they've got some wicked maternity wear here. You might clock something you could wear for Paula's hen night."

"What hen night?"

"Oh, c'mon, Paula. You've got to be having one," Ronnie challenged.

"Uh-uh!" Paula said, shaking her head.

"Why not?" Dawn asked.

"It ain't my scene."

Ronnie rolled her eyes. "Oh, for goodness sakes, P! Is Germaine having a stag do?"

"I reckon so."

"So, if he's having a night of sleaze and debauchery, why can't you?"

"Because I don't want one." Paula sighed. "I was thinking of a quiet meal—"

"A quiet meal? Do me a favour!" Ronnie scoffed. "Did I have a quiet meal for my hen night?"

"No. You opted for the red light district of Amsterdam," Paula said, shuddering at the memory. "I'm certainly not doing anything like that!"

"Paula, you're too dry-dry," Ronnie said. Then she grinned at Dawn. "We'll have to get her sorted, eh?"

Dawn laughed. "Where did you say they had maternity gear?"

"Downstairs, darling. And watch them steps, they're lethal; nearly broke up me neck earlier."

Paula and Ronnie watched Dawn descend the narrow metal staircase. When she was out of sight Paula said, "Mum's giving her a really hard time."

"How so?"

"You know last week, when Dawn babysat for you?" Ronnie nodded, so Paula continued, "Well, Mum found out she'd had Tony round and they'd ... you know."

"Had sex?"

"Ronnie!"

"Oh, come off it, Paula. Don't you think Dawn would've been on the news if she was pregnant and a virgin? But anyway, go on."

"Well, that's it. Mum went into one, and now she won't

have Tony in the house."

"Not even for Sunday dinner?"

"Not even for Sunday dinner."

"That's rough. It's not as though they've got their own place to be together and that. But how come mum found out? Did she catch them in bed or something?"

Paula raised her eyebrows.

"Dawn told me not to say, but I think you've a right to know. After all, she is your child."

"Jhelisa!"

Paula nodded grimly. "I'm surprised she didn't mention it to you."

Ronnie was getting exasperated. "What?"

"Apparently she told mum that she'd heard 'Auntie Dawn and Tony sexing.'"

Ronnie stared at Paula for a second and then burst out laughing.

"Ronnie! How can you laugh?"

"Oh, c'mon, you've got to see the funny side."

"What, like Dawn and Tony?"

Ronnie sobered up. "I know, I shouldn't laugh. I'll have a word with Dawn and try and talk some sense into Mum—"

"Don't you dare!" Paula interrupted. "Dawn didn't want me to say anything. Let her and Mum sort it out between themselves."

"She's our kid sister, Paula. We should help her."

"Yeah, well our kid sister is big enough to ask us if she wants our help."

"Well it's nice to know we can count on you, eh?" Ronnie snapped. Then, before Paula could reply, she looked past her and waved at someone.

"Ola!"

Paula turned and followed her sister's gaze. She remembered the funki-dred from Camden market; he had a record stall there. Paula had marvelled at his dress sense then, as she did now.

He was wearing a silver satin T-shirt and a pair of white bell-bottom jeans. He smiled at Ronnie and did a kind of shoe-shuffle bogle dance. You could get away with doing that in Freedom; in more conventional stores they would probably get the security guards on to you. That's how cool Freedom was.

He was with another guy who wasn't dancing. He had long dreads and looked a little scruffy. Paula recognised him too and quickly looked at the floor.

Ola kissed Ronnie on the lips.

"You remember Paula, my sister?" she said.

He didn't, but he kissed a shocked Paula full on the lips anyway.

"I thought you'd still be up in Camden," Ronnie said.

"I got a friend to take over while I checked you out in the coolest boutique in town." He surveyed the crowded shop. "And it's kicking, kicking, kicking!"

The guy with the dreads stepped forward. Paula had forgotten how lovely his smile was. It was the nicest smile she'd seen on anyone in a long time. It lit up his entire face.

He kissed Ronnie on the cheek.

"All right, Michael? You remember my sister—"

"Paula," he finished for her, then he gave Paula a peck on the cheek too.

She remained outwardly impassive but inside she felt a little giddy. She remembered feeling like this the first time she'd met him in Camden.

Ronnie switched records and started chatting away to Ola, so Michael looked Paula straight in the eye and asked, "Are you going to come tonight?"

The way he stressed the word "come" made Paula's cheeks burn. "Where?"

"There's a warehouse blues type thing going down — Club Uproar."

"Never heard of it."

"So?"

"So I'm making a special meal for my fiancé."

"Oh yeah? What kind of meal?"

"Malaysian."

"So, you a good cook?"

"Yeah."

"What else are you good at?"

Paula realised that he was checking out what she was holding in her hands. Hastily she dumped the white Lycra outfit on the rail next to her.

"You're not buying that?"

"No!"

"Pity."

Paula was relieved to see Dawn making her way painstakingly up the stairs with a bundle in her arms.

"They've got some wicked maternity gear down there. What d'you think of this?" She held up a black chiffon mini-dress that flowed out from the bust. It was perfect for Dawn; both Paula and Ronnie thought so and said as much. "I can't afford it, though."

Ronnie practically grabbed it from her. "Leave it with me, darling."

Dawn's eyes rounded. "You're joking! It's well dear."

"Like I said, I get a good discount." Ronnie didn't add that she felt indirectly guilty for causing Tony to be banned from their mother's house.

Dawn was in love with the dress. "I'll pay you back ..."

"Whatever," Ronnie replied, not intending to take a penny from her. Then she introduced Dawn to Ola and Michael.

"Well, we'd better make a move," Paula said immediately afterwards, nudging Dawn.

"We do?"

"Yeah," Paula said, fixing her with a glare.

"Oh, don't go yet," Ronnie pleaded.

"Ronnie, it's ram here and I still have shopping to do ..."

Dawn gave Ronnie a helpless look before following Paula towards the door.

Just as they were walking out of the shop Michael called out, "See you around, Paula."

Paula looked back. He was smiling. She felt a knot in her stomach and wondered for a split second what it would be like to share bodily fluids with him. Then she felt her engagement ring burning.

"What's with you and that guy?" Dawn asked as they strolled down the street.

"Who?"

"You know who. That Michael guy."

"Nothing."

Dawn dropped the subject, but not before remarking that, in all the years she had seen her sister with Germaine, she had never witnessed the vibes flowing from Michael in Freedom.

Back inside the shop Ronnie was grinning from ear to ear, and not just because Ola was doing one of his jerk-your-body-any-which-way (and don't care who or what you send flying) moves to Bill Withers's "Use Me Up". How he thought he had a hope in hell of hooking up with Nancy was anyone's guess. No, Ronnie was more amused by Michael's lust for Paula.

"I'm telling you, Quinones, don't be thinking you can have a little t'ing with Mary Poppins there. She's so uptight she can't even say the word sex without hyperventilating … and she's getting married."

"Ronnie, trust me. Your sister may seem all cool, all …"

"Sexless."

"Your words, not mine. And I meant to say sophisticated. But anyway, underneath that icy exterior there's a hot, bubbling volcano ready to explode."

"And you think you can lift it out of dormancy and catch

105

yourself some of that lava business? No chance. You're as bad as my guy Ola, tripping over for some girl you ain't ever going to get."

"WHAT AM I GOING TO DO when you go off and have your pickney in a couple of months, eh?" Verna Sinclair, the proprietor of Vee's Hair & Beauty Salon, sighed as she watched Dawn carefully spray Mrs Lewiston's newly cut and styled hair.

Dawn was proud of the fact that Mrs Lewiston had been prepared to wait over an hour to have her hair done by Dawn. It vexed Verna a little that it wasn't her whom people waited for, but she couldn't do anything about it. Dawn was younger and prettier, and had a real talent for styling that Verna had never possessed. Dawn brought in the customers. Verna wished it was possible for the girl to give birth on the salon floor and still be styling hair.

"You getting big, now. Sure you ain't carrying twins, love?" Mrs Lewiston asked as Dawn helped her put on her jacket, even though the July afternoon was way too hot to wear one. Verna had the fans going, but the mixture of steamers and chemical relaxers made the air muggy and heady. Several times that day Dawn had wondered if she would last till closing. Working six days a week was a killer.

"You t'ink of any names for de pickney yet, love?" Mrs Lewiston went on.

"Sade if it's a girl, and Hakim if it's a boy."

Mrs Lewiston shook her head as she fished around in her purse for money. "I don't know, the young people of today choosing them *H*african names, all this Haki-Shaki-Backi business. What's wrong with good West Indian names like Hortense, Hyacint' and Basil?"

"They ain't West Indian names, they're English," countered Latifah (formerly known as Sharon), who was setting the steamer for her client. "You're a victim of colonial brainwashing, Mrs Lewiston. Why d'you think I changed my name?"

"Oh, I thought it was in honour of your favourite rap idol," Dawn said cheekily, remembering how Sharon had debated whether to spell her new name Latifah or Lateefa.

Mrs Lewiston laughed as she handed Dawn money for the hairdressing. "And there's a little extra there for your pickney."

"Gosh, thanks, Mrs Lewiston!" Dawn exclaimed, stuffing the ten-pound note into the breast pocket of her sleeveless denim shirt.

As Mrs Lewiston was walking out of the door Tony burst in, nearly knocking her over. He apologised profusely, to which she accorded him a kiss of her teeth.

"Here comes the Romeo who impregnated my stylist," Verna sighed, looking up from the appointments diary, and the all-female salon (including Dawn) cackled with laughter.

Tony took it in good humour. But he was in an especially good mood. Today he and Dawn were going to look at a flat.

The estate was only a ten-minute walk away from the salon, but Dawn and Tony had taken the bus, as Dawn didn't feel like walking in this sweltering heat. Looking up at the bleak and sprawling mass of concrete, Dawn wondered why they had even bothered. There was no way she could live here, let alone bring up a baby.

"At least take a look at the flat. I mean, I know people who live here quite happily. It ain't fantastic, but it's somewhere we can live together, be together ..." He gave her swollen belly a gentle pat. "The three of us."

Dawn was unconvinced. And the straps of her sandals were cutting into her swollen ankles, which didn't improve her mood. She thought of where her sisters lived: Ronnie's trendy flat in Ladbroke Grove and Paula's upmarket apartment in Belsize Park. And here she was, contemplating living in a squalid flat on an equally squalid estate, notorious for its drug-ridden reputation (although Tony had told her not to believe the hype).

"You know why we got offered this so quickly. Who else would want to live here?" she moaned.

However, she allowed him to take her by the hand and steer her towards the entrance of the block that housed the possibility of a home. But the lifts weren't working, and the flat was on the sixth floor.

"I guess we'll have to forget it then," Tony said sadly.

Dawn sighed. She knew how enthusiastic he was about seeing the flat; he'd been jangling the keys throughout the bus journey.

"No, Tony, we're here now. Let's take a look."

"You mean it?" Tony could barely contain his joy.

"I must be mad, but yes."

So they began to trudge up the six flights of stairs, stopping for Dawn to rest and read the colourful graffiti along the way. But the hard slog upwards had given Dawn time to reflect, and when they finally reached the sixth floor she said breathlessly, "Tony, it's tough for me now at seven months. How am I going to do this when I'm just about to drop a pickney, or afterwards, with a buggy?"

"Oh, they'll have the lifts working by then."

"Yeah, right, and I'm Whitney Houston."

But the flat was not as bad as Dawn had feared. True, there was damp on the walls, especially in the kitchen, but it had two bedrooms, a bathroom and separate toilet, and a lounge.

"The view ain't bad," Tony enthused.

Dawn joined him at the window in the lounge and couldn't ignore the sight and sound of heavy traffic. "Yeah, there's no view like the North Circular Road, eh Tony?"

He moved behind her and wrapped his arms around her burgeoning waistline, turning her so that they faced into the lounge. He pointed to a corner of the room. "We could put the sofa there."

"What sofa?" Dawn teased him.

"The one we're going to buy from the wholesalers across the way," he replied. "And I'm going to strip the walls and repaint — or d'you reckon wallpaper'd be better?"

"We could get that wallpaper you can paint over," Dawn suggested.

Tony snorted.

"What's so funny about that?" She nudged him in the ribs.

"Nothing. I weren't laughing at that, I was thinking about something else."

"Yeah, what?"

"D'you remember that empty flat we used to go to?"

"It weren't on this estate."

"Yeah, I know that. But we had some good times there, didn't we?"

Dawn giggled, remembering years back when they used to sneak away from school during lunchbreaks to a vacant flat on a nearby estate, after a tip-off from one of Tony's friends who had discovered it. It was known as the "boom boom shack", and Trevor Mason had charged £1.50 per hour, even though the lunch break was only forty-five minutes long. It was the only place that couples like Dawn and Tony could go to make love in peace. When the council finally let the flat three months later, Dawn and Tony were back to her mum's sofa while she was out at work, and Trevor Mason had accumulated enough money to buy a criss pair of Adidas trainers, which at the time were the rage.

After all those years, Tony and Dawn were in the same situation: seeking out a place to be alone together. Maybe this flat was about to break the cycle.

"Imagine. We'll have the place to ourselves." He kissed her neck. "How about we christen it right now?"

Dawn glanced at the floor, which was bare and dusty. "How about I inspect the kitchen more closely," she said, gently prising his hands from her wide waist.

Tony groaned as she strolled out of the lounge. He had friends who were turned off by their women when they were pregnant, but for Tony it was the opposite. He fancied Dawn more than ever now she was carrying their child. Her hips and tummy were rounder, her breasts were fuller, and her skin had a golden glow about it.

They had dropped the subject of marriage, at least temporarily. Just as they had dropped the subject of his brothers and what they had done to the bouncer in Freddie's. Tony had been furious at being banned from Dawn's mum's place, but for her and the baby's sake he'd let that drop too. The baby was of paramount importance. They didn't need arguments that might jeopardise its well-being. Thus they had decided to channel all their energies into getting a place together.

The council had been a long time in coming, but this flat was what Tony had been hoping for, dreaming about for so long — a chance for him and his woman and their child to live as a family. And Dawn's mother, who had made it clear what she thought of him, could go to hell.

Yeah, Tony thought to himself, life was looking up.

Suddenly his thoughts were interrupted by a piercing scream from the kitchen.

"The damn place is teeming with them! How can you expect people to live there? I mean, keep food and cook there ... ? I've got a baby on the way, in case you hadn't noticed!"

The housing officer in charge of their case — a Ms Francis — twiddled with the keys that Dawn had thrown down on the counter moments earlier. "I realise there may be a slight problem with cockroaches—"

"Not slight. I'd say major. And you lot never said a word about it to us!"

Tony put his arm around Dawn's shoulder in an effort to calm her down; the housing office was crowded. But Dawn didn't care, she was disgusted, so Tony's arm was shrugged off.

They didn't have an appointment other than to return the keys, but Dawn was causing a scene. "Would you care to come into my office?" Ms Francis asked.

"No thanks. The only office I'm going to is the one for the local newspaper. I'm going to tell them what this council's up to. I had you lot snooping round my mum's yard, my boyfriend's mum's yard, asking all sorts of personal questions and making out that I got pregnant to jump to the top of the housing list. And for what? For a cockroach-infested, damp pit of a hole you see fit to call a flat! Well I'm sorry, that ain't good enough!"

"We've already advised you that, other than that estate, we don't have any suitable properties available. We have referred your names to a housing association who I'm sure will be in touch with you shortly ..."

This woman sounded like she had swallowed a complaints procedures manual. "And how soon is 'shortly'?"

"Well, not before the baby's born, I'm afraid ..."

"Oh, I know why that is! If I miscarry they won't have to do nothing."

"I'm sorry." The woman paused, fumbling with the keys. "Look, is there any way you can get a thousand pounds? If you can, you could participate in the shared housing scheme ..."

"Not unless I rob a bank or you give it to me," Dawn said

grimly.

Ms Francis sighed. She was a black woman about the same age as Dawn and Tony. But she could do little other than sympathise. "I'm sorry ... But your file will be kept open."

"Shove it up your backside!"

Dawn stormed out of the office.

Tony followed her after apologising to Ms Francis. It was boiling hot outside, and that wasn't only due to the temperature.

"How come you never backed me up in there?" Dawn hissed at him.

"From what I could see you was doing pretty good all by yourself."

"What's that supposed to mean?" Dawn stood in front of him, arms akimbo. "You saying I shamed you up?"

"No," Tony lied. Though he blamed her hormones and the heatwave for her loss of temper.

"D'you think it's acceptable that they want us to live in a dump?"

"Course not!"

"Could have fooled me."

"Yeah, well, ranting and raving ain't going to get you nowhere, Dawn."

"Yeah, well, neither will being a pushover."

"I ain't no pushover!"

Dawn pushed him to one side and started to walk off but Tony caught her arm. There were more people in the housing office than out on the street, but those few around glanced surreptitiously at the rowing couple.

"Listen," Tony said, "I stand up for myself, but only when it counts. What'd you think was going to happen by yelling in that place back there? Did you think we'd suddenly get a four-bedroomed house in Willesden Green? What's the point of getting all het up if it ain't going to get you nowhere? Life's tough enough as it is, man! And what did you want me to do anyway? Hit the woman?"

Dawn shielded her eyes from the sun's rays. They didn't say anything for a few seconds. Then Tony said softly, "I got carried away with the idea of us having a place together, you know."

"I know, it's tough. We hardly get any time alone together. Your mum's yard is pure ram."

"And she don't cook chicken as good as yours."

"Yeah, but that's a sacrifice I can handle. I couldn't stand not spending Sundays with you. It's the only day we've got."

Tony paused, then said, "Dawn, I know we've talked about it, but at least—"

"Tony, like I said, your mum's yard is pure ram."

"And you don't want to be near my brothers."

Dawn looked up at the sky. "We're going round in circles, Tony."

"All I want is for the three of us to be together." He placed a hand on her belly.

"That's what I want too. But we couldn't have lived in that flat, Tony. You understand that, don't you?"

"Yeah, I know," he sighed, pulling her into his arms. And they both felt the baby kick out within Dawn's stomach.

Pastor Raymond Duchess frowned at Ronnie and Dawn as they stood giggling behind Paula and Germaine. "If the bridesmaids would kindly stop laughing ... Marriage is a serious business, and this is a house of God ..."

As soon as he recommenced the rehearsal Ronnie started singing softly again, an improvised version of the tune made famous by Musical Youth: "Pas-tor Duchess pon de left 'and side, gimme de music mek me jump an' prance ..."

Dawn burst out laughing again.

This time Pastor Duchess had had enough. He pounded the service book in his hand.

"I'm sorry, Pastor Duchess," Paula apologised, turning round to reprimand her bridesmaids. "For God's sake, shut up!" Then she balked, because the pastor had growled at her use of the Lord's name in vain. She looked to Germaine for support, but he was laughing too, so she looked at the gathered assembly for support.

Her mum was knitting, Cameron was reading a newspaper, and Tony was playing hide-and-seek with Jhelisa between the pews.

"Oi, everyone! This is my wedding!"

Ronnie shrugged her shoulders. "Lighten up, P. It's just a rehearsal, the real thing's in two days time."

Paula glowered at her.

Then Pastor Duchess said, "You young people don't respect the sanctity of marriage these days. As the Lord says, 'Never taketh the union of man and woman as a joke.' It's no laughing matter. Not at all, not at all."

Dawn giggled. "Which lord a seh dat?"

The pastor glowered at her. "Him also believed dat a woman should be given away by her father or another such person who is suitable. Not fe de woman to march up de aisle all by herself 'cause she a feminist!"

Ronnie and Dawn cackled with laughter while Paula fumed.

"You cyan't find some uncle or male cousin before Saturday?" the priest ranted on.

"We spoke about this earlier, Pastor Duchess, and we agreed that it was all right for me to give myself away. It's not because I'm a feminist, it's because I've no choice. I come from a matriarchal family."

"And what about you?" The pastor swung his gaze upon Germaine.

"I agree with Paula. She should give herself away."

"My goodness! In all my forty years as a pastor I've never known anything like this."

Ronnie leaned forward and whispered loudly in Paula's

ear. "Oh my stars, P! Why d'you have to go and get a bad-tempered old goat like him for?"

"Shut up, Veronica!" Paula turned to Pastor Duchess. "Could we get on, please?"

The pastor cleared his throat and finally they managed to run through the wedding service. As Paula and Germaine said their vows, Paula wondered if she would feel too nervous on her big day to remember Germaine's middle name — until she remembered he didn't have one.

When Pastor Duchess had finished, he gave the bride-and groom-to-be yet another lecture on the sanctity of marriage. "It is sacred, sacred, sacred," he preached. Looking directly at Paula he went on, "You've been coming here to this church with your mother and sisters and your father — when he was alive, God rest his soul. I have watched you grow up and, even though of late I haven't seen you in this particular House of God ..." Paula blushed as he said this. "... I feel deep down in my heart that you've never been far away. So I am happy that you, and your young man Gerard—"

"Germaine," Paula corrected him.

"Er ... yes. Germaine ... Well, I am happy that you've chosen to sanctify your relationship in my church, and that I will be able to welcome you as members of my congregation as the Valentine family."

Paula squeezed Germaine's hand. She liked the sound of that. When they had first decided to get married she had thought she would keep her own name, as Ronnie had done. But after a while Germaine's surname grew on her, and she'd decided to have both names. From the day after tomorrow she would be known as Paula Smart Valentine.

Afterwards, they all stood outside the church. Shirley chatted to the pastor about the best way to grow marrows, Cameron and Tony discussed cars, Ronnie and Dawn sat on the wall plotting Paula's hen night, Jhelisa leaning between them. It was another sweltering hot day.

Paula squeezed Germaine's hand as they stood in the doorway of the small Pentecostal church. "D'you think it'll be like this on Saturday?" she asked him.

"Yeah, they reckon the heatwave'll last a few days."

"Great. That means I'll have sweat stains on my wedding dress. Be sure to use that extra-strong deodorant."

"Yeah, Paula."

"Well! If it's going to be boiling hot … You know, I'm wondering if there'll be enough room in that church."

"There's room for three hundred people."

"Yeah, but there's no air-conditioning … Germaine, what if I faint?"

"I can't see that happening somehow."

"What's that supposed to mean?"

"Paula, I know you. If you don't want to faint you won't. You can defy most things except gravity and death."

"Is that some kind of compliment?"

"I guess so."

Paula studied his face for a second, then dismissed the idea that he was mocking her.

Dawn and Ronnie were cackling loudly a few feet away on the wall. "They're up to no good," Paula said. "Talk about shaming us up in the church. I thought the pastor was going to chuck us out, refuse to marry us on Saturday. And then where would we be? No wedding! Could you imagine that?"

Germaine kicked at a few stones on the ground.

"I bet they're planning something gross for my hen night tomorrow. Kim's already got tickets for Basil Nastilove."

Germaine snorted.

"It's not funny, Germaine! Imagine me at one of his shows!"

"I hear the women that go are craven."

"Yeah? Well I'm not," Paula sniffed. "So, where are you going for your stag do?"

"I don't know yet. Cameron and Tony and some of the

guys from work are in on it."

"What about Conrad?"

"He's the one who's organised it."

"Oh, Germaine!" Paula groaned. "After how he's treated Kim ... and considering what an arsehole he is ... !"

"He was insistent. I couldn't refuse."

Paula straightened the collar on his blue linen jacket. "Just be sure to behave yourself."

The strip club was pretty run of the mill by Soho standards. Fortunately for the punters, Fifi the Swiss nun was not — once she was out of her habit and religiously swinging her 42-DD bust about the place.

"This was a terrible idea. Whose was it?" Cameron complained. He was sitting with Tony at a grubby table near the back of the dingy establishment.

"I think it was shinehead over there." Tony nodded at a skinny, light-skinned black guy with more hair in his moustache than on his head. "He used to deal with Kim. Give her two pickney and a whole heap o' grief. Goes by the name of Conrad Biddle."

"Jesus!" Cameron exclaimed. "I'm surprised Germaine's tight with him."

Conrad sat with Germaine at a table near the front of the stage (if you could call it that). Conrad was busy dealing with Fifi's large assets, trying to persuade Germaine to join in.

"I don't see how any man can come to a place like this and feel up woman. None can compare to my Dawn," Tony declared.

Cameron shook his head. Fifi was now sat on Germaine's lap. One of his colleagues had whipped out a camera and was clicking away while Conrad yelled, "Blackmail, blackmail!"

Tony and Cameron tried to ignore all this.

"How's t'ings running with you and Ronnie?" Tony asked.

"I'll be honest with you, it's still a one-day-at-a time kind of thing."

"But she's doin' good with her deejay t'ing, innit?"

"Yeah, she is." Cameron took a sip of beer. It had been watered down.

Lately, Ronnie had been getting more and more gigs, spurred on by the hot spell. Apart from Freedom on a Saturday afternoon, she was deejaying in a club not far from Soho on the first Thursday of every month, and doing the odd private party. Cameron couldn't really complain — before each gig she sorted out arrangements for Jhelisa if he couldn't take care of her himself and, most importantly, she discussed the situation with him first. It was all done by the book. But he couldn't help fearing that she would go over the limit one day, go off somewhere without telling him or not come back when she was supposed to. He dreaded that day.

"... The place was Cockroach City, man," Tony was saying.

"What?"

"The flat me and Dawn went to see the other day."

"It's tough."

"Yeah? You know about that then?"

"Hey, listen. Before I got into modelling and went to uni, I lived in squats, man."

"You lie!"

"It's the truth. My mum would've had a fit if she'd known."

"Yeah, I ain't surprised. But you was young and single then. I can't squat someplace with Dawn and a pickney."

"I'm not suggesting you should — unless it's a house with a pool on Millionaires' Row."

"Hey, maybe I should scout the place ..." Tony paused. "How come you jacked in the modelling? I mean, you was making 'nuff readies."

Cameron reflected for a second or two. "In the beginning it was great. I was just collared one day by some woman in Covent Garden who happened to be a talent scout for a modelling agency. The next thing I know — *bam!* — my face and body are doing things, I'm going to places you only dream of, meeting people you only dream of, and people are rating me for being a black male model on his way to the top."

"And that advert ..."

"Yeah, that advert. It got so I couldn't stand it." Cameron's eyes were drawn again to the stage. "Look at the way that stripper's getting pawed — that's how it was for me. You stop being a person, you become an object. Some people really go for that, but I'm not one of them. Unless you're at the top of your profession you get treated like dirt. And forget the glamour — it's hard work most of the time."

"I wouldn't mind it. One thing, though — you ever get touch up by some of them male designers? I hear most of them run on the gay side."

Cameron laughed. "Yeah, well, I had some moments."

"That also why you give it up?"

"No — I met Ronnie, who was probably the most genuine person to come my way in a long time. And once Jhelisa came along I decided to get into something more conventional. Truth is, I hated modelling and I wanted to get out." He nudged Tony. "This is getting nasty."

Fifi had just handed Germaine a bottle of baby oil. He was reluctant to do anything with it, let alone use it on the stripper, so Conrad snatched it out of his hands.

"You're not the groom!" Fifi (sounding more Swiss Cottage than Swiss) protested.

"Deff him for a real man."

Fifi groaned inwardly. She didn't want Conrad's scrawny fondle-happy fingers on her. She had earmarked Germaine — and not just because he was the groom. Then she was planning to move on to the gorgeous guy with the amber eyes and his cheeky-faced companion sitting at the back. But not this geek slobbering away in front of her.

"I'll give you ten pound if you give me some extra, baby."

Fifi scowled at him. "Listen, you scrote. I'm an exotic dancer, not a prostitute. And if I was to go with you it would certainly cost you more than a tenner." She snatched the bottle, and in doing so squirted baby oil all over Conrad.

"Big up, Fifi!" Tony cheered.

It wasn't late, but pretty soon Cameron and Tony had taken more than they could bear. As Ladbroke Grove and Harlesden were relatively close, they decided to share a cab. They went to phone for one while the rest of the stag party were either drinking themselves under the table or ogling the exotic dancer on stage.

They found the phones next to the toilets — which in this establishment were men only. But Germaine had already beaten them to it. "I didn't notice him slip out," Cameron remarked as they approached him.

They managed to catch the tail-end of his conversation. "Yeah … give it half an hour. I'm going to give the guys the slip." Then, sensing he wasn't alone, he turned and smiled at Cameron and Tony before quickly ending the phone call.

"I thought this was going to be an all-nighter," Tony said as Germaine replaced the receiver.

"I think my night here is done. Don't let on to the others, okay?"

"They're too far gone to notice," Cameron said.

"That Conrad's one demented bullock," Tony remarked. "It's hard to believe a nice girl like Kim would have been dealing with that."

"Tell me about it. But he's out of her life now," Germaine said.

Tony nodded. "So, has Fifi got you so whipped up you gotta get between the sheets with Paula?"

Germaine frowned at him.

"The phone call," Tony prompted.

"Oh, yeah. That. Well, you know how it is ... Listen, thanks for the support. I know it was a crap night."

"Don't worry. My stag do was crap too," Cameron admitted. "Ronnie thought it would be a good idea to have a joint hen and stag weekend in Amsterdam. The red light district was depressing, the sex museum was tacky beyond belief, and everyone got spaced out on spliff."

"That sounds pretty good," Tony said. He couldn't help thinking that Cameron was a bit dry sometimes. How he'd hit it off with Ronnie was anyone's guess. But, like they say, opposites attract.

"It'll be your turn soon," Cameron told him.

"Yeah," Tony said. But he knew it wouldn't be.

"Hey, I've got to love you and leave you, guys," Germaine said.

"Yeah, don't keep Paula waiting," Tony laughed.

"Why don't you share a cab with us?" Cameron suggested.

"It's a bit out of the way. I'll hail one from outside." He patted both of them on the shoulder before he strolled towards the exit.

"Does he think he's too good for minicyab?" Tony snorted.

"Nah, he's in a hurry to see someone."

"Yeah, Miss P."

Cameron didn't reply. He took a minicab firm's card from his shirt pocket and picked up the phone. He winced — the receiver was covered in baby oil.

Dawn and Kim stared at the spread Paula had laid on in her kitchen. There was mixed salad, potato salad, chicken salad, Mexican salad, Trinidad & Tobago salad (part of a Caribbean range being promoted at the local supermarket), sticks of celery, pitta bread, and assorted dips.

"It looks great. Real ... salady," Dawn remarked.

"It's *too* salady, isn't it?" Paula sighed as she poured some more dressing on the Mexican salad.

"No. You've got breadsticks and tortilla chips," Kim pointed out with her usual cheerfulness. "Anyway, we don't want to be too full when we go out tonight."

Dawn picked up a breadstick and dunked it in one of the dips. "What d'you normally cook for Germaine?"

"Oh, we're into Thai and Malaysian at the moment."

Kim and Dawn looked at each other sceptically.

"You should try it," Paula urged.

"Oh, right," Dawn and Kim said in unison. It wasn't the type of food they were doubtful about; it was Paula's culinary skills. Her lack of them was legendary.

Dawn glanced around the kitchen. It never ceased to amaze her how many gadgets Paula and Germaine had. A microwave, a dishwasher, a coffee machine and grinder, a food mixer that could have doubled as a cement mixer given the size of it. Then there was Dawn's favourite, something that Paula proudly declared was a state-of-the-art, heat-adjustable, hand-held mini-press. Dawn, however, found it easier to call it by its more common name: an iron.

Glancing around, Dawn could hardly miss the bouquet of flowers on the draining board. "You ought to put those in water. They from Germaine?"

"No, I got them from work."

"We gave her a great send-off," Kim said. "Dragged her down the wine bar, threw confetti over her ... but the girl let us down — she'd only touch mineral water, and she bought them herself cos she was scared we'd spike her drinks. Honestly, your sister, Dawn ..."

"I was never happy about having a hen night, let alone having one the night before my wedding."

"Tonight is Basil Nastilove's only London appearance," Kim said.

123

"Whatever. But I intend to remain in control. I don't want a hangover ... or, worse, to wake up in someone else's bed!" Paula guffawed.

"Somehow I don't see that happening," Dawn remarked.

"Oh, but listen, you lot go ahead. I've got white wine in the fridge, red wine, Martini, Gin, Vodka, Rum ..."

"Jamaican?" Kim interrupted.

Paula nodded and reached into a cupboard behind her to take down the bottle of rum. She poured out a glass each for Kim and Dawn.

"Don't tell me you're passing up rum?" Dawn cried.

"I told you, I'm not drinking tonight."

"One drink won't hurt. Jesus, it's your hen night. Anyone'd think you're being ordained as a flippin' nun!"

Paula ignored her younger sister and pointed to the card lying next to the bouquet from her colleagues. "You should read that."

Dawn picked it up and started to read the comments out loud: " 'The best thing about marriage is that you can get a divorce.' "

"Ain't that the truth!" Kim laughed. "Read what I wrote."

" 'Life's a bastard, and then you marry one.' Kim!"

"Well it's true! Imagine if I'd married Conrad."

"Apart from a dodgy surname you'd have had a whole heap of trouble," Dawn said.

"Maybe in Kim's case marriage would have been trouble," Paula began.

"No — definitely," Kim corrected.

"Whatever. But you see, I couldn't just live with someone for ever and ever. That wouldn't work for me." Paula poured herself a glass of natural lemonade.

"Oh yeah? How so?" Dawn demanded.

"The way I look at it, if you're living with someone you just don't make the effort. If you get married you do. I saw how my relationship with Germaine improved after we got engaged. We take each other more seriously now. Let's face it, it's harder to walk out on a marriage than a live-in relationship. But some men are just scared of commitment and don't meet their responsibilities."

Dawn took a slow sip of rum. "Oh really? And which men would you be talking about?"

"Oh, I'm not getting at you, Dawn. I know Tony's different."

"So you think you and Germaine will have the perfect relationship once you get married?" Dawn didn't allow Paula to answer. "I'm pleased, I really am. Because I was getting worried. Despite you going on about how good Germaine treats you and how committed he is to you, you keep speeching about how you hardly see him and spend time with him and all that. I mean, the man's always down at the gym, for crying out loud."

Dawn took another sip of rum. "See me now? I don't need to business with all that. Even though you may feel sorry for me because my man is not committed to me, don't fuss none. Because I left home tonight a very satisfied woman and I don't have no ring on my finger."

"Woah, ladies! Chill, chill," Kim interjected. "This is supposed to be a happy occasion."

Dawn picked up the relaxer kit she'd left on the draining board. "Come on, Kim, let me do your hair."

Paula pursed her lips as they left the kitchen. She couldn't understand why Dawn had been so touchy of late. Then she remembered an article in a magazine about pregnancy messing up the hormones and causing mood swings. But as she sipped her lemonade she reflected on how it bothered her that everyone made so much of Germaine's gym sessions. There really was no big deal.

"I mean, I'm proud of the fact that he works out a lot. We both do. Now he even trains more than I do. Really, I don't mind," Paula said for the zillionth time as she applied her make-up in front of the bathroom mirror.

Kim was perched on the edge of the bath towel-drying her hair. "Dawn didn't mean nothing by it."

"She seemed to be making out that he's more interested in the gym than in me. Or what ... that he's messing about with someone else?"

"Of course not!" Kim was indignant.

"What did she say to you while she was doing your hair?"

"Nothing. Just baby talk and that." Kim was lying by omission. Dawn had also vowed to spike Paula's lemonade with vodka. She hoped the alcohol would create an oasis in the dry, arid, desert that Paula had for a personality.

"You know," Paula said, "Tony and Dawn's relationship is what we all had as teenagers. But once you grow up you need something more mature and focused — emotionally, financially, not just physically. But to find a partner that can share in that is rare. It's like I say all the time — I'm fortunate to have Germaine."

"Yeah," Kim muttered.

Paula paused to apply her lipstick. Then she said, "You know, I never really knew my dad. He died when I was really young. But my mum's never had another man in her life — well, not seriously anyway. That's because of the marriage she had with Dad. It was so strong and powerful, you know? And that's what I'm going to have with Germaine."

The doorbell saved Kim from any further rantings from Paula. They heard Dawn answer it, and seconds later Ronnie's voice coming through loud and clear.

"Where's the virgin bride, then?"

Paula rolled her eyes and groaned. "Oh God, why did I agree to this?"

Then Nancy's laughter rang out, and Paula groaned louder. "And what did she bring *her* for?" She set her make-up down and walked out into the small passage.

Ronnie was standing there in maroon suede shorts and a matching suede halter-neck top, the outfit complemented by black suede platform sandals. Nancy had on a black velvet sleeveless catsuit and over-the-knee boots in black suede.

"Don't they look wicked?" Dawn enthused.

Paula sighed. These women were in their thirties. To her they looked like prostitutes. "Very, er … fitting."

Nancy grinned. "Yeah, I reckon black's appropriate for the occasion."

"You don't mind Nancy coming with us, do you?" Ronnie said. "She's feeling a bit down since she split from Miles."

"Miles? I thought your man was called Ty." Paula frowned.

"Oh that's old, old history. Miles is the third since him," Nancy explained happily. For someone who was supposed to be down she seemed remarkably upbeat.

"Jesus, it smells like an ICI chemical plant in here," Ronnie said, sniffing the air.

"I've just relaxed Kim's hair," Dawn explained.

At this point Kim strolled out into the passage.

"I don't know how you can use that stuff. It bitches up your scalp," Nancy said to her.

"I've been using it for years and never had no problems." Like Paula, the few times Kim had met Nancy had left her unimpressed. "Your hair looks good on you, Nancy, but if I had that style they'd probably take my kids into care."

Nancy gave her a funny look before Paula ushered everyone into the living room. She settled them down with drinks and took a sip of her "lemonade". Dawn and Kim exchanged glances and tried not to laugh as Paula took another sip without suspicion.

"So, how long have we got before Basil Nastilove and his crew?" Ronnie asked.

Kim glanced at her watch. "It starts in an hour. Until then

we can watch the man in action on video. You remember to bring it, Ronnie?"

Paula rounded on her sister. "What were you doing with it?"

"I lent it to Ronnie to prove it would be worth going to his show for your hen night," Kim explained.

"It's in my bag, Paula." Ronnie had many bags with her, so she had to point out the blue patent leather shoulder-bag by the side of the sofa.

Paula reached down, delved into it and took out the video. She studied the cover: Basil Nastilove was posing in nothing but a g-string. She made a good show of being disgusted, grimacing and making loud retching noises before tossing it across to Kim, who shoved it into the video recorder and switched on the TV.

"It's his latest one," she explained.

Everyone settled back to watch it. Paula, Ronnie and Nancy on the sofa, Kim on a chair with Dawn standing behind her tonging her hair.

When the video started to play, certain aspects looked strangely familiar.

"Hey, isn't that you?" Paula asked her sister.

Ronnie narrowed her eyes. "Oh shit, it's my wedding video!"

She made as if she was about to hurl herself on to the remote control to turn it off, but Nancy held her back. "No, hang on. Don't. This bit's a bit kinky."

Paula and Dawn had seen the video a couple of times before, but it was the first time for Kim and Nancy. This particular part of it featured Ronnie and Cameron dancing round a tree on Wormwood Scrubs. Though they were smiling away it was obvious that they were freezing to death. The theme tune to *Love Story* had been dubbed on and the picture had a kind of smoky effect to it.

By the end of the sequence everyone except Ronnie was on the floor, laughing hard.

"The guy was a film student at St Martin's. He came highly recommended," Ronnie defended, somewhat sourly.

"Is that why you told me the tape was mash up so no one could see it?" Nancy said between splutters.

"I knew you wouldn't appreciate the art-house effects."

"You mean asshole effects, right?" Nancy jibed.

"I'm telling you something," Paula declared. "There's no way I'm going to allow the videographer to put me and Germaine through such foolishness."

"Videographer!" the others spluttered.

"Paula, you're so *extra*," Dawn added.

"You should've got Miles to do it. He's excellent with a camera," Nancy said. "About the only thing he *can* do, really."

"But you and Miles aren't together any more," Paula said.

"So? It don't diminish his talents with a video camera. I should know," Nancy cackled.

"I can't keep up with your guys," Paula remarked.

"Hell, no," Nancy continued. "I'm into short sentences, not like you lifers."

"There's nothing wrong with a long-term relationship," Paula chided.

"Nah. It don't suit me. I prefer my tampons to last longer than my boyfriends." Nancy flicked a piece of imaginary fluff from her catsuit.

"Why's that?" Dawn asked her.

"Oh, you know me — I see a man and I like him. So I shag him senseless, then move on to the next. Ronnie was like that till she met Cameron."

"I was never as bad as you, Nance."

"Oh yeah?" Nancy mocked. "Anyway, I tell ya who I want to shag senseless."

"D'you have to be so coarse?" Paula complained.

"Go on, Nancy. Who?" Dawn asked.

"Michael 'Him Body Fit' Quinones."

"Who's he?" Kim wanted to know.

"This deejay me and Ronnie know. He's been in the States awhile, but he's back now. I don't know how long for, but I'm going to get me a piece of him before he goes."

"Make sure Paula don't get in there first," Ronnie laughed.

"Get lost! I wouldn't touch him with ..." Paula couldn't think of the word, so she finished simply, "I wouldn't touch him!"

"So how come you've met him?" Kim twisted her head to look at Paula.

Paula didn't get a chance to reply.

"What makes you think he's interested in Paula?" Nancy demanded. "I mean, she's hardly his type!"

"Thank you," Paula said, helping herself to a handful of tortilla chips.

She almost choked on them when Ronnie said, "He's always asking about her, that's why."

Everyone looked at Paula. She hastily swallowed down the rest of her lemonade.

"Secret admirer, eh?" Dawn giggled.

"Don't be ridiculous," Paula sniffed. Then she turned to Nancy and, in an effort to take the attention off herself, came out with, "I don't know how you can sleep around with all the diseases going about."

"I'm careful. I don't touch the guy unless he's wearing a helmet. D'you know you can get plastic condoms now? They don't have that after-smell like the rubber ones have."

"Really?" Kim queried.

Nancy nodded as she lit up a cigarette.

"Yeah. But apart from the protection, Nancy, I don't know how you can have one-night stands. I can't imagine having sex outside a loving relationship," Paula said.

"Oh here we go. Men can have sex without a relationship, but women can't. You know what the difference is between you lot and me? Say you get a whole heap of people in a gathering — like a barbecue or whatever. All the women will go off together and chat girl talk — make-up, clothes, babies … The men'll get together and chat about football and cricket and that. You know where I stay? With the guys."

"So, are you saying you're a guy?" Dawn laughed.

"I'm *like* a guy. I can have sex without being in love with the person. In fact I prefer it. Relationships are just a load of hassle." Nancy took a puff of her cigarette. "You know, I can't believe that you've never seen a guy someplace and just wanted to throw him to the floor and shag him senseless."

"Lord Jesus, the girl coarse!" Paula snorted.

"No, I'm serious. Haven't you ever met a guy — and he doesn't have to be good-looking or a piece of fitness — but it's just *there*, you know? You can almost taste the electricity, and you know that all he'd have to do is touch you …"

There was silence, half-embarrassed, half-captivated. Then Dawn announced, "I slept with Tony on our first date."

Paula and Ronnie stared at her as she tonged the last section of Kim's hair. This was news to them.

"See, the minute I laid eyes on him I wanted him. And it hasn't died down, even after eight years."

"Eight years!" Nancy exclaimed. "Hold on, what's his zodiac sign?"

"Scorpio."

Nancy nodded knowingly. "That explains it. Sex mad, them lot. Anyway, as we're on the subject of sex, where's the most exciting place you've ever done it?"

"Why are we on this subject?" Paula asked disdainfully.

"Paula, it's your hen night, get with the program," Nancy said. "I'll start. I bet none of you lot've done it out in the open."

"For real?" Kim asked.

"Notting Hill Carnival, three years ago. Did it in

someone's front garden. I didn't even know the guy's name. But he was definitely a Scorpio, he had a little scorpion on a chain. I won't say where he was wearing the chain! Anyway, a whole heap of people were walking past the whole time we were at it. God knows if any of them saw."

Paula could hardly believe her ears.

"Me and Cam like doing it on the washing machine once it's on the spin cycle."

"The washing machine?" Nancy sounded well impressed. "So what about you then, Kim? I bet you're a lights-out-in-the-bed kind of person."

"You shouldn't jump to conclusions."

"Oh yeah?" Ronnie smiled.

"The twins were conceived on the back seat of Conrad's old mash up car down by Tooting Bec."

"Age-old, but I'm impressed," Nancy said.

"When I found out I was expecting, we decided that if it was a boy we were going to call him Ford, and if it was a girl, Cortina."

"Lucky you didn't do it in the back of a Volkswagen or a Hyundai," Dawn quipped.

Kim didn't add the fact that, later on in their relationship, she had loaned Conrad the money to buy a brand-new VW Golf and hadn't seen a penny since.

"So how come you didn't stick with the names?" Nancy asked.

"Firstly, by the time I gave birth I didn't want more reminders of Conrad. I already had enough. Secondly — can you imagine twins called Ford and Cortina? Their lives would've been hell."

There were nods of agreement from the others. Paula felt sorry for Kim as she watched her move off the chair and remove the video from the machine. She was so plain and dumpy, the only person she could interest was a weedy stump like Conrad.

"You know Cortina is Spanish for curtains," Ronnie said

as Kim handed her the video. "Michael told me."

"What, does he speak Spanish?" Nancy asked in surprise.

Ronnie gave her a don't-be-so-stupid glare. "Oh my stars, Nance! My guy's fluent. His dad's from the Dominican Republic. Hence the surname."

"I thought he was from Dominica."

"I thought they were one and the same," Dawn admitted.

"No, no, no!" Ronnie exclaimed. "They're both in the Caribbean, that's the only similarity. You guys don't know your history or geography, know what I'm saying?"

"What about you, P?" Nancy asked.

"I knew they were two separate countries."

"No, we're talking about outrageous sex."

"Oh," Paula said flatly. Her mind had been on Quiñones. She'd been very interested when Ronnie had mentioned a little bit of his background. Without fully understanding why, she found herself wanting to know more. But she knew it wasn't her business to ask. So she deliberated Nancy's question for a few seconds and, against her better judgement, finally came up with, "One time we did it during the day."

"Where?" Dawn asked expectantly.

"Well, in the bedroom."

"Whose?" they asked in unison.

"Ours."

Everyone groaned.

Paula shrugged her shoulders. "Me and Germaine happen to think that any place apart from the bed is unhygienic."

Nancy shook her head. "I'm sorry, but that's just pure, unadulterated dryness."

"Leave my little sister alone," Ronnie said in mock anger. Then she asked Paula, "So, what are you wearing tonight?"

"A habit," Nancy muttered.

"My long black slip dress with a white body underneath."

"Oh, Paula. Are you out for a night of sleaze and debauchery or midnight mass at church? Good job I bought you something ..."

Ronnie picked up the Freedom bag she'd brought with her and handed it over to Paula, who opened it and peered inside. There was a large package, wrapped in shiny silver paper.

"What is it?"

"A pre-wedding present," Ronnie grinned. "Open it!"

They all watched as Paula carefully removed the paper. Her mouth fell open and Dawn gasped at the sight of what she'd unwrapped. It was the white hotpants-and-halter-neck outfit they'd seen on Ronnie's debut in Freedom.

"There's this as well, to go with them." Ronnie shoved another large Freedom bag over to Paula's feet. Paula pulled it open. Another gasp from Dawn. It was the pair of white knee-length lace-up boots.

"Ronnie, this is too much ..." Paula felt overwhelmed by the gesture, despite her reservations over the morality of the outfit.

"Hey, I get an excellent discount. Anyway, the boots are seconds. See the seam there? It's a bit crooked."

Paula couldn't see anything amiss. "But where would I wear something like this ..." Her voice trailed off as it dawned on her. "You mean wear this tonight? I couldn't!"

Ronnie shrugged her shoulders. "Is there a law against it?"

"I couldn't." Paula looked across at Dawn. "I couldn't wear this. Tell her."

"If you don't wear it I will, even with my big belly."

"Try it on," Kim suggested to Paula.

So she did. When she looked at herself in the full-length mirror in the bedroom she was pleasantly surprised. She

134

had expected to look like a right tart, but the hotpants fitted round her hips like a glove. The halter-neck part allowed for some cleavage, and the white boots laced up snugly round her calves.

When she sauntered back into the lounge everyone wolf-whistled. "That's more like it, girl!" Nancy bellowed.

"Basil Nastilove'll have you on that stage in no time, guy!" Dawn laughed.

Paula said nothing as she was busy downing another glass of lemonade.

Ronnie, being the only teetotaller, had volunteered to drive. You couldn't miss her car — a bright pink Citroen 2CV, and the only banger parked in the street.

"We can't be seen in public in that," Paula scoffed before letting out a loud burp. Most out of character.

"Who cares, as long as it gets us from A to B?" Dawn said. She looked stunning in the black chiffon mini-dress Ronnie had bought her. She'd finished off the outfit with black strappy sandals.

Ronnie opened the passenger door. Kim, looking unusually glam in a navy short-sleeved satin blouse and a pair of beige flared trousers, stood back. "I'll have to sit in front so I can give directions," she said. So Paula, Dawn and Nancy clambered on to the back seat.

"Lord Jesus, Ronnie! How many teddy bears died to line these seats?" Paula laughed.

"I don't know. But it only takes one idiot to sit in them."

"What a comedienne! But I bet the thing don't start," Paula scoffed.

Ronnie started the car first time. She gave her back-seat passengers a sarcastic grin and turned on the stereo, which was probably worth three times more than the car. Everyone started singing along to Cruise's "Party On", Paula's voice being the loudest.

"Oh my stars! She's a bit merry, ain't she?" Ronnie said to Kim.

"You've got Dawn to thank for that," Kim whispered. "She spiced up Paula's drinks a little."

"Excellent!" Ronnie smirked as she manoeuvred her car out of a tight space. "God, if they were any closer they would've needed condoms. Good job I'm a skilled pilot."

Kim laughed.

Ronnie paused before asking her a question. "So, Kim, back there when we was gabbing and that, you ain't said if you're on the job with someone, y'know what I'm saying?"

"Working full-time and with the twins, I ain't got the time or the inclination."

"Oh, cos I noticed it as soon as I saw you tonight."

"What?"

"The glow. You've got it, girl."

The club where Basil Nastilove was lined up to do his *thang* was across the river, down Brixton way, which was about a forty-five minute car journey at this time of night. But the way Ronnie was driving, the girls were on course to get there in record time.

"Ronnie, is this the South London Grand Prix or what?" Paula yelled as the car just made a junction before the lights turned red.

"You're the one who's been going on about seeing Basil Nastilove."

"I don't want to see him ... but we'll end up in the morgue at this rate anyway," Paula countered.

"Or the local nick," Nancy added.

Then it looked as though Ronnie was going to miss a turning. "Take this road on the left," Kim instructed, and she took the corner in fourth gear.

Paula, Nancy and Dawn got thrown across the back seat.

"Ronnie!" Dawn screeched, thinking of the danger to her unborn child.

"Is my driving making you nervous?" Ronnie asked, all innocence and virtue.

"No, but I think maybe the view's different on your

side," Kim said, gripping the dashboard.

An hour later, Nancy was on her last cigarette.

"It's not her fault the petrol gauge is busted," Dawn said in Ronnie's defence.

Kim swivelled round in the passenger seat. "But we're going to miss it!"

"Who's hen night is this? Yours or Paula's?" Nancy snapped.

Paula stuck her head out of the window. She could see Ronnie in the distance, trudging back with a can of petrol. It was lucky they'd been near a petrol station when the car had broken down. A bit unlucky to be on a busy major road, mind.

"Here you go," Ronnie said when she reached the car. She opened the back door and tossed a pack of cigarettes at Nancy. Then she gave the others a hapless smile. "I'm sorry about this. Some hen night, eh?"

Paula shrugged her shoulders. "Don't stress yourself." The others exchanged glances. They had never seen her so mellow.

Ronnie opened the petrol cap and poured in the contents of the can. Then she jumped back into the car.

"At last!" Nancy said.

Ronnie turned the ignition but nothing happened. She tried again. Dead. Nancy swore. Ronnie tried three more times, but nothing.

"It does this sometimes," Ronnie said, opening her door.

"Where you going?" Kim asked.

"Well, it's like this: if we rock the car it might get going."

"What d'you mean 'rock'?" Dawn leaned forward.

"Just rock it from side to side."

Nancy got out the car. "She's keen!" Paula giggled. But Nancy started to walk away.

Ronnie called out, "Where you going?"

137

"I'm calling a cab."

Everyone got out of the car.

"There's no cab office round here," Dawn told her.

Nancy put out her cigarette and stomped back. "I know 'nuff people round here, you know. I used to live here with Trevor." She spoke his name with emphasis, but none of them could remember who the hell he was. "Anyhow, any of them see me …"

"I ain't taking no cab. I've got all my records in the boot." Ronnie was doing a stint at a happening place — Club Uproar — later on.

So in the end, Ronnie and Paula stood on one side and Nancy and Kim stood on the other. Together they rocked the car from side to side about four times, while Dawn stood nearby, thanking her lucky stars she was pregnant and therefore exonerated from this shameful episode. They had cars tooting at them and guys stopping to look, wolf-whistles, the lot. But none of the bastards offered to help.

Then, after what seemed an eternity, Ronnie decided to try starting it again. This time the car spluttered into life. At last they were on their way again.

But when they finally arrived at the venue it was choc-a-bloc with cars.

"Where am I going to park?" Ronnie wailed.

"Let us out here, then find a scrapyard." Nancy was still vexed from the car-rocking session.

"You can be a moody cow sometimes," Ronnie chastised.

"I don't think you should bother parking anywhere," Dawn said. "Look."

Outside the club, a bouncer was arguing with a group of women. "Oh my stars!" Ronnie exclaimed. "Don't tell me it's full!"

"Yeah, but my girl Kim's got tickets right?" Nancy said.

"Sort of …" Kim said.

Everyone rounded on her. "What d'you mean, 'sort of'?" Nancy demanded.

"I didn't have time to come down and collect them, so I had some set aside. There shouldn't be a problem."

"You'd better hope not," Nancy snapped.

"I thought you didn't want to see him," Kim challenged.

"Listen, I got myself all dress up with somewhere to go. I don't care if it's Basil Nastilove or Zippo the clown, I want to be in the house."

So Ronnie double parked the car and everyone got out to see what was going on. The music and whistling coming from inside hinted at what was on offer.

They made their way to the front of the queue, ignoring the evil-eyed glares. "You've got to let us in, I booked in advance," Kim shouted out to the bouncer, trying without success to mask the desperation in her plea.

"Where's your tickets?" He grunted rather than used human speech.

Ronnie leaned close to Dawn and said, "Okay, there are probably some very articulate bouncers around somewhere, but how come you never come across them?"

Dawn, remembering the incident that had occurred at Freddie's, did not reply.

"It was a verbal booking," Kim was saying.

The bouncer held up his hands and shook his head. "It's a roadblock in there."

Paula shoved Kim out of the way and confronted the bemused bouncer. "But it's my hen night and I want some nasty lovin' from Basil."

"Lord Jesus, is that my uptight sister?" Dawn cackled.

The bouncer shrugged his shoulders. You could tell from his expression that there was no way he was going to let them in unless they all performed oral sex on him.

"So, what do we do now?" Paula demanded sulkily as she kicked a poster of Basil Nastilove in his g-string.

"Go home," the bouncer suggested. "And kick that again and you'll be sorry."

"This is all your fault," Nancy snarled at Kim. "You

should've booked properly."

"It's my fault; my car broke down." Ronnie jangled her car keys. "Step aside, ladies. Let me chat to the man, see if I don't get us a squeeze,'

And Ronnie could get a squeeze from an iron sponge.

Basil Nastilove had been born Winthrop Norman Basil thirty-five years previously, but he had been aged a perpetual twenty-nine for the three years since he'd started his troupe. He kept his body honed and trim, a habit he'd acquired from his days as a professional footballer. The stripping and dancing had come at a time when his footballing career was going down. His girlfriend had gone to see the Chippendales with some friends, and had told him that he could do it better than them. So he gave it a try. Now, after three years, the girlfriend had become his wife and manager, and he was raking it in by taking off his clothes in front of craven women. He got a kick out of making them scream, as did his troupe members, the equally well-toned Romeo and Marco. Basil didn't feel threatened by the pair, who were respectively seven and nine years his junior. He knew that his prized possession, the one he took out at the climax of every show, was the biggest, blackest and finest in the country. And that was why the women craved him.

He watched Romeo and Marco doing their stuff from backstage. They were making a particularly good job tonight of warming up the women for him with their raunchy ragga routine.

They were almost done when Derek, the bouncer tapped him on the shoulder. "Check out a girl in a black catsuit with a blonde afro. Apparently she's up for anything."

Basil nodded. He hoped she was pretty.

Then the intro to his theme tune, Buju Banton's "Make My Day", came blasting out from the sound system. Cue

Basil Nastilove on stage, cape flapping to the tumultuous welcome from his female fans, just as Paula and her party, precariously carrying their drinks, were fighting their way through the horde of women to get a better vantage point.

"Jesus, he's done up like Superman," Kim remarked, taking in Basil Nastilove's black catsuit and gold cape.

"Check out the bulge, girls! Funny place to keep a beach ball, y'know what I'm saying?" Ronnie added.

"Ugh! He is nasty," Nancy remarked as Basil threw his cape into the eager crowd.

"That's his name, stupid," Dawn retorted, placing a protective hand across her stomach. Like the others, she was getting jostled on all sides by women desperate to catch his cape.

"No, I don't mean that kind of nasty. I mean he really is *nasty*. Nasty like genital herpes."

"You don't know a man when you see one, Nancy. If I didn't have Germaine I'd go for him up there," Paula declared. All she could see was six-two of nubian hunkdom.

"Dawn, whatever you put in her drink is working overtime, y'know what I'm saying?" Ronnie whispered.

Dawn nodded. Maybe she had overdone it with the vodka. "Ronnie, I've been meaning to ask. What did you say to that bouncer to get us in?"

"You'll see."

A woman old enough to be someone's grandmother caught the cape and waved it in the air like it was some kind of trophy.

"You get all ages in here," Dawn observed.

They watched the routine in silence for a while. In spite of themselves, Basil Nastilove had them as captivated as the rest of the audience. His hips seemed to have a mind of their own as he thrust them forwards, slowly peeling off his black catsuit to reveal a broad and hairy chest. At this point the crowd went really wild and there was a massive surge.

Nancy felt herself being shoved forwards. The spell had

been broken. "Oh, stuff this! I'm moving out of Crush City, man!"

She had just started to back away when a spotlight appeared from nowhere and began searching the packed hall. Regulars to the show — and there were many — knew that this was the moment when Mr Nastilove, now gyrating in just a g-string, invited a willing participant from the audience to help him remove it. Pandemonium broke out as women desperately sought to be selected, until finally the spotlight fell on Nancy, much to her surprise.

This feeling of surprise quickly transcended to shock, then to horror as it dawned on Nancy what was expected of her. She balked at the thought, and frantically considered how to find a way out of the situation.

But she didn't need one. Her hesitation was someone else's gain. She was shoved aside by another woman, and her eyes bulged when she realised who it was.

"My girl, you were rampant!" Nancy said for the hundredth time. Although it was almost midnight the heatwave was holding and it was still very warm outside. "You'd have had that thing in your mouth if he'd have let you!" She narrowed hers eyes. She couldn't quite form the image in her mind of Ronnie's uptight sister peeling off Basil Nastilove's g-string with her teeth.

Nancy didn't want to mention the fact that she was very impressed. After all, it was she who had the reputation for being wild and craven, and she didn't want to lose her title.

"I didn't know you had it in you, Paula," Kim chimed in.

"I thought I was going to go into premature labour," Dawn remarked.

Paula was unrepentant. "Hey, it's my hen night. I'm entitled to fun. I bet Germaine got up to worse. Ronnie, you told me what Cameron said about the strip place they went to." Although a little voice somewhere inside her head was telling her she'd acted outrageously, a much bigger voice told her not to give a damn. For the first time in living memory, Paula felt free — and, above that, she truly felt herself. Now she wanted more action. "So, where to next?"

The girls glanced at each other. Then Ronnie said, "Like I said before, I've got to deejay down Club Uproar. I was going to take just Nancy with me as I didn't reckon the rest of you would be up for it."

"Of course we are!" Paula declared. "Kim, your kids are round your mum's, aren't they?"

Kim nodded.

"No excuse then." Paula looked at her pregnant sister. "Dawn?"

Dawn felt a little tired but she reckoned she had a few more hours in her yet. Besides, she was worried about Paula. "Yeah I'm in." She linked her arm in Paula's. "Someone's got to keep an eye on you."

Ronnie's Citroen was parked outside what looked like a disused, dilapidated warehouse. You could hear the funky sounds drifting out from way back. There was a naff neon sign above the entrance, and a long, disorderly queue of trendy clubber types outside.

"This place is kicking," Ronnie enthused. "It's got three floors of music and a chill-out lounge."

Paula looked across at the club. She had never set foot in a place like it, but there was a first time for everything. "So, what are we waiting for?"

They got out of the car.

"We ain't going to get in. I mean, just look at the queue." Kim was shaking her head.

"Kim, I got us into Basil Nastilove. This place is a piece of Sara Lee. I'm the deejay, remember?" Ronnie, weighed down by her boxful of records, marched up to the front of the queue. The bouncers simply stepped aside and let them all file in. The people standing in the queue were none too pleased.

Inside, the place was ram and it was barely half past midnight. It was obvious that Ronnie and Nancy were among friends, judging by the amount of hugs and kisses they got from people milling about the entrance.

"How much, Ronnie?" Dawn asked, checking her purse for money.

"I beg you, do put your coffers away. It's free, babe," Ronnie announced. And sure enough, the stunning, Latin-looking girl who was taking money on the door waved them through.

Ronnie explained that she wouldn't be doing her stint until around two o'clock, so they could all bop together for a while. In her opinion, the best floor was the middle one. They had to clamber up a metal winding staircase to get to it. *Clank clank clank* went their shoes, then Dawn got one of her heels caught in a groove and launched into a lengthy cussing session.

Amazingly, Paula approved of Ronnie's choice, but that probably had more to do with her alcoholic consumption than her social preferences. The walls were sprayed with "The Right Groove", and a jazzy beat was playing when they walked in. But Dawn and Kim weren't too impressed. They liked their ragga. They immediately volunteered to get the drinks in.

A familiar funki-dred in a satin T-shirt and faded flares came up behind Ronnie and put his arms around her. She turned her head and kissed him on the cheek. He had to shout to make himself heard. "So, what's occurin'?"

"Ola, babe. Feelin' good feelin' wicked! Take my vinyls from me, will ya?" she hollered back.

"Who are you with?"

"Ola, you remember Paula ..."

He didn't, but he smiled at her appreciatively.

Paula blew him a kiss. "It's my hen night."

Ola's eyes grew round. "Really? Well we're gonna do our set soon, so stick around."

He took Ronnie's box of records and turned to Nancy to kiss her full on the lips. "Looking the business, Nance."

"He's got a nice arse," Nancy said as they watched him disappear into the crowd.

"And he couldn't take his eyes off you," Ronnie remarked.

"Treat 'em mean, keep 'em keen," Nancy laughed.

Paula was tapping her feet impatiently to the beat. "C'mon, let's get boppin'."

Nancy exchanged a bemused glance with Ronnie. "What she on? Cos whatever it is I want some," she shouted in her ear.

They had to push their way through the crowd to get on to the dance floor. Ronnie was a brilliant mover. Paula tried to copy her steps but found them difficult to follow, so she invented some of her own. She was like a woman newly released from prison, really strutting her stuff.

Nancy was impressed. "You're almost as good as Ronnie."

Normally that kind of remark would have offended Paula, but tonight nothing could mar her exuberant mood.

Kim and Dawn managed to find them a few minutes later. They were armed with bottles of beer (Paula had finally succumbed) and a glass of orange juice for Ronnie. They stopped in their tracks and stood, mouths agape, not quite believing the sight in front of them.

"Paula!" Dawn managed to utter.

Paula reached forward, grabbed hold of her arm and swung her about. Then a blonde next to them with long hair started tossing it in time to the beat and Kim got a faceful. Unusually for her she lost her temper. She cussed the girl down in patois, then turned to the others and said apologetically, "This ain't my kind of place. I think I'll catch a cab—"

"No chance! Just enjoy yourself, Kim. Get into the beat," Paula cajoled.

"I don't like this kind of music." She smoothed down her trousers. "And I look out of place. I mean, if I'd have known I'd have come in just my bra and knickers like everyone else."

"Kim, you sound just like my mum," Ronnie chided.

Then the record stopped and a familiar voice announced, "This one's for the girl in the white hotpants suit who's getting married tomorrow. *Que peña*!"

Ronnie, Nancy and Dawn squealed and pointed at Paula. Then it seemed like everyone else was staring at her as well. When she heard the wolf-whistling she wanted to die. Up in the deejay booth Michael Quinones was smiling at her while Ola started the record.

"What does *que peña* mean?" Dawn wanted to know.

"It's Spanish for 'what a pity'," Ronnie explained.

As it dawned on the crowd what the dedicated record was there were more wolf-whistles.

"What's this?" Paula asked Ronnie.

" 'Je t'aime'. You know, that song from the sixties with that French guy and Jane whatsername."

Never mind gyrating with Basil Nastilove, Paula couldn't have been more shamed up if she'd been standing there stark naked.

"The beat on this is the business," Ronnie continued. She started moving her body in a kind of winding motion, her skinny little hips jerking this way and that. Paula started chuckling, more out of nerves than anything else. Then it turned to laughter.

Ronnie took one of her hands and Dawn took the other and the three of them twisted from side to side in a semi-bogle style in time to the beat.

"You can see why that Michael's in demand," Dawn said to Paula, who glanced over at him.

He had a whole heap of women around him — in

demand all right, but it wasn't hard to see why. Those lazy good looks could be a heart-stopper. He was so different from Germaine. Not that her fiancé wasn't good-looking. He was — perhaps *too* good-looking. He had a very clean-cut look, close-shaven hair, no stubble in public, whereas Michael looked like he'd just got out of bed. Maybe he had.

Paula was so busy checking him out that she didn't realise the record had changed until she heard whoops of joy from Dawn and Kim. It was serious ragga time. They both got down and did their stuff; and if you thought the kind of crowd in that place wouldn't be into that you'd be wrong. Everyone got it on.

Pretty soon the place became even more packed and much, much hotter. And the girls were downing more bottles of beer except Ronnie, who'd changed from orange juice to mineral water. For someone who had recently cried off alcohol, Paula was getting merrier by the minute — in fact she was close to crossing the thin line that exists between being unsober and being drunk. It wasn't long before she felt that if she didn't get some air she'd pass out. She asked Ronnie where the loos were. Both Ronnie and Dawn offered to accompany her, but she could see that, like Kim and Nancy, they were well into the music. So she insisted they stay put.

It was roadblock in the toilets. Paula could hardly get through the door. And once she did, she couldn't get close to a mirror. Some of the girls seemed well out of it, others were doing repair jobs on their faces.

A girl moved aside and Paula managed to catch a glimpse of herself in the mirror. She looked like she'd just come out of a sauna; the sweat was dripping off her. There was an automatic hand drier fixed to the wall, with an adjustable nozzle you could set to cool your face. As soon as it was free Paula made a dive for it. She closed her eyes as it blasted her face with the nearest thing to fresh air she could get.

She would have stayed under there a good while longer if it hadn't been for the bad vibes she was getting. Sure enough, when she turned round there was a sea of hostile faces all waiting their turn.

"D'you reckon that air's fresh?" one girl asked her friend.

"No, it's recycled," Paula told her as she walked away.

She emerged from the toilets smirking at her own joke and walked straight into Michael. Even though it was hot and sweaty, he smelt of Polo. (Despite her attempts to change him, Germaine only wore Giorgio.)

"Did you follow me?"

Of course he had. He smiled at her — that beautiful smile. So she smiled back. He didn't move or say anything, so she went to sidestep him. But he blocked her way by putting his arm up against the wall. She made to duck under it, and he held her gently but firmly by the wrist.

"I want to talk to you."

"Shouldn't you be back there spinning your tunes?"

"We've finished for now."

Next thing she knew he was steering her towards a door by the stairs, marked 'Private'.

"Where are we going?"

"You scared?"

She thought about it for a second and decided that she wasn't. So she shook her head.

"Good." He nodded in approval, like she had passed some kind of test, then propelled her through the door. They went down some more stairs, wooden this time, and arrived at yet another door. This one was marked 'Members Only'. Michael pushed it open and led her inside.

It was a smoke-filled room, neither big nor small, and was almost like somebody's front room: soft lights, people lounging around on couches and large cushions, mellow soul music playing in the background. This was definitely the 'chill out' room, and you had to be cool to get in here.

But being cool was no problem for Michael Quinones. He was greeted with smiles and nods all round as soon as he walked in.

He nodded at a space in the corner with some piled up cushions, and motioned for her to sit down. Paula obliged, crossing her legs yoga style.

"D'you want a drink?" he asked.

Paula scanned the room for a bar. There wasn't one, but there was a fridge on the other side of the room. "I'll have whatever you're having."

She watched him saunter across the room, bend down and take out two bottles of beer. There was a bottle opener on top of the fridge, and she watched him open them. In all her years she had never seen someone carry out that function quite so sexily.

He strolled back and handed her a beer before slumping down next to her. "Cheers," he said, clinking her bottle with his.

"Yeah, cheers."

She watched him as he took a gulp. He had a big Adam's apple, and she took in the way it bobbed up and down as he swallowed. The whole thing seemed unreal, as if she were outside her own body watching herself. Hastily she gulped down some beer.

"So, talk to me," he said softly.

Paula grimaced. She was tongue-tied, having difficulty in thinking straight. It could have been because of the beer. Or it was the way Michael was rubbing the tip of the beer bottle against his bottom lip. She took a deep breath and said, "I'm getting married tomorrow."

Michael let out a low, dirty laugh.

"What's so funny?"

"That's obvious." He looked her up and down appreciatively, making her cheeks burn. "What are you doing in here with me?" he continued, his deep brown eyes penetrating hers.

149

Paula took another sip of beer and, even though she felt all hot inside, said coolly, "I'm just chatting."

"For now ..."

He made a slight movement towards her and she shifted away from him a little.

"So, how did you get into deejaying?"

"You won't be able to avoid the inevitable by changing the subject."

She bit her lip. "I think I will. Anyway, I'm interested in what you do."

"It's like this ..." He rolled the beer bottle around his lips again. "You're in front of a crowd. They can't see you, but you're responsible for their pleasure. You have to know what they want and when to play it. If you play the wrong tune it's like a cold shower. If you play a killer tune too soon it happens too fast. You have to build it up. Slowly. Get them in the mood. Each tune has to be better than the last, so that you make the people so excited that they scream. But people can't keep that emotion for ever — it's too exhausting — so you have to bring them down again, just as slowly as you got them going. But you make it so that, any time you want to bring them up to that highest level again, it's still possible."

His words hung irresistibly in the air like a long-promised orgasm. They were sitting real close, their legs touching. Paula glanced around the room. A couple on a nearby couch were snogging away. She took a swig of beer. It was no good. She was gone on this guy. She remembered what Nancy had said about meeting a man who has such an impact on you that you want to shag him senseless there and then.

Some beer had trickled down her chin. Michael reached out and wiped it away with his finger. Then, just as he opened his mouth, all set to do something with hers, Ola burst into the room.

"Michael, man! We're on!"

It was two in the morning. The chill-out room was the only sanctuary in a club which was otherwise ram. Ronnie was chatting happily away to Michael Quinones. She had gone down a storm during her stint, impressing everyone with her selections, and consequently she had a pocketful of business cards and a number of deals in the pipeline. Her mix of Marvellous Lee's "One and Only" had nearly brought the roof down. People left, right and centre were telling her to get it on vinyl before somebody else did. And Michael had the contacts. He was her hope.

Nancy had made Ola's dreams come true, and was now snogging him in a corner. Dawn and Kim were crashed out side by side on the sofa.

Paula had decided to go and dance, find the moves that would help her get Michael Quinones out of her head. She slipped away without anyone noticing. Almost.

She went down to the basement this time. It was much smaller than the middle floor, but less packed. The music was hardcore hip-hop. A couple of guys who'd drunk too much Canei noticed her stroll in alone and thought their numbers had come up. Maybe guys was not the right word — they couldn't have been more than seventeen. Anyway, they latched on to her, tongues hanging out ready to catch a fly if one came their way.

"Where you from, babes?" asked the smaller of the two, with more gold in his teeth than had been dredged up during the California gold rush.

Paula wanted to dance unhindered. "The People's Republic of Mind Your Own Business."

They didn't take the hint. "Check her. She thinks she's Janet Jackson!" said the other one, a boy so thin he'd probably need paperweights to hold him down on a breezy day.

Gold Teeth grinned. "Yeah, she's like Janet Jackson all

right — Janet's backside, that is!"

"Look, just leave me alone."

"You don't wan' that really, sweetness. You want a piece of us, innit?" Thin Boy said, touching her arm.

"I'm not into bestiality."

Her aggressors looked blank.

"You'll find it in the dictionary under B. It means doing unnatural things with animals. I ain't into that."

Paula looked about her. As no one seemed interested in helping her out, she left the floor.

But the little gits followed her out. "Hear her!" Gold Teeth snarled. "You shouldn't have worn that little t'ing you got on. You ain't got the tits for it, guy!"

Then someone said, "I don't think that's true."

Michael Quinones was standing there, looking very relaxed and sure of himself, but something about his stance hinted that he was ready to use force if he had to.

Paula's two admirers kissed their teeth and sauntered off back into the basement dance floor, knowing when they were beaten, and Michael flashed Paula a brilliant smile that made his eyes twinkle.

Dawn stretched and yawned on the sofa. She gazed around: Kim was snoring gently beside her; Ronnie was lying on some cushions a few feet away, chatting away to the gorgeous Latino girl who had been taking money on the door.

"Ronnie, where's Paula?" Dawn asked, rubbing her eyes.

Ronnie looked up. "I dunno."

"Oo's Pawla?" asked the girl, who in fact wasn't Latin at all: her name was Tracey MacFarlane, she hailed from Plumstead and she had the dialect to prove it. Her dark hue was down to mammoth tanning sessions at a south-east London beauty salon.

"Our sister. The one who was sitting on the couch

earlier."

"Wha' — in the wickid 'ot pance?" Tracey said. "I saw 'er go off 'bout ten minutes ago."

"Where's Michael?"

"He wen' off an' all," Tracey replied helpfully.

Dawn buried her head in her hands. "Oh God. What have I done?"

Ronnie crawled over to her. "Maybe you've done her a favour."

Dawn stared at her. "How'd you work that one out?"

"Look, I always knew that inside that stuffy, uptight body of hers there was a real human being fighting to come out. Well, girl, maybe you just released it."

"I didn't — the alcohol did."

Ronnie took Dawn's hands and squeezed them. "Dawn, I really like the Paula we've got here tonight. I wish she could stay that way."

"Great — so you want her to be an alcoholic." Dawn shook off Ronnie's grip.

"Don't talk soft! I'm just saying I thought the change in her tonight was a definite improvement on the old model, y'know what I'm saying?"

"Yeah, well, a person should make their changes when they're stone-cold sober, not tanked up like she was."

Dawn struggled off the couch and began to pick her way through the people between her and the door.

"Where you going, girl?"

"Where d'you think?"

Ronnie scrambled to her feet and hurried over to her sister. "Wait! Wait. Listen, you ever heard of kismet?"

"Yeah, he had an album out on the Greensleeves label a few years back."

"I'm serious, Dawn. Hear me out. Maybe this is P's destiny. It's like she's not going to make a huge mistake and get married."

"Ronnie, a lot of people thought Cameron was making a

huge mistake by marrying you. How would you have felt if someone had prevented you from becoming his wife? Would that have been kismet?"

Ronnie had no answer for that.

"You'd better wake Kim up," Dawn advised before leaving the chill-out room.

THE WEDDING DRESS WAS LAID OUT on Shirley's bed. It was pure off-white silk, with tiny pearl buttons running down the back and sleeves reminiscent of upside-down thin-stemmed crystal glasses, and it flowed out from the waist right down to the floor. Paula picked it up and, with the greatest care, stepped into it. She drew in a breath when she saw herself in the mirror.

"So, did they or didn't they? Like my man Hamlet says, that is the question and me wan' know de answer."

Ronnie was standing behind Dawn in the kitchen, preparing to tong the back of her sister's hair. They were both wearing their bridesmaid's dresses.

"You've taken liberties with the quote, Ronnie, but I hear what you're saying. And since you're asking I reckon they did." Dawn thought of the embrace Paula and Michael had been locked in when she'd found them near the basement bar at Club Uproar.

"Nah, babes. According to my girl Nancy, if they had we would've heard Paula's orgasmic screams all over the club."

"How come Nancy knows?"

"Not from personal knowledge, though the girl tried from time. No, she got chatting to one of his former bedmates."

"Bedmates! I might've known he had a harem," Dawn

155

said, shaking her head. "Oh God, if they did do it I hope they used a condom."

Ronnie paused to style a perfect curl. "Listen, girl, the CK didn't go down — and I'm talking carnal knowledge here, not Calvin Klein, you know what I'm saying?"

"How can you be so sure? It was ages before we reached." Dawn winced as the tongs lanced her neck. "Ouch, Ronnie! Watch it with them tongs, man!"

"If you stopped wriggling about ... My stars, the worse person to style hair for is a hairdresser."

"I should've got Latifah to do it."

"Yeah, and you would've had initials carved into your head, my dear." Ronnie started to tong another section of Dawn's hair. "Like I said, I don't think nothing went down. Besides, I rang Michael."

Dawn's mouth fell open. "What — you phoned and asked him? When?"

"When you was doing Paula's hair. He told me nothing went down, they just talked, and I believe him."

"Yeah, right. What else?"

"He said he hoped everything'll go all right."

"That's all?"

"Well what else is there to say? It's between him and Paula now anyway. In fact it's dead and buried. A last-night-before-loss-of-freedom kind of thing. He's off to the States tomorrow."

"Maybe Paula should have second thoughts about this wedding." Dawn brushed a lock of hair away from her face and picked up a mirror from the table. "You're doing it all wrong!"

"I'm doing it how you wanted!"

"Ronnie, if I'd wanted a bird's nest I'd have climbed up a tree and got one!"

Dawn pointed to the photograph she had ripped out of the Spring/Summer edition of *Black Hair & Beauty* magazine. Ronnie groaned and began to redo the curl she had just finished.

"You want to know something else?" Dawn said. "Tony reckons that Germaine's gym trips are just a cover."

"For what? Him got another t'ing going?"

"What d'you think?"

"Oh, I don't know. Why'd Tony get that idea?"

"At the stag do, Germaine—" She stopped short as Shirley marched into the kitchen from the front room, pulling a weeping Jhelisa behind her.

"Ronnie, deal with your pickney!"

Jhelisa ran over to her mother and wrapped herself around her legs.

"What's wrong, darlin'?"

"Granny said she'd cut off all my hair," Jhelisa wailed.

"No, I said I'd cut it off if you didn't sit still."

"You were hurting me!"

Shirley kissed her teeth. She had yet to dress, let alone do her own hair.

Ronnie squeezed Jhelisa's shoulder with her free hand. "D'you want Mummy to do your hair when she's finished doing Auntie Dawn's?"

Jhelisa screwed up her nose and shook her head. "I want Auntie Dawn to do it."

Ronnie rolled her eyes as Dawn chuckled and the doorbell rang. "I'll get it," Shirley offered, seeing as she was the most able.

It was Aunt Delia. She bounded into the room followed by Shirley. "Look what I got you girls!" she beamed, reaching into a Marks & Spencer carrier bag. She pulled out two floral coronets and a smaller one intended for Jhelisa.

Ronnie groaned. "I can't be doing with that, Aunt D."

"And why not?" Shirley demanded.

"I'm allergic to anything naff."

"What d'you mean by naff?" Aunt Delia had never heard of the word.

"Don't worry about it, Delia. Ronnie will wear it,"

Shirley said.

Delia placed the coronets on the table, then bent down in front of Jhelisa. "Give me a twirl, precious."

Jhelisa obliged without hesitation. She adored her peach satin dress. It was just like being a grown-up.

"You look wonderful, precious!" Delia said, clapping her hands. She rose and addressed the older bridesmaids. "How do you two feel in your dresses?"

"Mine's a bit loose round the waist," Ronnie admitted.

"You lost weight since the last fitting? Heh, but you's so maaga anyhow."

"And mine's a little on the tight side," Dawn confessed.

"An' you was complaining before that it was too big!"

"Yeah, but how was I to know I'd get as big as this in my seventh month?"

"And you, Shirley? You going to church in your housecoat?"

"Don't mind me," Shirley said as she checked the teapot. "Lord! Is this a brew or a stew?"

"You're better off chucking that out, mum. It's been there ages," Dawn advised, stifling a yawn.

"You look exhausted," Delia observed.

"They was out partying till six this morning," Shirley explained with disapproval in her voice.

"True?" Delia was surprised. "Must've been some hen night!"

Ronnie tapped Dawn's head with a comb as if in agreement.

"So, where's the bride?"

"Getting dressed," Ronnie replied.

"What? None of you's helping her?" Delia cried.

"She said she wanted it that way," Shirley explained. She had been a little hurt when Paula had insisted on being alone while she put on her dress.

Delia, however, was never one to take a hint. "I'm going to go and check everything's all right."

But she didn't need to, because at that moment they heard Paula coming down the stairs. Seconds later she walked into the kitchen, complete with veil.

Everybody gasped. For a few seconds no one spoke a word, until a choked Shirley said, "You look so beautiful, Paula." She blinked away a tear. "You know, if your daddy could see you now, getting married, he'd be so proud."

"The girl favour top model!" Delia remarked, causing giggles from Ronnie and Dawn.

"No, she favour me and a lickle piece of their father, like all me girls do."

"I couldn't do all the buttons at the back," Paula said.

Shirley was immediately upon her and doing up buttons. Her hands were shaking. "You know it was a real scandal when me and your father got together. People didn't know what a young girl like me could see in a man of forty-t'ree, married and him head big like a wharf dog."

"Yes, sir. Him a heinous creature, but kind," Delia added softly.

Shirley gave her cousin a funny look, then continued. "Anyway, he divorced his wife for me and there was a lot of bitterness. She couldn't have pickney ... That's why we came to the UK, to get away from all the aggravation and start a new life here, with all the opportunities and that.

"But, you know, your father was a big old deputy headmaster back in Kingston, and when we came here he could only get work as a bus conductor on the number fifty-two!"

"Within five years him dead," Delia said, shaking her head. "You know, I never use that bus route, out of respec'."

"Aunt D, you live out in East London, the fifty-two don't go nowhere near you," Ronnie pointed out.

"Yes, but it's the t'ought that counts," Delia said solemnly. "Anyway, hush up an' listen to your mother."

Shirley had done up the last of Paula's buttons. "Yes, Ronnie, you were five, Paula you were barely t'ree, and I was t'ree months gone with Dawn. The doctors said it was a heart attack that kill him. But I know it weren't no heart attack, it was heartache. Heartache and shame. And his family back home said him brought it 'pon himself. I had to use what savings we had for his body to be sent back for burial. God rest his soul. Since then I been struggling to make ends meet working for the council."

Her daughters had been listening to the story intently. Shirley didn't usually like to talk about their father, but today was an emotional occasion. And now that she had finished telling them about him, none of them knew what to say.

It was Jhelisa who broke the ice. "Auntie Paula looks like a princess. I want to look like that one day."

Paula motioned her to come forward, then bent down and kissed her.

Delia studied her movements. "D'you t'ink I did the adjustments right, Paula?" She pulled the back of the dress tight, causing Paula's stomach to heave slightly.

Shirley frowned at her. "Are you all right?"

"I'm okay. Just feeling a little queasy, that's all," and she gave them a fake smile that they all knew was not genuine.

"It's nerves," Dawn stated, knowing that Paula was badly hung over. She had no idea what else her sister was feeling, because while she'd been styling her hair into an elegant chignon Paula had talked about everything but the night before.

Ronnie nodded. "You know what I'm saying? I was sick for a week before my wedding, remember?"

"Yes, but that was morning sickness," Shirley pointed out as she smoothed out the creases she imagined on Paula's dress.

Then Mariah Carey came on the radio.

"I love this song. Turn it up, Mum," Paula requested, tapping her feet to the rhythm.

Shirley pushed the fader up on the radio and "Dream

Lover" blasted out on almost full volume. Soon the kitchen was filled with the sound of everyone singing along to the tune, Paula's voice ringing out the loudest.

Germaine pulled up outside the terraced house in Norwood. He had told his parents he was getting ready by himself at the flat. But he wasn't in his morning suit, he was wearing jeans and a T-shirt.

It had taken him almost an hour to get here, thanks to the crosstown traffic. Now he was sitting outside and sweating — not because of the hot sun threatening yet another scorching day, but because of the decision he was about to make.

He took a deep breath, got out of the car, and ambled up the path to the door. He took another deep breath before he rang the bell, then took a step backwards and waited.

It was a quarter to one, and Pastor Duchess was surveying his church. It was just how he liked it — full — however, he recognised only a few of the parishioners. The rest were outsiders, the "sometimish" people who saw the inside of a church very occasionally, the kind who went to church only when there was the promise of nourishment afterwards, be it a christening, a wedding or a funeral ... the kind of people who knew how to hog table. There was a parable about it somewhere. Pastor Duchess couldn't recall it word for word, but it was something like "Them who hog table have no manners them ..." That was the gist of it. Pastor Duchess liked to translate the teachings of the bible into a language his parishoners would understand — in fact, he often thought he should receive one of those Plain English awards the government was always on about.

He glanced at his watch again. The service was due to start at one, but there was still no sign of the groom. Pastor

Duchess frowned. If there was one thing he hated it was lateness.

He stepped down from his pulpit and walked towards the front pew, where Cameron and Tony were chatting. "So, where's the groom?" he demanded.

"I've got no idea, Rev," Tony replied.

"Pastor, if you don't mind." He addressed them in his most authoritive voice. "Your women are the bridesmaids, right? Well they should be here. And the best man — where is he? *Who* is he? He wasn't at the rehearsal."

Cameron started to explain. "They wouldn't release him until today—"

"You mean he is a convict?" the pastor asked in surprise. Not that he had anything against the fallen — anyone could be saved in his church.

"No, he's in hospital. Broke his leg playing football a week ago. But he should be coming, Germaine's picking him up."

"As I said, I can't abide tardiness."

"Yeah, but we ain't on Greenwich Mean Time no more. It's Black People Mean Time, innit?" Tony grinned.

Pastor Duchess was not amused. "The Lord said if one is truly pious, one is hardly tardy to the House of God, and—"

He was cut short not only by Cameron's and Tony's laughter, but also by the sight of Shirley and Delia rushing down the aisle. Pastor Duchess appreciated the effort both women had made with their pretty hats and flouncy dresses, but that was as far as it went for him. He looked, but never touched — he was a true man of God. Besides, his wife would kill him if he did more than look. Nevertheless it was hard to believe that Shirley had never remarried after her Evan had been called upstairs all those years ago.

"Pastor, Paula'll be here soon ..." Shirley's voice trailed off when she saw the empty spaces in the front pew. "Where the hell is Germaine?"

Pastor Duchess gave her a sharp look for her blasphemous language, but Shirley didn't pay any attention. She needed to know what was going on.

Germaine stood in the middle of the living room and stared at the photograph on the mantelpiece: a young woman cradling her twins.

Kim walked in, carrying two mugs of tea. Germaine waited until she had set them on the table, then grabbed her by the waist and pulled her towards him.

"Germaine!"

But he covered her lips with his. They stayed locked together like that for what seemed like an age but was in reality just a few seconds. Then Kim pulled away from him slightly.

"It's not too late to change your mind," she said. "You could still make it to the church."

"No, Kim. Like I've told you, my mind's made up. I'm not going to marry Paula. If I did, I'd be making the biggest mistake of my life, her life, and yours."

Kim shuddered. The impact of his words both terrified and excited her. She had almost fainted when he'd appeared on her doorstep. Throughout their five-month affair she had never allowed herself to think of him not marrying Paula. And each time they had made love she'd promised herself it would be the last. But there was always a next time.

When he had phoned her during his stag night wanting to come round she had wanted to be strong and firm and say no, but she hadn't been able to; she needed him too much. When he hadn't shown up she had felt a mixture of relief and disappointment. He was going to marry Paula and that was that.

It had made going to Paula's hen night that little bit easier. Of course she had felt guilty, but she was able to put on a front. Even so she'd felt a pain so deep that sometimes during that night she wondered whether she could stand it. It only eased when it evolved that Paula had gone off with someone else — a deejay.

"Are the twins asleep?" Germaine whispered in her ear.

She nodded. Marlon and Monique had been up and about since she had collected them from her mother's first thing that morning. Then Germaine had arrived and they had been all over him. Germaine loved playing with them, but it had been difficult talking to their mother while they were around. He was glad that now there was peace and quiet.

"I want you to come away with me."

"Germaine, we've been through this. It's impossible. There's the kids ..."

"I want all of you to come with me."

Kim moved away from him and leaned against the wall. "Where would we go? And what about Paula?"

"Paula doesn't want me, she wants the status. That's what she's always wanted, that's why she picked me out."

"Germaine, that's not fair! She loves you."

"We both know that's not true."

They were silent for a few seconds. In her mind, Kim went over Paula's hen night again. The way she had carried on with that deejay was hardly the behaviour of a woman deeply in love with the man she intended to marry. Even so, she didn't deserve the blow that Germaine was about to serve on her.

"You can't just not turn up. It's your wedding day!"

"I've written her a letter."

"I can't believe that! A letter?"

"It's the only way I can do it, Kim. In the letter I told her everything I've told you."

"I don't like to think of her at the church waiting for you. It's not right."

He strode across to her and pressed his forehead against hers. "Can you imagine how she'd be if I faced her?"

Kim's brief pause proved that she saw his point.

"Kim, right or wrong, I'm not marrying Paula. I want to be with you and the kids."

"Why?"

"Because I love you. I love the way you laugh, the way you talk, your gentle way, your eyes, the lashes, the way they curl up. I love the way you make me feel — like I've known you all my life. If you don't believe me I'll prove it and I'll keep on proving it. Come with me, Kim, let me show you how much I love you.

He kissed her, softly at first, then more urgently. Kim recalled how the affair had started. It was the night Conrad had invited a few of his friends round to watch a boxing match on the satellite TV. Kim hadn't even known who the fighters were, and she didn't care. The fact was, even though Conrad had walked out on her months earlier, he'd been using the house like he still lived there. Kim wouldn't have minded if it was because he'd wanted to see his kids, but no — it was to do his laundry (his bedsit didn't have a washing machine), to work on the car that was clogging up the driveway (his bedsit didn't have a drive), or to watch something on Sky Sports(his bedsit didn't have that either).

But that night Conrad had taken things too far. It was one thing for him to come round when he pleased, but another when he invited three or four of his friends around without warning her, let alone asking.

So Kim had gone up to the bedroom that she'd once shared with him and cried. Cried because she had been so stupid. Then someone had knocked at the door: Germaine, one of the invitees. He'd explained that Conrad had told him and the others that he would be babysitting for Kim the night of the big fight, that they could come round and watch it and keep him company at the same time. He'd said he felt terrible that it had all been a lie, and that he wanted to leave there and then. But Kim had asked him to stay.

After the fight Conrad and the others had left, leaving

the place a pig-sty. Germaine had stayed behind to help her clear up. One thing had led to another, and he'd kissed her. At first Kim hadn't known whether it was out of pity or lust. Maybe it was a mixture of both — but by the time he'd led her to the bedroom she'd no longer cared — about anything, not even Paula, her best friend. All she'd known was that with Germaine she didn't feel fat, she didn't feel plain, she just felt loved.

He'd spent the night with her, and the next morning they'd both agreed it had been a mistake and sworn never to repeat it. But deep down both of them had known that it hadn't been a mistake and it would be repeated. Over and over.

Germaine's voice brought her back to base. "Come with me, Kim," he pleaded softly as he began to unbutton her blouse.

Paula stood in the doorway of the small Pentecostal church, not able to believe her ears.

"How would you like me to break your other leg?" she snarled at the young black man, his right leg in plaster up to his thigh.

Christan Paul, Germaine's best man, shrugged his shoulders helplessly.

"I'm telling you the truth. I phoned his parents earlier and they said he'd left ages ago. He was supposed to pick me up, but when he didn't show I thought I'd make my own way down. I'm going to kill him, though. You ever tried hailing a cab when you've got a bruk-up leg? I mean, it's hard enough to hail one if you're black, but a black man on crutches — you're talking definite mugger," he said sarcastically. "I mean, you can just imagine it can't you? Tell me, how am I supposed to rob a cyab? Mash him with my stick? Take the money and hobble? Jeez, some people have too much imagination."

166

"Look, I'm not interested in your little problems. Just tell me — are they here?"

"Who?"

"His parents!" Paula practically screamed at him.

"No, they've not arrived."

"He must've had an accident," Paula concluded. "Yes, that's it. Let's ring round the hospitals. Maybe he's being operated on as we speak, maybe he's in the morgue—"

"Paula, calm down." Shirley had her arm around her.

"How can I calm down? He might be dead ... And if he isn't he will be soon!"

Ronnie and Dawn stood by her side, unable to think of anything to say. During the car ride Paula had been in the same high spirits as they all had. Driving through NW10 in a white Bentley, blasting out Dawn's Mary J. Blige tape, they'd almost lost their voices screeching along to "Be Happy".

Then they'd arrived at the church to find Shirley waiting outside. "Germaine's not arrived yet," were her words. Paula hadn't been worried — Germaine was often late — so the driver had taken them round the block.

Then they'd done it again, and then again. After the last circuit Paula had stomped out of the car, not caring about her dress getting creased or crushed. Dawn and Ronnie had eased themselves out, the hot weather making their dresses stick to their skin. Ronnie had pulled out Jhelisa, who'd needed the toilet desperately. Cameron had volunteered to take her, just in case Germaine turned up and Ronnie was needed. They could do without a flower girl, but not a bridesmaid.

"I don't believe this!" Paula wailed now. "What's happened to him?"

Pastor Duchess strode out from the church into the brilliant sunshine. "I'm sorry, but it's been forty minutes. I've got another wedding due at two ... Look, their guests have even started to arrive."

They followed his gaze to the people starting to pile out of their cars, all dressed up for a wedding. A different wedding.

Paula stood there trembling. She thought she would either burst into tears or scream her head off. Before she had even thought why, she dropped her bouquet of flowers and slowly removed her veil, throwing that down too.

She knew Germaine hadn't had an accident, just like she knew she wasn't going to have a wedding.

"Could someone take me home?"

Nobody knew what to say except Shirley.

"Tony and Dawn'll take you. We'll stay here to ..." Her voice trailed off, but everyone knew what she was about to say: "... tell everyone it's off."

Just as Dawn and Tony drove away with a dumbstruck Paula in the back seat, Germaine's parents pulled into the end of the narrow road now packed with cars. Mrs Valentine suggested to her husband that she should be the one to do the talking as she could keep calm in such situations, being a dental nurse and everything. Then, as they cruised past the church still looking for somewhere to park, their eyes fixed on the bouquet and veil in Shirley Smart's hands.

"Oh Lord!" Mrs Valentine sighed.

Paula looked long and hard at her watch. It was exactly seven hours twenty-eight minutes and twelve seconds since Germaine had jilted her.

Jilted.

The numbness was starting to wear off, and Paula sat up on the bed. She wasn't sure how she'd ended up here in her old room. She didn't even know who had undressed her and then dressed her in an old track suit. She couldn't remember any of it. It was Dawn's track suit, so it was probably Dawn who'd done all those things. People had been in and out of the room. Her mother — several times — Ronnie and Dawn, Delia ... Each of them had gabbled away, but Paula hadn't heard a word they'd said. They were just voices. The only time she had been alert was when her mum had told her that Mrs Valentine wanted to see her. Paula had refused point blank. She couldn't face it, couldn't face what she knew Mrs Valentine had to say. Her son had jilted her, but at that point Paula didn't want to know why.

She looked about her. This had been her room for practically all her life before she'd moved in with Germaine. Beneath her bed she had started collecting for her "bottom drawer": towels, cutlery, dinner sets ... It had got so she had more stuff under the bed than in the rest of her bedroom. But she had known when she met Germaine that things were going to be serious. He was the one.

She glanced at her watch again. It was now seven hours twenty-eight minutes and forty seconds since Germaine had jilted her. The reception would have been getting under way by now. She scratched her hair distractedly, and suddenly remembered that her workmates had showered her with confetti yesterday afternoon. It had taken her ages to get it all out of her hair. She didn't have that problem now.

A lump came to her throat, and she thought she felt tears but none came.

She could hear voices downstairs. They're all talking about me, she thought. She wanted to move but her body seemed reluctant to allow it. But she knew she couldn't hide away in this room for ever, so she literally pushed herself off the bed and padded softly out of the room.

She went downstairs, bracing herself for the reception she would receive when she walked into the kitchen. Sure enough, they all stopped talking when she entered. Her mother, her sisters, Delia ... Kim wasn't there, and that had surprised her. They were supposed to be best friends.

She was about to ask if she'd been round when her eye caught something else: outside, Jhelisa was playing football in the garden with Tony and Cameron like she didn't have a care in the world. And she didn't. Like the others, Jhelisa was no longer wearing her wedding outfit. It was almost as if nothing had ever happened.

"Sit down, Paula," her mother urged.

Paula shook her head.

She didn't want to sit or stand or do anything but maybe curl up and die somewhere, just like an animal does when it knows the end is near. Germaine had treated her like an animal, like a puppy given as a Christmas present then cast aside days later.

Her eyes fell to the table, and focused on the white envelope Dawn had been holding when she'd first entered the room.

"Is that for me?"

"Yeah, but—"

"Give it to me."

"Paula, maybe you should ... I don't know," Shirley sighed as Dawn handed Paula the letter.

"The Valentines left it," Ronnie explained.

There was general cussing from around the table, but Paula wasn't interested. She headed for the door.

"Where are you going?" her mum demanded, concern in her voice.

"To read my letter."

As Paula walked out of the room she heard the scrape of a chair followed by her mum saying, "I don't think she should be alone."

Then she heard Dawn reply, "Leave it for now, Mum. I think she still needs time on her own..."

She mounted the staircase, not taking her eyes off the envelope. It was clean and white and crisp. Germaine had written her name on the front in his neatest handwriting. On the landing she decided she couldn't wait till she got to her bedroom.

She ripped it open. Germaine's tidy script covered just

one page.

Paula,

I can only imagine your reaction when you read this letter. I've thought about what to write. In fact all I've done lately is think. I've thought about how wrong we are together, how miserable and depressed I've been.

I haven't been Germaine Valentine since I met you. I'm losing myself, and if I don't do something about it I'll be lost completely. I don't want that.

The one thing you couldn't give me, Paula, was the permission to be myself. Now I've met someone who can give me that. I expect that you'll hate me, and although I don't want that, I can live with it. But try not to hate Kim.

Neither of us intended this to happen. But it has.

Sorry.

Germaine.

Paula's eyes kept returning to the name of her best friend. She felt a painful sensation, like she had just been kicked in the stomach. Her head was whirling. Kim ... and Germaine?

Kim!

She leaned against the wall at the top of the stairs. Her mother's bedroom was opposite, and the door was ajar. She hadn't paid any attention to it when she had gone downstairs, but now it had her full attention. There, hanging up against the wardrobe, was her wedding dress.

Paula marched into the room. She went to the dressing table and in the second drawer found what she was looking for: a pair of scissors.

With deliberate but ferocious strokes she slashed the dress over and over. She didn't realise she'd been screaming until several pairs of arms relieved her of the scissors and restrained her on the bed. The wedding dress was still hanging on the wardrobe, but it was ripped to shreds.

RONNIE HAD JUST PUT a frozen Chicken Kiev in the oven when the doorbell rang. Jhelisa ran out of the living room, where she had been watching *EastEnders*, to answer it.

"Ask who it is first!" Ronnie reminded her.

She heard Jhelisa bellow, "Who is it?"

It was Nancy. Ronnie heard her daughter open the door, and seconds later both of them came bogling into the kitchen. Nancy had dyed her hair again. This time it was scarlet red.

"New style, Nance?"

"Flaming red because I'm feeling flaming good!"

"So, Nancy, it feels good to go almost a week with the same bloke, does it?" Ronnie laughed.

"Honestly, I know it's a cliché, but I never thought I could feel like this for someone." She clutched Ronnie's arm. "I'm in love. Really and truly, head over heels in love with Ola."

"Yeah, but he's been after you from time."

"I know, I know … but he was always like my kid brother. I mean, he's only twenty-five. I'm thirty-one this year."

"So he's your toy-boy. It's no big deal."

"I know. But this love thing's kind of weird, you know? Now, when I walk out of the supermarket, I not only have to remember if I've got all my shopping with me but my bloke as well!"

"Whoa! This sounds serious! You go shopping together?"

"Ronnie, he's moved in with me."

"Wow! We're talking fast moving Intercity train here!"

"I've known the guy for eight years."

"But you've only been *sleeping* with him since last week, y'know what I'm saying?"

Nancy pouted. "Be happy for me, Ron."

"I am, Nance. It's just that it's happened so quickly ..."

"Look, I simply got talking to the guy in Club Uproar, and for the first time what he was saying made sense. Normally with Ola you don't know what the hell he's talking about. But that night I did, and I still do. So please be happy for me, Ronnie. I mean, look at your sister — she'd been with Germaine all them years and look how it quickly it ended for her." Nancy cast a quick glance at Jhelisa, then looked back at Ronnie. "Speaking of which, I know you told me the deal over the phone, but I've got to hear it again. I can't believe he dissed Paula for that heifer Kim!"

"Sshh!" Ronnie warned her. She turned to Jhelisa and said, "Give Mummy and Auntie Nancy a kiss good night before you go to bed."

The little girl curled her lip. "Oh! I don't want to go, Mummy. I'm not tired. I want to wait up for Daddy."

"Daddy's working late tonight, peaches — much too late for you to stay up."

Jhelisa kissed and hugged Nancy, then did the same to her mother with a little reluctance.

"Now, now," Ronnie said. "Don't be like that with me. You've got playgroup tomorrow and it's past eight."

The youngster gave her a proper hug and kiss, then skipped out of the kitchen.

"So, Cam's going to be late back tonight?" Nancy asked with a twinkle in her eye.

"Yeah. So we can spliff and chill for a while."

Nancy giggled and tapped her bag, which made a clinking sound. "I've got some cherry brandy. It was s'posed to be for your sister's reception — which I was going to gatecrash, as I wasn't invited ... But anyway, that don't matter none seeing as what happened."

"Yeah, and I'll tell you about it. C'mon!"

Nancy glanced about the kitchen. It was a mess: the table hadn't been cleared of Ronnie and Jhelisa's plates and cups; the pot Ronnie had used to burn the rice and peas her mum had given her over a week ago was still in the sink, festering like a nuclear waste dump. "What about all this lot?"

Ronnie hustled her friend out of the kitchen. "It can wait, girl. The spliff can't."

"What I don't get is how Kim could come out on the hen night and that. I mean, that is *sick*. I know I've done some bad things in my time, but never something like that." Nancy paused to pass the spliff to Ronnie. "Could you imagine if I'd run off with Cameron on the day you was supposed to be marrying him?"

Ronnie inhaled the joint and exhaled real slow. "Nancy, you wouldn't be sitting here with your own set of teeth, girl, I can tell you."

"But Kim ... ! I mean, she's a bit dry in terms of style and that, but she's basically a nice girl, easygoing — a doormat, even. And she ain't even that pretty; she could definitely do with losing a few pounds. I mean, compared to Paula, she ain't even in the same league. So why did he do it?"

"Girl, it's the question we've all been asking, you know what I'm saying? It tells you something, though ..." Ronnie passed the spliff back. "Quiet people have their music on the inside."

"What d'you mean by that?" Nancy frowned as she inhaled.

"Apparently it's what my gran used to say — my mum's

mum. See, my dad was this quiet, respectable deputy headmaster, right? Married for almost twenty years, fine, upstanding member of the community and all that. Then — scandal! He starts having an affair with my mum, who's much younger and a real local beauty. All the men were after her." Ronnie paused to take a sip of orange juice. "See, everyone was shocked that my dad could've done something like that because of his taciturn nature, but according to my gran everyone has music going on."

"What d'you mean — music?"

"Music represents feelings, emotions and all that. Most people have it on the outside, like they're in an orchestra or something, but quiet people have it on the inside — until it comes out, and then it's like a Reggae and Soul weekender, big daddy speakers, call out the noise-control people from the council, you know what I'm saying?"

"So Kim's like your dad?"

"Yep, she's one of them quiet people. And, hey, I ain't dissin' my dad or nothing; without him running off with my mum, me and my sisters wouldn't be here, you know. Jhelisa wouldn't be here, Dawn's unborn baby and all that. But I sometimes wonder about his first wife. How did she feel when he left her?"

"Kind of like how Paula's feeling now." Nancy shook her head in disbelief.

They were silent for a while as they passed the spliff back and forth. "Hey, at least one good thing came out of the whole mess," Nancy said finally as she poured herself another glass of cherry brandy.

"What?" Ronnie stubbed out the spliff-end on a plate from St Lucia that Cameron's mother had given them one Christmas. It gave her a certain satisfaction to use it as an ashtray.

"You're going to be doing Club Uproar every Friday night."

Ronnie smiled. She had gone down a storm on Paula's

hen night, not only with the crowd but also with Terry Liston, one of the club's owners. Before they had gone on their hunt for Paula he had approached Ronnie and dropped the deal. And he had mentioned a possible regular Saturday-night spot at a new club he was opening down Camden way. "Yeah, things are happening for me."

"What about that Marvellous guy?"

"You wouldn't be chatting about my Cameron, would you?"

"No, the other Marvellous. Michael was chatting about getting him to do some vocals ..."

"Oh that." Ronnie said it like it was no big thing to be cutting a track in a studio. "I don't know where I put that damn card he gave me. How am I supposed to contact the guy? Normally I keep all my business cards together ... But Michael's not back till next Tuesday. I should've found it by then."

"It'll turn up." Nancy took a sip of her drink. "What did Cameron say when you told him about working Friday nights?"

"Nothing. I ain't told him yet."

"Ronnie, you know how stressed he gets with the hours you do now. Don't you think you should mention it? I mean, you start tomorrow."

"Jeez! Talk about changing your tune. What happened to 'Stuff the guy, do what you like'?"

"Hey, I'm in my first proper relationship, I'm learning how to be considerate and to think of the other person."

Ronnie laughed. "Roll up another spliff, darlin'!"

Nancy took out a little tin from her bag and opened it. She glanced up at the clock on the wall. It was twenty-five to nine. "Uh-oh! I've got to get off soon. I told Ola I'd be home by nine."

"Jeez! He's got you housetrained too. You've only been here five minutes! Stick around till Cameron comes and then I'll drop you. He shouldn't be long ..." and as she said the words there was the sound of keys clanking in the front door. Knowing Cameron's aversion to marijuana, Nancy hastily stashed her little box back into her bag.

It was a waste of time, though. As soon as he walked through the door and into the living room, Cameron was hit by the mingling odours of spliff and cherry brandy.

Ronnie leaped up and kissed him. "How are you, gorgeous?" She pinched his behind.

"You know I don't like you smoking that crap in here, not with Jhelisa around."

"She's in bed," Ronnie assured him.

"Hi, Cameron!" Nancy smiled her sweetest smile.

"Nancy," he replied grimly.

Then he turned heel and headed towards the kitchen.

Ronnie rolled her eyes at Nancy before following him.

"I suppose you don't like Nancy being here either." She was speaking to his back as he stood in the doorway, surveying the kitchen with a look of disgust.

"No. Especially not with Jhelisa around."

Ronnie squeezed past him. "Cameron, she's my best friend."

"She's a waste of space and a bad influence."

"You're talking to me like I'm Jhelisa."

"No, she's more mature." He opened the oven door and peered inside. "Is this supposed to be dinner?"

Ronnie joined him and looked at the dish on the middle tray. The Chicken Kiev had completely dried out. "At least it ain't burnt," she muttered.

Cameron didn't reply as he put on some oven gloves, removed the dish and chucked it in the bin. The bin was underneath the sink, so he got a good look at the burnt pot dumped in the washing-up bowl.

"Ronnie, I've got to go." Nancy had appeared in the doorway.

"Hold on, Nance," Ronnie said. Cameron was leaning against the sink. "Sweetness, you don't mind if I run Nancy home, do you? Leave all this mess. I'll sort it out when I get back. Oh, and I'll stop by the chippy and get you a portion and a pattie."

She pecked him on the cheek. "See ya."

"Yeah, laters Cameron." Nancy smiled.

By eleven o'clock Cameron had given up waiting for Ronnie to come home and had made himself a fried egg sandwich. He washed the plate and pan he had used, along with all the washing up Ronnie had left behind. He didn't even bother to phone Nancy's. He knew she was there and would be for a long time to come. Besides, she should be the one to call him. But then again things like that never occurred to Ronnie.

By quarter to midnight he was in bed. Some hours later he heard the front door being shut quietly. He looked at the clock on the night table. It was three-thirty.

When she came into the bedroom, Cameron rolled over on his side and made like he was asleep. He felt the bed dip, then her breath on his face as she checked to see if he was awake. Finally he heard her sigh, and shortly afterwards her gentle snores. He envied her. He wished he could fall asleep like that, but he knew that tonight, like many other nights, he wouldn't.

Dawn lay still on the examination table, squeezing Tony's hand as Jennie, the midwife, spread yellow liquid over her extended belly. She ran the scanner over the bulge, and Dawn and Tony looked at the screen in awe.

"There, you can see the baby's head … There's its legs," Jennie explained in her Aussie twang, pointing to various parts of the shadowy image. "Just perfect."

Tony grinned at Dawn. "He's looking good."

"*She* is, you mean." Dawn was certain she was going to

have a girl. "With boys you get fat all over, with girls it's just your belly, and that's how I am."

Tony frowned. "I thought it was the other way round."

"No … I'm right, Jennie, aren't I?"

"I'm staying out of this one, guys," Jennie laughed. The first time she'd met Dawn and Tony she'd had them down as a teenage couple. It had been a surprise to discover their real ages — just three or four years younger than herself. She liked the fact that Tony had attended all the ante-natal classes and all the scans. They were obviously into each other. All too often the mothers-to-be came on their own or with their mothers or friends, but rarely with the father of the child.

"Now, Tony, are you going to be at the birth?" Jennie teased, keeping her eyes on the screen.

"Of course he is!" Dawn cut in before he could reply.

"Yeah, but it's going to be gory isn't it? I mean, that film you showed us was …" Tony couldn't think of a strong enough adjective to express his repulsion.

"Don't be such a big girl's blouse!" Jennie laughed. "If you can watch *Silence of the Lambs* or *Seven*, you can watch a baby being born! Of course, having said that, my partner had to be drugged before he could face our little one being born." She saw the look of horror on Tony's face and laughed. "I'm having you on, love!"

She turned off the monitor. "Okay, now I'm going to check the baby's heartbeat."

"What's your baby called?" Dawn asked her as she placed the stethoscope on her belly.

Jennie paused to listen to the heartbeat. Then she smiled. "Beating just fine." She reached over to pick up a chart. "She's called Narelle."

"Never heard of that one," Tony remarked.

"It's quite popular in Oz," Jennie explained as she filled in the chart. "Now, we're going to get you cleaned up, Dawn, and then we'll have another sample of liquid gold from you."

Dawn screwed up her nose. She hated urine tests. "Look what I have to go through, Tony."

Tony stroked her hair.

"Any problems, Dawn? Swollen feet?"

"Yeah, but that's due to this heatwave. And I've got a bit of eczema on my back, but other than that everything's fine."

"Hmm, your ankles don't seem too bad," Jennie said as she examined Dawn's feet. "We can prescribe you a lotion for that, and cream for your eczema. As for the heatwave — there's not a lot we can do about that, I'm afraid. Personally I love it, it's even hotter here than it is in Sydney at the moment."

"For real?" Tony asked.

"Yeah. But then again it's winter down under." Jennie grinned. "Try and keep your feet up, and stay away from the carnival."

A few minutes later Dawn and Tony walked out of the hospital and into the bright sunshine, holding hands affectionately. They crossed the road and began to amble towards the car park.

"How's Paula?" Tony asked as he put on his shades.

"Same way. She's still at home," Dawn replied. She was glad she'd worn a sleeveless cotton dress; it was another scorcher of a day. The heatwave was definitely holding on.

Tony grunted. "Still no word from Germaine?"

Dawn shook her head. "Just that he's in Birmingham with Kim. Even with this bump I'd like to go up there and mash the two of 'em up, boy."

"What's Paula going to do?"

Dawn shrugged her shoulders. "It'll be a week tomorrow since it all happened. The girl ain't hardly left her room. She's not even been to the flat."

"That's rough, man, rough." Tony shook his head.

They strolled along in silence for a while. Then Tony

asked, "What d'you want to do now? We could go to the park for a bit."

"That'd be nice, but I've got to get back to the salon. I've got a week before my maternity leave, and Verna still ain't got no replacement for me."

She took out the bottle of lotion from the paper bag she was carrying. "My feet are killing me. I hope this stuff they gave me works."

"If you're feeling bad you shouldn't be working."

"I'm okay. Honestly, don't fuss so." She squeezed his hand. "You got nothing to do today?"

"Today, just like every other day," Tony sighed.

Dawn rested her head against his shoulder. They had almost reached the car.

"You know Claude went to Jamaica last night ..."

Dawn lifted her head. "What for?"

"What d'you mean 'what for'? He went for a holiday."

Dawn stopped dead in her tracks. "You sure he ain't running away from something?"

Tony carried on walking, but slowly. "It's just for a while, till things cool down some."

"Oh God! What's happened? Is that guy dead?"

Tony stopped and stared at her hard. "No! Nothing like that — he's still in hospital. It's just that Claude thinks someone may decide to go to the police and front up his name."

"For God's sake, Tony! Why didn't you tell me this before?"

"I didn't want to upset you before you had the scan done. I didn't want to spoil things."

"Tony, I hate things being kept from me! Now you *have* spoiled things."

Tony tried to put an arm around her, but she stepped out of his reach.

"What about Duane? Is he hiding away too?"

"No!"

"And what about you?"

"What about me? I ain't involved."

They began walking again but without holding hands.

"Tony, I don't like this, I really don't. What if someone decides to give your name?"

"But I wasn't involved."

"Yes you were. We both were. And we both know who did that guy in. We're withholding information. We could be accessories."

"Oh please, you've been watching too many cop shows, Dawn."

"Don't make fun of me, Tony."

"I ain't. But anyway, what kind of person would I be if I grassed up my own brother? Furthermore, you ain't supposed to testify against a relative in court."

"Now who's been watching too many cop shows?"

They had reached his car. Tony unlocked the door for Dawn, and with some difficulty she eased herself into the car. The seat was hot from the sun. She wound down the window.

"Claude asked me to do him a favour," Tony said as he got into the driver's seat.

Dawn was having difficulty getting the seat-belt around her bulge. "Why don't he do us all a favour and stay in Jamaica?"

"He's my brother, Dawn. I don't diss your sisters, regardless of what they do."

"Yeah, well, to my knowledge neither of them has put someone in intensive care." She thought of the Paula–Germaine–Kim triangle. "Well, not yet anyway. So what's this favour anyway?"

Tony turned the ignition. For a change it started first time. He wound down his window, carefully, so the handle didn't fall off. He'd been meaning to fix it.

"Well?"

"He wants me to look after his flat. I was thinking maybe

183

we could move in ..."

"What?"

Tony shifted the car into first gear. "Why not? It's going to be empty. He reckons he might not be back until Christmas."

Dawn let out a sarcastic laugh. "I ain't staying there, no way!"

"Dawn, what are we going to do when the baby arrives? Your mum won't let me in your house, there's too many people in mine. And the council and the housing associations ain't exactly falling over themselves with accommodation for us. How am I going to spend time with you and our baby?"

"We'll work something out. But I'm telling you, I ain't setting foot in that flat, Tony."

"But why not?"

"Your brother — and I'm sorry, but I'm going to have to diss him — is into all kinds of devious things."

"He ain't!"

"Drugs ..."

"Just grass—"

"Receiving and handling stolen goods ..."

"He didn't know that at the time."

"Tony, if one of my friends asked me to look after various makes of TV and video recorder — several at a time, without saying where they came from — I'd be a little suspicious."

"He thought they were Dixon's rejects."

"No — they were part of Operation Bumblebee," Dawn corrected. "And what about his guest appearance on *Crimewatch*?"

"That wasn't him! Half the black men in this country have been pulled up because they were allegedly seen on that programme. The police are always on our case, anyway. Two of my brothers are already inside. Besides, Claude's never been involved in credit card fraud!"

"Oh yeah, I forgot — he ain't into non-violent crime."

They had hit the main road, still busy with mid-morning traffic. Tony turned on the radio. Jazzy Jeff's "Summertime" filled the car.

"So, because of his so-called reputation, you won't move in?"

"Tony, I'm scared to move in."

He gave a snort of disbelief.

"I am! I don't care what you say, but he's into all sorts, your brother — and that means he's dealing with dodgy people, and not all of them'll know he's away. What if they come round and we're there — me pregnant, or after, with the baby?"

"You make it sound like he's a yardie or something."

" 'Or something' is right. And how d'you know this guy him and Duane done in don't have friends?"

"They'd have done something about it by now. It's been over five months."

"And the poor guy's still in hospital."

Tony wiped the sweat from his brow.

"Look, Dawn, I can see your reservations, but the way I see it we're between a rock and a hard place. It kills me to think we can't live together as a family once the baby's born." He glanced across at her. She was staring out of the window. "Dawn?"

She looked at him and gave an exasperated sigh. "Just take me to the salon, Tony."

Paula stared at her reflection in the bathroom mirror. She didn't like what she saw. Her complexion was dry and almost grey in colour. Her eyes were puffy and red from too many tears and insufficient sleep. Her hair looked like — and when she put her hand to it, felt like — straw. Neither her mother nor Dawn had told her she looked like crap, but she knew that's what they thought.

When Ronnie had come round two days ago (or was it three days? Paula's timing was way off base now) she had suggested that Paula do something about her appearance. It had been kind of like a pep talk. She'd even left her some Chanel nail varnish. Paula hadn't touched it.

Now, looking in the mirror, Paula saw herself for what she really was: a twenty-seven-year-old woman who'd thought she had it all but in reality had nothing. Everything in her life was just for show: her job, the flat ... hell, *definitely* her friends, judging by the behaviour of a certain fat bitch from the Midlands. And as for the man to whom she had given her all for so many years — he was simply a freak show.

She threw cold water on her face and dabbed it dry. Tiny specks appeared on the towel. She examined them more closely: it was her skin.

"Damn! Who's the freak?" she said to her reflection. "I'm not going down with this, no way!"

She turned on the bath taps and added some of Dawn's lemon bath oil. As the water ran, she washed and then exfoliated her face with some other stuff Dawn had left lying around. Then she brushed her teeth with the spare head of her mum's electric toothbrush. She eased herself into the bath and leaned back until the water came up to her neck. Then she relaxed. She had the house to herself. Shirley had gone to work and Dawn had an appointment at the ante-natal clinic. Paula assumed that, from there, Dawn too would go to work.

Closing her eyes, she began to think of the two things that had been occupying her mind since last Saturday. First there was Germaine. He had written in his letter that she'd made him miserable. That she'd stopped him from being himself. If that was the case, she dreaded to think what "being himself" entailed. When she'd met him he hadn't had a clue how to dress; he'd spent his money in Top Man, Burton's and C & A. She'd introduced him to Paul Smith,

Hugo Boss and Armani. During their relationship he had been promoted three times, because she'd encouraged him to go for it. She'd given him wider cultural tastes: Japanese and Thai food, *Carmen* at the Royal Opera House. His muscular, toned frame was down to her too. It was she who had encouraged him to join the gym; now he was fit enough to try out for *Gladiators*. It was she who had made their home beautiful and classy, with parqueted floors and Persian rugs, the antique bookcase they had bought from a shop in Camden Passage, the art deco fireplace, the mahogany kitchen. None of those things had been Germaine's idea.

And he couldn't have asked for a more in-shape woman. She worked out regularly to keep her body trim and toned. She had her hair kept in condition by one of the top black stylists (no offence to Dawn), her skin was in beautiful condition thanks to regular sessions at a West End salon, where she got her legs and underarms sadistically waxed too, so Germaine never had to brush against a stray body hair. Most of her clothes were designer, and she never wore tight jeans because she knew that, even for a size twelve, her backside was on the big side. And it wasn't just her looks. She had a 2.1 honors degree from Leeds University in Business & Finance, and was a qualified chartered accountant. She could talk about everything from Anita Baker's singing technique to the political, social and economical ramifications of a unified Germany ...

So why, oh why, had he humiliated, debased, degraded and demeaned her by jilting her at the altar for Kim?

Kim, of course, was the second thing that occupied her mind. Kim — who was so dry she should have a desert named after her. Kim, the woman who was a full six dress sizes bigger and hadn't changed her fashion since her teens. Kim, the woman who, even with a decent haircut and make-up, still resembled a hippo's backside. Kim, who was so weak and spineless that everyone treated her like a doormat. Especially Conrad, the dickless git she'd allowed herself to be impregnated by, and was eventually dumped by. Kim, with her whiny, nasal Brummie accent that irritated everyone after ten seconds of listening to it.

Why? If it had to be anyone, why her?

Paula banged her fist on the side of the bathtub. A letter wasn't good enough. She wanted some real answers.

She hauled herself out of the bath and reached to the side where Dawn kept her shampoo. She would wash and tong her hair, and then she would pay the lovebirds a little visit. She had been to where Kim lived before moving down to London. It wouldn't take more than an hour and a half to reach Birmingham. Maybe two hours, with one stop on the way.

The flat looked exactly as she had left it the morning after her hen party. There was a pile of letters on the floor. She gathered them up and checked through them. Most of them were bills, but there was one from the bank addressed to her. She opened it. It was a letter stating that, on condition she provided them with a marriage certificate, the bank would be delighted to change her account details to Ms Paula Smart Valentine.

Paula glowered at it for a second before crumpling it up and dumping it in the bin. Thank God she hadn't written to the tax office yet about her prospective change in status. She tossed the rest of the post on to the table in the living room and walked into the kitchen. Nothing had been touched.

But as soon as she entered the bedroom she knew instinctively that someone had recently been here. She was proved right when she slid open the closet door. Some of Germaine's clothes were gone, but most of them, mainly the designer suits and jackets, had been left hanging. It might have been Germaine, or maybe his parents; they had a key.

She checked the bathroom. His electric shaver had gone,

as had all his toiletries ... except the bottle of Ralph Lauren she'd bought him for Christmas and he'd never used. He'd claimed he was allergic to it. She now knew that his allergy wasn't due to the aftershave. She went back into the bedroom and wondered why he hadn't taken all his clothes. Well, she would save him the trouble of coming back for them.

She went into the kitchen again and rummaged through the drawer until she found a large pair of scissors. Then she set to work on his suits.

Fifteen minutes later she surveyed the bedroom floor. Every item of clothing Germaine had left now lay in tatters. She bundled the remains into three black bin liners ready to put in her car.

She would have started on his records and CDs, but decided to save that for her next therapy session.

She took off Dawn's track suit and put on a navy-blue halter-neck top and matching flares, throwing on a pair of navy buckskin trainers and a pair of shades. She gave herself the once over in the bedroom mirror. She knew she looked good. She wanted Germaine to know what he was missing when he saw her.

There was so little traffic that Paula was able to do a steady eighty m.p.h. all the way up the M1, (although sometimes she was closer to ninety). When she got on to the M6 the traffic was even lighter.

The windows were wound down and she had soul music blasting out in an attempt to keep her mind off her mission and on her driving. Before she knew it she had hit the outskirts of Birmingham and was following the signs to the city centre.

Paula had been to Birmingham on several occasions, mainly for work, when she would stay in one of the hotels in the middle of town. But her first visit had been for a social reason.

It was not long after she'd started at Stennard & Blake and had befriended Kim. Kim had been invited to a friend's wedding, and as Conrad couldn't be bothered to accompany her, Paula had offered. They'd stayed over at Kim's mum's place, a small terraced house in a suburban street, much like her own mother's. The wedding had been duller than dull, and the pair of them had sneaked off to a wine bar in the city centre and got blitzed — one of the few times Paula ever had. She laughed at the irony of it all. Here she was, again in Birmingham, again because of a wedding. But this time it was one that hadn't taken place.

During that first visit Paula had teased Kim about the city, calling it a dump, run-down and drab. But on subsequent visits she had seen that Birmingham was evolving. Now, driving through its centre, she could see that the place had not just changed, it had been transformed. There were statues and water fountains, snazzy new buildings and office blocks. It was lunchtime, and the streets were busy with workers and shoppers. There was a fresh feel to the place that Paula hadn't noticed when she'd visited the first time.

But Paula wasn't here to admire the architecture. She was on a mission, and had to get back on it.

It took her several wrong turns and a near collision with a double-decker bus before she found herself heading in the right direction. It was more through fortune than anything else that she found herself passing Birmingham City football ground. (It was even more fortunate that it wasn't a match day, otherwise the road would have been clogged up.) Kim's mum lived only minutes away, in Bordesley Green.

The Asian grocery stores she passed on the way reminded her of where she'd grown up in Harlesden. As she drove by the police station she dropped her speed from forty to thirty. Then, a little further on, she took a left turn, and seconds later she was pulling up outside the Oliver house. She sank down in her seat.

Paula didn't known how long she'd been sitting there, contemplating her next move, but it could only have been a few minutes before she saw a vision in her rear-view mirror that made her heart jump. A couple were strolling down the street. The woman was pushing a double buggy, and the man had his arm around her shoulders. They were laughing. Paula took a deep breath, counted to three, then stepped out of the car.

The pair, startled, stopped dead in their tracks.

"You make a lovely couple." Paula smiled, but her eyes were narrowed.

"What are you doing here?" Germaine asked with a steady voice. Kim could only stare in disbelief.

"I've come to make a delivery."

Germaine and Kim exchanged glances as Paula went round to the boot of the car and opened it. Out came the three black bin liners.

"You'll find your clothes in there, what's left of them."

Germaine and Kim looked at the bags. Sitting in their buggy, the twins did the same.

"Haven't you got anything to say for yourselves?"

Germaine and Kim exchanged glances again. Then Kim said, "Let's go inside and talk this through."

Paula glared at her.

"Oh, it speaks! Well, I tell you something. I ain't interested in your hospitality, friend. Whatever you've got to say you can say it out here. And I don't give a shit if your neighbours hear *WHAT A TEEFIN', DEVIOUS BITCHTRESS YOU ARE!*"

"Paula, cool it," Germaine said, his voice still steady. "Now, what I did — what *we* did — was wrong. But, like I said in the letter—"

"Yeah, you're a real poet laureate, Germaine." Paula kicked one of the bin liners and both twins jumped. Kim knelt beside them as if to protect them. "But a letter isn't good enough! You want to know what you put me through? What you put my family through? How am I supposed to face people at work after what you two have done? You bastards!"

She kicked another bag, sending it rolling a couple of paces. Out of the corner of her eye she saw a net curtain twitching.

"You two come strolling down the street, so in love, like you don't have a care in the world, like you don't care that my life's in tatters! I never knew — and I'm swallowing what pride I have left now — I never knew what it was like to feel suicidal ..."

She broke off, not trusting her ability to prevent the tears.

"Now you know how I've felt the last few months — no, years," Germaine said softly. Kim, still kneeling by her babies, glanced up at him.

"You? Suicidal?" Paula exclaimed. "Don't make me laugh! You couldn't have had it better, Germaine, and you know it. I did everything in my power to make you happy."

"No, you made yourself happy, not me."

"That's just bollocks!"

"Paula, listen to him—"

"You can shut your mouth, bitchtress! I ain't speaking to you ... yet."

Kim straightened up slowly.

Paula turned her attentions to Germaine again. "We had everything going for us, Germaine! Why'd you have to throw it all away?"

"What we had was *image*, Paula. We had material things. If those bags contain what I think they do, then they belong there. I would've thrown them in the bin myself if I'd had time. Everything we've done has been for image. Or should I say, *you've* done. And it's my fault, a lot of it, because I went along with it. I bought the designer gear even though I didn't really want to. I joined the gym — again, I was happier playing football on a Sunday morning. I ate at trendy ethnic restaurants when all I really wanted was rice and peas. I went for promotions at work that I wasn't really interested in; I went to operas that bored me to tears, not to mention Swedish film festivals, when the only thing Swedish I'm into is IKEA. And I moved to Belsize Park when I would've preferred Peckham Rye."

Paula glowered at Kim but continued to address Germaine. "So, you pick the first heifer that opens her legs for you? You could have at least chosen someone who doesn't need to put a bag over her head. Look at Miss Dumpling there, backside so big, if de gal let off fart northwards we'll see Nart' England and Scotland blow away."

Kim winced and Germaine touched her hand.

"That's you all over, isn't it? You judge everything by appearances. I fell for Kim because she lets me be myself. She's warm, she's kind … she's everything I want. And I love her."

Paula shuddered. It was like he'd stabbed her with his words.

"Oh really? So when did it start?"

Germaine gave his new love a reassuring glance, then faced his embittered and jilted fiancée, clearing his throat before answering her question. "That time I went round to watch the boxing."

Paula shook her head, taking it all in. "Did Conrad make up a threesome?"

Kim gripped the handles of the buggy.

Germaine frowned at Paula. But she didn't care.

"Why did you wait until the altar to do this?"

"I was all set to marry you, even though I knew it was wrong. But on the day I woke up and felt I couldn't do it. I sat down for ages and asked myself what I was doing. Then I got in my car—"

"And ended up at her place. I think I know the rest."

Paula looked at Kim. "So, all those times Germaine was supposed to be at the gym or in a meeting, he was in your bed? Did you do it to get back at Conrad? Or have you harboured some mother of a grudge against me all these years? What kind of a woman are you?"

"Paula, I never meant this to happen. It's got nothing to do with Conrad or you. It's to do with me and Germaine. It happened. We'd been friends awhile before you came along."

"You're not going to tell me you had a thing going on, that he was your man till I took him?"

"No. No, I'm not. We were friends, and we stayed friends. People always assumed you and I were the best of friends. But when I had problems you were never there for me. I went through hell when Conrad left me. But what did you do? Nothing. You had your wedding, and that was it. You didn't give a shit about my feelings. You kept telling me I should lose weight. How many times did you accuse me of eating for Jamaica? I know you thought I was too fat to be your bridesmaid. You made fun of my accent, my clothes, my hair ... When I started going out with Conrad you told me to my face that you weren't surprised he was going with me as he was so ugly. You said these things, bad things, and I never spoke out. But all this time my best friend was never you. It was Germaine. He was the one who was there for me and always has been."

Paula paused, taking this in.

Kim was close to tears and Germaine touched her hand again. This time the show of affection was too much for Paula.

"So, is that what you want, Germaine? This fat bitch and another man's kids? God, you must be cracked! Well, you deserve each other." She grabbed the third bin liner and hurled it at them. It glanced Kim on the shoulder and hit Germaine in the chest, causing him to take two steps backwards. The twins cried out in alarm and more curtains twitched.

Paula had planned much worse for these two Judases. She had planned to knife them, pepper them with bullets and give them a caustic soda bath, among other treats.

But in the end, all she could do was head for her car.

She had opened the door when she felt a hand on her arm.

"Where are you going?"

She glared at Germaine. "What do you care?"

"I care about what'll happen to you if you drive back to London in your state."

"Don't flatter yourself. D'you think I'd crash into a pylon because of you?"

"We've still got things to sort out. The flat—"

"Do it through my solicitor," she growled, even though she didn't have one.

"That's probably best."

Paula shook her head in disbelief, then climbed into her car. Germaine stepped away as she started it up and revved the engine.

"You bastard! I've half a mind to ram you and your heifer there!"

Without a backward glance, Paula pulled away from the kerb and drove down the street so fast she left a trail of skid marks.

By the time she hit the motorway she was crying so hard that her tears were almost blinding her. She eventually pulled into a layby and sobbed loudly for almost an hour. And the one thing that kept the tears flowing was the realisation that everything Germaine and Kim had said about her was true.

Finally she got back on to the road and continued. The traffic was fairly heavy — not that she noticed. In fact, she didn't notice anything around her until it was too late and her car had drifted out of the middle lane into the hard shoulder. It hurtled out of control once the wheels struck the grass verge.

A few seconds later all that remained of the BMW was crushed and twisted metal, with Paula inside it.

THE MILK BAR WAS A SMALL CAFE not far from the Angel tube station. From the outside it looked innocuous, almost hidden behind its own plain brown door, but once you entered you were hit by the continental feel of the place, with its zinc counter that served as a display cabinet piled with Danish pastries, French croissants and German apple strudel. The counter staff would serve you with freshly pressed orange juice, mineral water, rich espresso or creamy cappuccino at a reasonable price. Thus it was popular with students from the nearby City University. The café's customers didn't sit down at tables but at long wooden benches, each seating around six people comfortably, ten if you weren't fussed about being squashed. In a corner near the entrance, there was always a stack of current magazines and newspapers piled high. The place had a mellow, chill-out feel to it that Ronnie adored. So it was here that she had arranged to meet up with Michael and Marvellous Lee.

They were already there, seated near the back, when Ronnie arrived. Ronnie waved to them and ordered a freshly pressed orange juice and a Danish at the counter. Then, balancing her order precariously, she ambled over to them and kissed each man on the cheek.

"Sorry I'm late, guys." She nodded towards a passageway. "Why don't we go out to the garden?"

The men followed her outside, where there were a few

197

more benches and a lot more people. They found a space on a bench close to some bushes which provided some shade from the midday sun.

Marvellous Lee took in Ronnie's appearance. She was wearing an orange tank-top and dark blue denim shorts that showed off her long, slim legs. "You're looking good, Ronnie," he said.

"Thanks. You don't look so bad yourself," she replied. And it was true — he looked much better than she remembered, in a plain grey T-shirt and taupe-coloured jeans. Shame about the Jesus creeper sandals, though. "You know, I searched high and low for your number, till I back-tracked over what I was wearing the day we met."

Marvellous began to recount every item; Ronnie was a little taken aback. "… and a suede jacket."

"Yeah, your card was still in the pocket."

"Well, I'm glad you called me." He glanced about him. "This place is cool, Ronnie. How'd you find it?"

"*Time Out* listings," Ronnie replied. "Check out Sleepy Head."

Michael stifled his yawn. "Sorry. I'm still jet-lagged. I only got back last night." He took a sip of his double espresso. "Well, let's get down to business."

Marvellous Lee had already heard the mix. Around the beginning of the month a friend's daughter had been to a trendy club in Soho where it had been played. She'd described to Marvellous the deejay, and the description fitted Ronnie. Marvellous had intended to go down there, but found out that Ronnie did sessions only on the first Thursday of every month. He hadn't relished the idea of waiting until September, so when Ronnie had called him last Sunday out of the blue he'd thought all his Christmases had come at once.

Because hardly a day had gone by since their encounter, on a freezing cold day in January, that he hadn't thought of her.

Another friend of his, who had read Law but failed the bar exam, had advised him to sue Ronnie for copyright. But Marvellous didn't have the copyright: he'd sold it during the cold winter of '74, when he hadn't been able to pay his gas and electricity bills, only to suffer a long-lasting power cut during the huge strike of that year, which had meant he'd ended up using candles anyway. The publishing company to whom he'd sold the copyright had gone bust eight and a half months later. So, as far as he knew, no one now had copyright. But if he wanted it back he would have to pay to have it registered — with money he didn't have.

Besides, he'd liked the idea of working with Ronnie. Very much. And this Quinones guy seemed to know what he was talking about. Marvellous had done some asking round after Ronnie had phoned him. Quinones was highly rated, and by all accounts was making waves in the States. He also had good connections: he'd assured Marvellous that both Choice and Kiss would pick it up and give it decent radio airplay.

But what Marvellous liked the most, even more than Ronnie, was the idea of being in a studio again, this time being the frontman. Before Ronnie had turned up, Quinones had told him that he had some studio time already booked for the following weekend — the weekend before the carnival. When Marvellous had asked why they didn't simply release the mix Ronnie had done, Quinones had laughed, saying he wanted the quality of fresh vocals, like Dawn Penn when she'd redone "You Don't Love Me" a while back.

There would be no money upfront. All of them would give their time for free and then take their cut from the royalties — which both Ronnie and Quinones were sure would come in, if only modestly — from record sales. Every time Ronnie had played the mix in a club it had gone down a storm; people were asking her if they could buy it anywhere.

So Marvellous saw no reason why he shouldn't go for it — and not just the record.

After they had decided how to proceed with the project Ronnie stood up. "Well, guys, I've got to love you and leave you," she said, glancing at her watch. "I've got to do some shopping before I pick up my little girl from playgroup." She stood up; her shorts were sticking to her legs. "I tell you, this heat … ! I'm having to use sun protector on Jhelisa."

"And how's that husband of yours?" Marvellous asked her.

"Fine," Ronnie smiled, trying to forget the row they'd had about her working both Friday and Saturday nights. Sometimes it seemed that all they'd done lately was fight. "Hey, listen, my friend Nancy's having a birthday bash on Sunday. You're both invited."

"That's a shame," Marvellous Lee said as he stood up, "I'm doing a gig in Amsterdam."

"Sounds good," Michael said, also rising.

"Nothing big. Just back-up for an old friend. But it pays the bills sometimes. Plus my expenses get covered. Maybe with you guys I might get out of my council flat."

They parted company at the Angel. Marvellous decided to browse around the antique shops in Camden Passage, knowing he couldn't afford to do more than look.

"You know he's after you?" Michael said as they watched him go.

"Yeah, but I ain't encouraging him," Ronnie replied. "He is kind of sweet, though."

Michael yawned.

"You look well mashed."

"I'm going to get me some shut-eye, man."

"You still staying at your mum's?"

He nodded. "I'm going to get the Northern Line to Stockwell and walk it to Vauxhall."

"You're lucky you've got a straight journey. I've got to face the Euston Road."

"You drove down? Jeez, you must be nuts, guy!"

"Yeah, well, I ain't big on public transport. If I can't get there by car I don't reach."

Michael laughed. Then he said, "You know that party at Nancy's?"

"What about it?"

"D'you reckon your sister'll go?"

"Which one?"

"You know who I'm talking about."

"Yeah, let me stop. But Paula's pretty bad at the moment."

"I can imagine."

"No, you don't know the latest." She had Michael's undivided attention. "She made the mistake of driving up to Birmingham to see her ex and his new job ... You remember Kim, don't you?"

Michael nodded.

"Anyway, she got so stressed out that she had a crash on the motorway."

"Was she hurt?"

"Got away without a scratch, although she was pretty shaken up. The car's a write-off, though."

"I'd like to see her, Ronnie."

"I'll see what I can do."

They kissed each other on the cheek, and Michael entered the tube station as Ronnie strolled off towards the private housing estate where she'd illegally parked her car.

Dawn and Shirley had just got off the number 266 at Jubilee Clock when they bumped into Lurlene Marshall. It was starting to get dark, but the air was still warm.

"You been shopping? At this hour?" She was looking at their Mothercare bags.

"Brent Cross closes late," Shirley replied curtly.

"Me know, dear. How you keepin', Dawn? You due any

day now, innit?"

"A few weeks. How are you?"

Lurlene sighed. "Me all right. I'm jus' going round to my Tony's with some t'ings." She lifted up her bags. They rattled with what sounded like cutlery.

"Where's Tony living?" Shirley asked.

"Him lookin' after Claude's yard for a while. Didn't you know?"

Shirley shook her head.

"You moving in after you have pickney, innit?" Lurlene said to Dawn.

"Er ... yeah," Dawn lied, avoiding her mother's eye.

"That'll be good. You can finally be a family together. Innit, Shirl?"

Shirley snorted.

"I don't know why you didn't have Tony run you to Brent Cross. You shouldn't be carrying them bags, Dawn. Should she, Shirl?"

"It's okay," Dawn insisted.

Lurlene Marshall seemed totally oblivious to the fact that Shirley couldn't stand her son. "I would've had him pick me up, but I want to surprise him. Should I tell him to expect you later, Dawn?"

"Not tonight, I'm a bit tired."

"Yes, dear. You put your feet up. Make the most of it before pickney reach. Innit, Shirl?" Lurlene cackled, revealing her golden treasures.

"Be sure you don't get mugged for your teeth," Shirley warned her.

"Oh my cheese! You t'ink I go anywhere without my screwdriver? Just let anyone try and ..." She stopped as an 18 bus turned into the road. "There's me bus! I'll be seeing you."

"Not if I see you first," Shirley muttered as Lurlene scuttled off to the bus stop in her patent high-heeled court shoes. "That woman's weave looks like its been attached with Scotch tape. Lord, the woman coarse!"

"At least she lets me in her yard," Dawn pointed out.

"Look, he didn't respect my yard ..."

"Yeah. Well, we've been over this before, mum." Dawn didn't want her day spoiled. It had been her last day at the salon. Verna had organised a whip-round and they'd bought Dawn a carrycot. Not a cheap one either. Dawn had been overwhelmed. Then she'd come home, and on seeing the gift her mum had insisted on taking her to Mothercare to get some accessories to go with it. Shirley had spent almost two hundred pounds, and Dawn had been even more overwhelmed.

"Yes, well, it seem Tony has his own yard now," Shirley said. "How come you never said?"

"You heard Lurlene. It's not his place, it's his brother's."

"But you're moving in after the baby's born?"

Dawn didn't like Shirley's tone of voice. "Maybe."

"Nice of you to have said."

"It's not definite."

"But Lurlene Marshall knew about it."

"Tony must've told her. I didn't," which was true.

"How long is Tony's brother going to be away for?"

"I don't know."

"It must be longtime, or you wouldn't be thinking of moving in to a place with pickney just for a few days, innit?"

"Like I said, nothing's definite."

"Dawn, I don't like this. I mean, you're going to be responsible for another life; you have to start being certain about things." She sighed, thinking about her girls. Lately everything seemed to be going wrong: Ronnie was being her usual irresponsible self, going out to clubs every night, it seemed, even though she had man and pickney. And Paula ... Lord knows what that girl had been through lately! Germaine, that rotten no-good sonofabitch, ran off with that girl who favour horse-teet' hog-face bullock, caused her baby to nearly kill herself on the motorway. And now here was Dawn, her baby, about to have her own baby with nowhere of her own to bring it up.

"Surely the council will come up with something."

"Mum, we've been through all this," Dawn repeated, then paused as a thought occured to her. "Would you let Tony move in after the baby's born?"

Shirley's answer was to pull a face.

"Right then? What choice do I have?"

Shirley relented a little. "He can come round to see his child, but I'm not having him live under my roof."

"Thanks. That's a great help."

Shirley opened her mouth to cuss, but seeing Dawn waddling along with her swollen belly stretching the material of her cotton maternity dress, she changed her mind. Instead she said, "I'll run you a nice bath when we get home, and then we can finish off that ackee and saltfish from yesterday."

"Great," Dawn said. Like that solved everything.

"Nancy lives here?" Paula asked in amazement.

Ronnie had pulled up outside a huge Victorian house in Westbourne Grove. "Yeah, she shares it with a heap of other people who seem to come and go."

Paula tapped her fingers on the dashboard distractedly. "Ronnie, it was nice of you to drive all the way out to mine and pick me up and everything, but I really don't feel I'm up to this."

"Up to what? It's just a party. In fact it ain't even that. It's a select gathering to big up Nancy's three-one."

"Yeah, a select gathering of people that probably know all my business. I know Nancy's got a big mouth."

"Listen, girl, hibernation's for hedgehogs and bears. Besides, it ain't the season for it." She patted Paula's knee. "And anyway, you look wicked, star."

Paula was wearing a pair of black crocheted bell-bottoms

and a matching batwing top that Ronnie had got her on discount from Freedom.

"So do you."

Ronnie smoothed down her flared brown suede mini-dress. "Smart sisters on the rampage — well, two of 'em anyway, seeing how Dawn didn't feel like busting her bulge tonight." She opened the driver's door. "C'mon, girl."

They got out and tottered up to the house. It was a warm night, but not as warm as it had been of late. Maybe the heatwave was finally starting to cool down. The funky music and laughter coming from inside was so loud that when Ronnie rang the doorbell they didn't think anyone would hear it, but a Chinese girl answered almost straight away. She had dyed red hair cut into a crop, and looked like she was ready to go into an oven, the amount of silver foil she was wearing.

"Natasha! How are you, babes?" Ronnie gave the girl a big hug.

"Hi, I'm all right, darlin'! Come in, come in!" She gave Paula a big smile as she let them in.

Paula couldn't believe her coarse cockney accent; but then she recalled how many people she'd met in her life who had been stunned that she didn't have a heavy West Indian accent.

Natasha was looking at her as if she recognised her from somewhere, and Paula wondered if the girl had been at Club Uproar that night. Sure enough, Natasha said, "You're the one who got jilted in't ya?"

Paula glowered at Ronnie.

"Listen, mate, you're better off, I'm tellin' ya," Natasha added as she closed the front door.

There were people everywhere — in the hallway, going up and down the stairs — and Ronnie seemed to know all of them. Natasha ushered them into the front room. It seemed like half the crowd from the Uproar chill-out room was there. With the amount of spliff in the air you could get a high from just standing in the doorway.

Nancy was relaxing on a bean bag by the window gently rocking Ola's head in her lap. She leaped up when she saw them, causing Ola's head to thump against the bare floorboards.

"Hey! Hey! Hey!" she squealed as she hugged them.

"Happy birthday, darlin'!" Ronnie said. Then she produced a Freedom carrier bag.

Everyone watched as Nancy opened it and pulled out a pair of orange and red checked trousers that Paula thought might have been designed for Rupert the Bear. But Nancy loved them — after all, why else would she be clutching them to her chest?

"Happy birthday, Nancy." Paula produced a bottle of cherry brandy. "Ronnie says you like this."

"Sure I do, darlin'!" Nancy took the bottle and stepped over to a table serving as a makeshift bar on the other side of the room. She then placed the bag containing her trousers behind where Ola had set up the sound system. If it was this loud with just the hi-fi playing, Paula dreaded to think what it would be like once the sound system got going.

"What d'you think of the walls, Paula?" Ronnie asked. "They were buttercup yellow the last time I was round, which weren't long."

Paula gazed at the walls. Since then someone had obviously decided to paint black stripes down them. "Different."

"What'll you two have?" Nancy asked as she poured herself a glass of the cherry brandy. "I know you're tee-total, Ron. What about you, Paula?"

"Coffee," Paula said.

Nancy gave her a funny look. Then she shrugged her shoulders. "Come with me, then."

Paula followed Nancy into the kitchen, which was down the hall from the front room.

"You did say coffee, right?"

Paula glanced at the cups festering in the sink. "Actually, you got a can of something?"

Nancy went to the fridge and took out a can of Coke — diet, which Paula couldn't stand, but it was better than nothing.

"You know, I'm sorry about what happened," Nancy said as she handed Paula the drink.

Paula took the can and opened it. "Yeah, right."

"Hey, listen, I know we ain't ever been the best of friends, but I'm being sincere. I really am sorry."

Paula studied her face and saw that she was being genuine. "Thanks."

"I never knew what it was like to fall in love. I mean, I used to be a real love-'em-and-leave-'em kind of person, y'know?"

"How come you're talking in the past tense?"

"Ronnie must've told you about me and Ola."

"She says you're together." Paula took a sip of the Coke and winced.

"Together! Honey, we're in *love*." Nancy giggled.

Paula frowned at her.

"No, I mean it. Here I am, thirty-one years old and in love for the very first time. I've never had a maternal bone in my body, but now I want his baby."

Her giggles turned into laughter, and Paula wondered whether she was stoned. Nancy's laugh was more like the cackle of a dirty old man. The thought made Paula start giggling.

"What are you two snickering about?" Ronnie was standing in the doorway.

Nancy bit her lip, trying to suppress her cackles.

"Nancy's in love," Paula sniggered.

And that set the two of them off again, while Ronnie looked on, bemused. She hadn't seen Paula laugh like this since her hen night. The last person she would have expected to break the drought was Nancy.

"Well, my dear," Ronnie said, "they reckon it's time we brought out the cake and started praying we have enough candles to put on it."

"Look who's here, Paula."

Paula looked to where Ronnie was pointing. Leaning against the doorway in a pair of black leather jeans and a grey T-shirt was Michael Quinones. His face broke into a broad smile. Nancy rushed over to him and he gave her a kiss and a bottle of red wine. Then he punched fists with a couple of guys and waved to Ola, who was now spinning the decks in the corner. Finally, he sauntered over to where Paula and Ronnie were sitting.

"I bet you had no idea he'd be coming," Paula said sardonically.

"You know I'm into happy reunions," Ronnie managed to get in cheekily before Michael reached them. "Where are your vinyls?" she asked as he squatted in front of them.

"I wasn't planning on taking a busman's holiday." He pecked Ronnie on the cheek.

"What's that?" she asked.

"A guy who drives a coach for a living don't want to go on a coach holiday, right?"

"So you don't want to deejay when you're chilling out at a party." Ronnie heaved herself up. "I'm going to get me a drink. You two want anything?"

They didn't.

Michael filled the space Ronnie had vacated, and found himself sinking.

"What is this thing?"

"It's a bean-bag bed. Same concept as the bean bag, only bigger." Nancy had explained it to her earlier. It reminded Paula of a beached whale. "How was the States?"

"Happening — unlike your wedding."

Paula glared at him. "Bastard."

"You sure you're talking to the right guy?"

Paula didn't answer him.

Nancy's cake had been demolished hours ago and Ola had mellowed down the music. The guests had mellowed too, and were lounging about the room on anything they could find, smoking spliff and drinking beer. Ola decided to create a romantic vibe and put on "Turned Onto You" by the Eighties Ladies, and there were murmurs of approval from all round. Nancy swayed seductively over to Ola and wrapped her arms around his waist.

Michael had his eyes closed. "I love this tune."

"I can see that," Paula smiled.

Michael opened his eyes. Then he touched her hair lightly.

Paula liked that.

"I've had Club Uproar on my mind ... Think what might've been, if—"

"Yeah — if."

"So, what happened with the wedding?"

"He didn't want me."

Michael sighed and moved his hand to her chin. "A crazy man."

"Maybe not," Paula said softly.

"What makes you say that?"

He ran his finger over her lips, making it hard for her to answer his question.

"I don't want to talk about it."

He smiled, and she had to draw in a breath. "What d'you want to do instead?"

She thought for a moment. "I want to call a cab and go back to my place. Interested?"

A wide grin spread across his face. But as he opened his mouth to speak she placed a finger on his lips.

"Don't answer that."

Then she replaced her finger with her mouth, and played a deep, probing tune with his tongue.

They didn't care if they had an audience.

Five minutes later Ronnie and Nancy watched them climb into the back of a cab.

"I think I've started something," Ronnie smiled as the cab sped away.

Paula scooped a spoonful of coffee into the percolator and poured in the water. She rubbed her forehead. Michael was still asleep in her bed — the bed which, until a few weeks ago, she had shared with Germaine.

She switched on the radio. The weatherman forecast yet another hot day. She sighed. She had showered a half an hour ago and was already starting to feel sticky. Although that probably had more to to with the situation she was in.

She had woken up to find Michael's arm flung across her naked torso. Then, when she'd crept into the living room, she'd found their clothes strewn all over the floor and a used condom by the sofa. She'd piled up all their clothes and left his by the side of the bed. Then, after showering, she had put on her smart cream shift dress, registering with gloom that she was due back at work today.

That had been enough to be getting on with — but then she'd added Michael to her already mixed-up head. She had virtually raped the guy last night, and now he was in her bedroom. What was she going to do with him?

The percolator began to make gurgling noises, so she switched it off and poured herself a cup of coffee.

"That smells good."

She felt his arms slip around her waist and forced herself to look at him, praying he was wearing some clothes. He was: her white towelling robe. She could have lent him Germaine's, only that was on a rubbish tip somewhere in the Midlands.

"You mind if I take a shower?" Even in her bathrobe he looked good.

"Sure." She forced a smile and prised his arms off.

"What's up?" He was studying her face.

"Nothing."

"You seem kind of offish."

Paula put the cup to her lips. "It's my first day at work since ... you know."

"You sure that's all?"

Paula took a sip of the coffee. It scorched her mouth. "Michael, about last night—"

"Is this gonna be an F &D?" He took a step backwards.

"A what?"

"A fuck and dump."

Paula was lost for words.

"Usually it's me who does that."

"Michael, I ... It's just that I'm really mixed up at the moment. Up until three weeks ago I thought I knew exactly who I was, where I was and what I was. Now I don't have a clue."

Michael mulled this over for a couple of seconds. Then he gave her a half-smile and left the room.

She found him in the bedroom pulling on his boxer shorts. Her bathrobe was on the bed. "What are you doing?"

He looked at her intently. "You don't want me here, that's obvious."

"Look, I just need some space. Things are happening so fast."

"Hey, if I'm not mistaken you were the one who wanted things to go fast. I've got the marks to prove it." He turned his back to her and she gasped when she saw the scratches.

"I've got some Germolene ..."

"I don't want antiseptic cream, Paula. God!" He sank on to the bed. "You had me going last night. I mean, *really* going. Well, anyway, I hope I exorcised the ghost of your ex-fiancé."

"You make it sound like I used you."

"Tell me then, what was last night for you? What did it mean?"

"I don't know."

"You're even embarrassed to have me in your place now. Like the magic's worn off. Or you've woken up to find it's me and not whatsisface lying beside you."

"That's not true. If you must know, I was into you from the moment I saw you down at Camden — no, it was in Freedom when you got me thinking. But I thought that with you it was lust and with Germaine it was love. Now I know that, with the latter, love was just something we played around with. But with you, I still don't know if it's only lust. Okay, I initiated last night, but if I led you to think this was going to be more than ..." She broke off suddenly.

"More than a quick fling, one-night stand kind of t'ing," he finished for her.

"Do you want more than that?"

"I'm going to lay myself open and hope you'll have mercy on me — but, yes, I do want more than just one night. I've had my fill of women and thrills too, but I never found the real deal. I don't know if you're it but you're definitely close, and I wouldn't mind finding out for sure." He ran his fingers through his locks. "So, you had a thing for me all those months ago when we first met?"

"Yeah."

Paula wandered back into the kitchen and added some cold water to her coffee.

A few minutes later he was standing fully dressed in the doorway, watching her. "I guess the timing's off base, right?"

She turned to him.

"No, don't answer that. See you around, Paula ... Maybe."

And seconds later he had gone. Paula gulped the coffee down.

She should have felt relieved.

The impressive offices of Stennard & Blake took up a whole block abutting a square by Moorgate tube station. For two weeks Paula had been dreading the moment when she walked through its swing doors, and as soon as she did it her fears were confirmed.

Everybody was polite to her. Nobody mentioned the wedding that never was, much less Germaine or Kim. And that was what galled her the most: everyone's efforts to make out that nothing had ever happened. But she knew that, as soon as her back was turned, the whispers, the debates and the moralising would continue.

In the days before her return Paula had told herself that she would be the subject of gossip for a couple of weeks until the next scandal. Every two weeks was an accurate guide. But sitting at her desk, trying to sort out the mess that had piled up on it in the time she'd been away, Paula wondered whether she would ever cease to be the topic.

The only person who seemed prepared to mention any of the turmoil that had been her recent life was Roger Harcourt. Not long after she returned he summoned her into his office. "I don't know if you've heard, but me and Susanne are engaged," he blurted out. "I know it's a bit tactless to say it, given the circum ..." His voice trailed off.

"Congratulations," Paula said drily, wondering how many men Susanne Hurry would shag between now and their wedding day. Poor Roger. He had no idea what he was letting himself in for.

"Please take a seat, Paula."

And as she sat there opposite his desk, she felt herself sinking into the sumptuous leather of the chair when he told her in a soothing but patronising voice that he hoped she had recovered from the strain of recent events. The expression on his face told her that he obviously thought her accident had been a suicide attempt. Then she wanted to disappear completely when he informed her gently that Germaine had put in for a transfer to the Birmingham office, which had been accepted, and that Kim's letter of resignation had arrived three days before.

"Everybody's rooting for you, Paula. Let's put this mess behind us, shall we?" He cleared his throat. "By the way, I've been talking to some of my colleagues in the New York office. Have you ever been there?"

Paula looked at his hair, which was thinning on top, and hoped she would make it to the toilet before throwing up.

"You're going to the States? Wow!" Ronnie stopped trying to restart the barbecue, and peered at Paula over her shades.

"I didn't say that. I said that, if I put in a transfer, it would be treated favorably. There's a difference."

"I'm telling you, girl, if it was me I'd be on the first plane out!" Ronnie started valiantly stoking the coals again.

"You're doing that all wrong," Dawn said. She was leaning against the fence holding her plate of rice and chicken. The chicken was delicious. Shirley had seasoned it with herbs and spices and then let it marinade in the fridge for two days.

"Okay, Miss BBQ, you try!"

Dawn nodded at her plate. "My hands are full." Then she glanced at Paula. "Can me and Tony stay in your flat while you're out there?"

"Jesus! You two have me packed and at the airport! And not so loud — I haven't said anything to Mum yet."

"Don't fuss none. She's in the kitchen showing Jhelisa how to make dumplings, cos Ronnie can't."

"Watch it, Dawn." Ronnie waved the poker at her. "So, why you hesitating?"

"It's a big move. So much has happened lately, I don't want to make a rash decision. Besides, look at the motives.

They want me out of the way because I'm an embarrassment to them."

"You've done nothing wrong. It's that bastard and your so-called friend who are the shame merchants. I still say we go up there and—"

"Ronnie, for someone into love and peace you're showing very violent tendencies."

"What they did to you was wrong, Paula," Dawn said.

"Yeah, well. It's done."

"I think you've OD'd on chill pills, cos I don't know how you can be so calm. If Cameron ever ..." Ronnie swallowed her words and poked vigorously at the coals. She had a fire burning. Almost.

"Speaking of whom, it ain't like him to miss Sunday lunch," Paula remarked, eager to change the subject.

"Yeah, well I don't know where the guy is. I got in late from the club and he was asleep, and when I woke up this morning he'd gone. I half expected to see him here."

"That ain't like him, going off somewhere without saying where. That's more your style," Paula said.

Ronnie nudged her. "Remember who's holding the red-hot poker. But you're right — it ain't like him."

"Aren't you worried?" Dawn asked her.

"See, that's where *I'm* mellow. He wants to list me as a missing person if I disappear for five minutes. But me, I don't panic. I like to give people space."

"Cameron needs space?" Dawn asked.

"Nah, don't get the wrong idea. It's not a legally binding contract that he eats at his mother-in-law's every Sunday. Chill, girls, chill."

Paula and Dawn shrugged their shoulders. Then Dawn stuck out her protruding belly. "Hey, Paula, I hope you don't go before this one's born."

"I'm probably not going anywhere, so don't jump to conclusions. Anyway, I thought your housing problems were sorted. Isn't Tony's brother's flat free? I thought you'd be staying there."

"Don't you jump to conclusions either," Dawn retorted.

"What's the deal?" Ronnie wanted to know.

"There is no deal. I just don't like the idea of staying in Claude Marshall's flat. I don't like Tony staying there either. The less connection we have with that guy the better."

"Yeah, Tony and Claude are connected. They're related. Closely related," Ronnie prodded the coals a couple more times. Finally they had started to burn.

"Hallelujah!" Paula cheered. "But, Dawn, if — and I stress the *if* - I do go anywhere, you're welcome to stay at my place until it's sold."

"Sold?" Dawn and Ronnie asked in unison.

"Yeah. I just want it out of my hair. And Germaine's taken a pay drop transferring to Birmingham, so I guess he needs the money."

"Let him and his bitch starve," Dawn said as she prepared to take a forkful of rice.

Paula ignored her and picked up a covered tray from the garden table. She peeled back the foil. It was more pieces of chicken. "Didn't mum get any sausages? I love barbecued sausages."

She began to place chicken legs on the barbecue rack. "Makes a change, though, doing this for Sunday lunch."

Dawn sighed. "I wish Tony had come."

"Mum said she invited him," Paula said.

"Oh yeah, but what kind of an invite? 'He can come if him want'! Tony don't want to know. He says that the only way he'll set foot in this house is if she apologises for how she's treated him all these years. And I don't blame him. But can you see Mum apologising? It's a good thing there's a heatwave on; lately we've had to meet up in the park just to have some time together. Just like when we were bloody teenagers!"

"What will you do once the baby's born?" Paula asked.

"I really don't know. In fact I'm trying not to think about

it. One thing I do know, this situation can't go on."

"Well if things are really bad and you don't have anywhere, you can stay at my place."

Dawn's mouth fell open; Ronnie's eyebrows flew up in surprise.

"You can have the big bedroom. I'll take the small one."

"But, Paula, there'll be three of us, including a baby. Babies cry a lot." Dawn thought of how meticulous Paula was about her furniture and things. Tony was very clumsy. "And if you want to sell the place, it ain't going to look good having us lot in there."

"Look, it's genuine. Until the flat sells, you can stay."

Jhelisa came tottering out into the garden with a plateful of freshly fried dumplings. Paula strolled over to help her carry them to the table.

"You know, I can't get over her," Dawn said.

"You and me both, girl. You know she sexed Michael?"

"What! When?"

"Last Sunday."

"At Nancy's place?"

"No, they snuck off round hers."

"So they've got a thing going?"

"Nah. She ain't interested in a relationship. I got this from Michael, not her, by the way. She's gotten into keeping things to herself, lately."

"I feel my ears burning," Paula said from the table.

"I was telling Dawn about the recording session."

Paula gave them a sceptical look. "When is it?"

"Next weekend. It's going to be wicked, I'm telling ya!" Ronnie enthused. "We're using the studios in Willesden High Road."

"You're kidding!" Paula exclaimed.

"Hey, 'nuff big people use it," Ronnie said in defence.

Shirley walked out into the narrow garden carrying two large bowls of salad. She had spent the morning tending to her flowers and herb patches. It had been therapeutic. "You know what I was t'inking?" she asked.

"What, Mum?" her girls replied.

Shirley placed the bowls on the table. "This is the first time in ages that I can remember us having Sunday lunch without you girls having your men here."

"Thanks for reminding us, Mum," Paula sighed.

Cameron was sitting in the kitchen when Ronnie and Jhelisa got back.

"Daddy, Daddy! We had a barbecue at Granny's and I made some dumplings!"

"Did you, sweetheart?" Cameron kissed her on the cheek as he hugged her. "Why don't you go into your bedroom and tidy your things away. It'll be bedtime soon."

"All right." She kissed him and Ronnie before skipping out of the room.

Ronnie leaned against the doorway. "What's up, Cam? Where've you been?"

"I need to talk to you."

Ronnie strolled over and sat next to him. The kitchen was spotless. She had left it in a mess before leaving for Shirley's. He had obviously cleared it up. Hence the mood.

"I left the place in a tip, didn't I?"

"Yeah, as always."

"Look, I woke up late and got behind on everything—"

"You asked me where I've been."

Ronnie tapped the table lightly. "Yeah?"

"But first, tell me how it felt."

"What?"

"How did it feel to wake up and find me gone, without knowing where I was or when I'd be coming back?"

Ronnie shrugged her shoulders. "I just assumed you'd gone out, had some engagement you'd told me about but I'd forgotten. But I knew you'd be here when I got back."

"Yeah, well, I don't have that luxury. Sometimes I know

where you are and who you're with, but there are lots of times when I don't. And there are times when you tell me where you're going and when you'll be back, but you don't stick to it. And I think we've had this conversation before."

He got up abruptly and walked to the window. "You want to know where I went? I went for a walk."

"What — for the whole day? Must've been a marathon!"

"That's right. I did some thinking. I do that when you're not here. And, let's face it, you're hardly ever here — which means I've done a lot of thinking."

Ronnie braced herself. "Go on."

Cameron rested his forehead against the window. He'd done this many times when Ronnie had been out. Too many times, asking himself how long he could go on. "I've had it, Ronnie. I can't take any more."

"You're leaving me?"

"The last few months, we haven't been together. We've led separate lives. Let's face it, things haven't been the same since—"

"I went off to Paris," Ronnie finished for him. "You're leaving me? For how long?"

Cameron swung round and faced her. She was incredible. "How long?" He almost choked on a laugh. "Let's see now ... How long are you going to be like this — partying and clubbing the night away?"

"It's my job, Cameron! I get paid to do it. Look, I didn't complain when you used to go off on modelling shoots and I wouldn't see you. And you used to love clubs and that. We had a great time."

"Yeah. And the key words, the words you keep saying, are 'used to'. See, that life was fine back then. We didn't have Jhelisa. But when we became a family our lifestyle should have changed."

"Nah, man, you're making out that I should have stopped home and had your dinner waiting on the table when you reach from work, innit?"

"Give it up, Ronnie. You know what I'm on about. You make all your choices, all your decisions, without thinking about your family. Yes, Ronnie, you have a husband and a child! Technically, that's a family. But you're still living your life like you're single. That's what I can't take any more."

"So you're leaving? That's what I call a family man!"

Cameron lashed out at the nearest thing to him, which happened to be the chair he'd been sitting on. He kicked it hard, sending it skidding across the floor, finally crashing against the oven.

Ronnie stared at him in disbelief.

"Don't you ever — *ever* — mock my credentials as a family man! You're hardly in a position to. And don't even *think* about telling me to chill!"

Ronnie rose slowly from her chair. "What about Jhelisa?"

"I want full visiting rights."

"Visiting rights?" Ronnie repeated. That was the jargon solicitors used in divorce cases.

Cameron had regained his composure. "Maybe I should go for more, I don't know." Then he stormed out to the hallway and into their bedroom.

Ronnie hurried after him. "Where are you going?" She was looking at his two suitcases. "Not to your mum's?"

"No. I'm going to stay round my cousin Joe's till I find a place. His address is in the book if you need to contact me, and I'm always there for Jhelisa."

For once in her life, Ronnie's words failed her. She could talk her way into any exclusive club, party or restaurant, on to the trendiest guest-list, but she couldn't find the words to stop her husband from walking out of the door.

As the front door closed, Jhelisa appeared in the hallway in her Barbie nightdress. "Mummy, is Daddy coming back?"

"I hope so." Ronnie hugged her. Her throat felt lumpy. She coaxed her daughter quickly back to bed because, for the first time in a long while, she knew she was going to cry.

TONY SANK INTO THE SOFA and picked up a copy of the *Evening Standard* he'd left lying on the floor. He went straight to the classified advertisements and scoured the jobs section. He circled two ads for security guards with the first thing that came to hand — a silver pen Dawn had given him for his twenty-first birthday. He carried it everywhere with him.

They had spent the day together at her mum's place, just as they had done every weekday since Dawn had gone on maternity leave. The evenings and weekends were the difficult times. Dawn still refused point blank to come round here — to Claude's flat, and even though sanctions had been lifted at Shirley's place he could no longer trust his reactions to her snide comments. Maybe his intolerance towards Shirley stemmed from the fact that, even though he was the father of her grandchild, she still treated him like dirt.

One thing Shirley Smart would not succeed in doing was keeping him from witnessing his child's birth. He'd told Dawn that there were only two places he would be: with her or at Claude's place (even his own mother had to visit him, not the other way round), so if she went into labour when he wasn't around she was to phone him no matter what.

He picked up the remote control from the arm of the settee, pointed it at the TV, and flicked the power button. Claude was into his gadgets. Apart from the TV he had remotes for the video, the hi-fi system and the living room curtains. The whole place was like a British Telecom showroom. He had phones in every room, including the toilet. And he had three answering machines, none of which Tony had been able to set up, so he'd had to rely on the call-back service on the rare occasions he had left the flat, to know if Dawn had called.

The nine o'clock news had started. He flicked through the other four channels but nothing held his attention for more than a few seconds, so he went back to the news. He had been surprised to find that his brother didn't own a satellite dish, but Claude had said that the council were putting in cable TV down their street, so he'd wait for that.

The news droned on. It was at times like this that Tony wished he had Dawn here. They had to get a place of their own soon. When he'd been round at her mum's place today, Dawn had told him that Paula had offered to put them up if they couldn't get a place of their own. Tony had been drinking a glass of tropical fruit juice at the time, and had nearly choked on it. He could hardly believe that her stuck-up buppie sister would have them in her plush flat. As it was, he could count on one hand the number of times he'd set foot in it, and even then he'd been afraid to touch anything. But Dawn had said that Paula had really mellowed since she'd been jilted. He'd have to take her word for it, as he hadn't seen Paula since that day.

He reached for the hi-fi remote and pressed the power button. He'd left a swingbeat compilation cassette in the tape deck, so he tapped play and switched off the news, and the hip-hop version of BioE's "One More Time" kicked in. Dawn loved this tune. She should be here now, Tony was thinking as he tapped his feet.

He didn't hear footsteps coming up the stairs, but he did hear the doorbell. He slid off the settee and without hesitation went over to the front door. He didn't wonder why the intercom hadn't buzzed; for some reason he thought it was Dawn or something to do with her.

As soon as he opened the door he knew he was wrong, but it was too late to do anything about it. The man in the ski mask standing in front of him had already drawn his revolver and was about to pull the trigger.

Dawn was in the kitchen helping herself to a cold chicken leg from a bowl in the fridge when the telephone rang in the hallway. She heard her mother leave the front room to answer it.

Dawn took a bite out of the chicken. It tasted good. A day after the barbecue and there were enough leftovers for a week; but then again, at the rate Dawn was bingeing, maybe they would last just a day or two.

She was preparing to take another bite when Shirley walked in. "Dawn, we've got to go to hospital."

Dawn laughed. "Why? I'm not in labour."

"That was Lurlene." Shirley took Dawn's free hand. "Tony's been shot."

As Paula ran a bath she could have sworn she heard the phone ringing. She turned off the taps — it was the phone, and she had forgotten to switch on her answering machine. She cursed whoever it was on the other line. She needed this bath badly.

She had spent another day at the office as the centre of the gossip, and being pressurised by Roger Harcourt to come to a decision about going to the States. After work she had gone to the gym to try to work off some of the tension she was feeling, and one of the instructors (who thought he was God's gift but was actually God's mistake) had asked her out, "seeing as you're now single". She had told him, in a voice loud enough for everyone in the musculation room to hear, that she wasn't good company at the moment and, besides, she'd rather wait until his dose of genital crabs had cleared up. Then, when finally she'd arrived home, she'd microwaved a foil-wrapped frozen pie and it had exploded before the pre-set three-minutes were up.

So, right now, she really needed to unwind.

The phone was still ringing as she left the bathroom. She wondered if it was Michael. If it was, she didn't know what she was going to say to him. Her feelings on that score were still mixed up. She knew he did something for her, but she also knew she wasn't ready for a relationship on the rebound. Then she wondered if it might be Germaine. But that was doubtful. They made all their communication these days by letter.

Finally, fed up with speculation, she picked up the receiver.

"Paula, it's me — your mother."

"I do know who you are," Paula smirked. "There's a whole heap of noise. You calling from a phone box?"

"I'm at the hospital with Dawn."

"She's in labour?"

"No, not yet, though the shock might bring it on. It's Tony — he's being operated on. He might not pull through."

Paula took a second to absorb this, her heart pounding. Her sister didn't deserve this.

"What hospital are you at?"

Shirley told her and Paula said she would ring Ronnie. Then she hung up and punched the memory button to call her sister. She swore when all she got was the answering machine: Ronnie was probably out partying somewhere and Cameron was probably in bed.

"Sit down, Dawn," Shirley said as she handed a weeping Lurlene a plastic cup of tea.

They had been waiting outside the operating theatre for ages, and Dawn hadn't sat down the whole time. She couldn't while Tony was in there. He was critically ill, that's all the doctors would say, and she knew that meant he might not live to see his child. She had just about managed to stay still when the doctors, seeing her advanced pregnant state, had given her a check-up. Afterwards they too had told her to sit down. But she couldn't.

"Where's Duane?" Lurlene whimpered. He was difficult to get hold of at the best of times.

"You left a message. I'm sure he'll reach," Shirley assured her, her eyes not leaving Dawn. Other than her fidgeting, her daughter seemed somehow *too* calm. Their next door neighbour, old Mr Tanner, had driven them to the hospital, and throughout the journey Dawn had not panicked. And since their arrival she had hardly said a word except to ask the doctors of Tony's condition. Even when they had told her it was serious and that the next few hours would be critical she hadn't broken down, nor shed a tear.

Shirley got up and walked over to her daughter. "You should sit. Are you sure you don't want anything? Tea?"

Dawn glared at her. This woman had treated Tony like he was a piece of dirt, banned him from her house and done everything in her power to split them up. Something in her snapped. "I don't want anything except for you to go."

"What?"

"You heard me. Just move from me, take your pretend sadness and get out of here. I don't want you around me, right? I don't want someone who wishes Tony dead to be here."

Lurlene, tears streaming down her cheeks, looked up at them.

"Dawn, don't say such things," Shirley gasped.

"I'm just telling it like it is. You've never liked Tony; you treated him like shit. You wanted me to have an abortion when I fell pregnant. Your own grandchild! Then you wouldn't even let him in the house. You're always telling me I'll end up a single mother, and now it looks like I might. It's just how you wanted it, isn't it?" Dawn pushed her. "I can't stand the sight of you, you evil woman!"

Most of what Dawn had said was news to Lurlene, and she didn't like what she'd heard. She flung her cup of tea down and started screeching obscenities at Shirley so loud that a couple of nurses came running over to sort them out.

Shirley and Lurlene were instantly building up to a full-scale row. Dawn burst into tears and one of the nurses hurried over to her and put an arm around her.

"Let's sit you down …"

Dawn was looking down at herself. "I can't."

The nurse followed her gaze. A clear, sticky substance was travelling down Dawn's bare legs. Her waters had broken.

Ronnie smoked the last of her joint and stubbed it out in her Citroen 2CV's ashtray. Then she chucked the entire contents out of the window and on to the kerb.

She had spent the last two hours driving around in circles. After she had dropped Jhelisa off at the play centre this morning she had gone straight back to bed and stayed there for most of the day. She couldn't get her head around Cameron leaving. He'd walked out before, but never like he had done last night. She had never seen him so angry.

She had left the answering machine on all day, as she hadn't wanted to speak to anyone except Cameron. Michael had rung and left a message about the recording session the following week. Nancy had called to ask her if she wanted to do to a club with her and Ola. But Cameron hadn't phoned, and her pride wouldn't allow her to call him.

At around five-thirty she had panicked about picking Jhelisa up. Then she'd remembered that when she'd dropped her off she had arranged for her daughter to sleep over at her classmate Sabrina's house, as Ronnie couldn't face thinking of an excuse to give for her daddy's absence.

Then, at around eight, she had become tired of waiting for him to ring and she'd gone out. It had crossed her mind to drop by Paula's, but she'd changed her mind half-way down the Harrow Road. She hadn't felt like admitting that her marriage might be over to someone who had herself just been jilted. She would have preferred to talk to Dawn, but of course she lived with their mother, and Ronnie wasn't ready to face Shirley with her troubles — troubles that Shirley believed were of her own making. Ronnie had cursed the fact that her youngest sister didn't have a place of her own.

In the end she hadn't gone anywhere. She had simply driven around until she'd found herself in the West End. Then, when she had got tired of driving round Trafalgar Square, she had driven home.

She eased herself out of her car and looked up at her flat. She didn't need to see that the lights were out to know it was empty.

The first thing she did after letting herself in was roll herself a joint. She could see the red light flashing on the answering machine, but she needed to feel mellow before she played back the messages. Maybe then she wouldn't feel so depressed that none of them were from Cameron. She knew instinctively that he wouldn't have called.

Finally, taking a deep lungful of spliff, she flicked the playback switch.

Another message from Nancy.

Then Paula: "Ronnie, me and mum are at the Central Middlesex with Dawn. She's in labour. And Tony's in the operating theatre. He's been shot. Could you get down here?"

Ronnie stubbed out the joint in the plate from St Lucia and grabbed her front door and car keys from the table.

"Dawn, can you stop trying to push? It's not time yet."

Jennie was stroking Dawn's forehead as she endured

another contraction.

"I can't! I can't," she gasped, gripping each side of the bed. As the pain seared through her she cried out Tony's name.

"Don't you want me to get someone in with you? Your mother or your sisters ..."

"I don't want them! I want Tony!"

Dawn began to cry again. She had been in labour for three hours and no one would tell her how Tony was. All she knew was that he was still being operated on. She couldn't concentrate on her breathing, and the gas and air were barely taking the edge off the pain.

Jennie squeezed her hand until the contraction wore off. "I'd give you an epidural but you're too close to delivery, Dawn."

"I want Tony," she sobbed.

"Tony will pull through. But Dawn, he can't be with you right now. Are you sure you don't want your mother here? She's outside."

"No!" Dawn shouted.

Jennie tried again. "You shouldn't go through this alone. What about your sisters?"

Dawn managed to nod before another contraction hit her.

She crouched on the bed and panted as Jennie had taught her to. She was covered in sweat and her mouth felt so dry that she thought it would crack. Ronnie and Paula were either side of her, holding her hands.

She felt another contraction building up.

Jennie was at Dawn's feet. "Okay, Dawn, you're going to have to push now ..."

"Oh God, I can't do this!"

Ronnie cradled Dawn's head. "Yes you can, girl."

"I can't ...," Dawn's voice dissolved into a growl of

agony.

Paula winced as her sister dug her nails into her hand, but didn't cry out. Dawn's pain was far greater than hers. "Push, Dawn, push!" she urged.

"Go on, girl," Ronnie chanted.

Dawn summoned every bit of strength she could find and pushed. She kept pushing, even though with each attempt her body felt like it would rip apart. She heard Jennie say that she could see the head, and pressed her head down on Ronnie's shoulder and twisted Paula's fingers and, with a loud groan, she pushed for the last time.

Shirley sat on a chair in the corridor of the maternity wing. Three other women had gone into labour at around the same time as Dawn. Their partners and families were bustling about in a state of nervous excitement, but Shirley had stayed in the corridor throughout.

She had broken down when Dawn had refused to have her there while she gave birth. It broke her heart to think of her child, her baby, going through that ordeal under such distressing circumstances without her. Ronnie and Paula had tried to spare her feelings by saying that Dawn was in shock and didn't know what she was saying, but Shirley knew the truth. Her daughter hated her — hated her for the way she had treated Tony.

She was a hypocrite. When Evan's family had treated her with the same disdain, the same scorn, the same abhorrence, hadn't she vowed never to do the same thing to whomever her future offspring fell in love with? Her own parents had disowned her after her marriage; now she was facing the same from her daughter.

"Mum! Mum!"

Ronnie and Paula were hurrying towards her, laughing and crying at the same time. "She's had a boy!"

Shirley's spirits soared. "Can I see her?"

"Not yet, she's resting at the moment," Paula said.

"Lucky cow. She had a five-hour labour — mine was fifteen!" Ronnie flopped down next to Shirley.

"Yeah, well, I'm sure she'd rather have had a long labour than a short one, not knowing what's happened to her young man," Shirley said sombrely.

Ronnie chewed her lip. "Any news?"

"He's out of the operating theatre. They've moved him into intensive care. I got that much out of Lurlene. Could the two of you tell her that Dawn's had the baby? I don't think she wants to see me."

"You going to stay here?" Paula asked.

Shirley nodded, then watched as they strolled down the corridor arm in arm.

Daylight was starting to break through the gloom outside the windows. Shirley heaved herself up from the chair. She would wait. She couldn't leave this ward without seeing Dawn.

An hour later, Dawn and her baby were moved into a screened-off area of the maternity wing.

Tony was still on the critical list, but his condition had stabilised. Jennie had told her to try and get some sleep, but Dawn knew she couldn't. She had to absorb the fact that she had given birth and Tony had almost died on the same day. He still might die.

She gazed down at her son, tiny and helpless, lying in the cot beside her. She was too exhausted to cry, but every time she looked at the baby, so perfect and beautiful, she thought of Tony and it caused her eyes to mist over.

A nurse pulled part of the screen back. Dawn wondered for a minute where Jennie was, but then remembered she'd gone home half an hour ago.

"There's someone here who wants to see you. Now we don't normally allow visitors—"

"Tony?"

Then Dawn's heart sank. The question had been absurd.

"It's your mother."

Dawn closed her eyes a second.

"She says she won't leave till she sees you."

Dawn gave the nurse a weak smile and nodded. Then she heard the nurse tell Shirley she could only stay a minute or two.

Seconds later Shirley appeared. Dawn noticed how haggard and drawn she looked, like *she'd* just given birth. She stood at the foot of the bed for a while, just looking at Dawn, then she stepped across to look into the cot and smiled.

"Can I hold him?"

Dawn nodded and watched Shirley pick him up. He stirred once in her arms, but stayed asleep.

"He's beautiful," Shirley said, almost in a whisper. Then she gazed at her daughter with tears in her eyes.

She placed the baby back in his cot and grasped Dawn's hand, the one without a drip attached to it. Then she bent and kissed her on the forehead. "I'm sorry," she said, as the nurse reappeared from behind the screen.

The three bullets had hit him in the shoulder, the abdomen and the thigh. It was fortunate for him that some neighbours, on hearing the shots, had called the police and an ambulance. More than fortunate — it had been crucial to the point of saving his life. He had lost a lot of blood by the time they arrived, but he probably would have lost a lot more if several people hadn't ventured out of their doors and used whatever they could to stem the flow.

When the emergency call had been made, an armed response team had happened to be in the area on an unrelated matter. After a car chase along the North Circular Road, during which shots had been fired, Tony's alleged assailant had crashed and was now under police guard in the Whittington Hospital in Archway. His condition was not serious. The police were anxious to speak to Tony.

They weren't the only ones.

But, at half past nine, four hours after the birth of the son he had yet to see, Tony went into heart failure.

Dawn and Lurlene stood outside the operating theatre and listened to what the surgeon had to say. When he had finished, Lurlene collapsed in a heap on the floor, but Dawn remained impassive. She glanced up at the clock on the wall opposite. It was ten minutes past midday. After almost fourteen hours of not knowing, she now knew. She leaned against the wall to steady herself and watched the surgeon help Tony's mum to her feet. Then the surgeon asked her if there was anyone she wanted to call. Dawn shook her head. She needed to absorb the news, let it truly sink in.

Ronnie sat at the kitchen table nursing a cup of tea that had long since gone cold. She heard the telephone click, then moments later Paula ambled in wearing one of their mother's bath robes, a nylon number in ultraglow yellow.

"God, you look awful."

"Thanks, Ronnie. You don't look so bad yourself." Paula tightened the belt on the dressing gown. "Boy, they didn't stop bitching when I told them I wouldn't be coming in today. Well, if it's a crisis, Harcourt goes to me. Him favour backside."

"Where's Mum?"

"Asleep."

Paula turned on the radio and reached across to put the kettle on, ignoring the teapot next to it.

"There's tea in the pot," Ronnie told her.

Paula lifted the lid and screwed up her nose. "When did

you make it — last year?"

Ronnie shrugged her shoulders.

Paula frowned at her sister. She was still in the same clothes. "How long have you been up?"

"I never went to bed."

"I know what you mean," Paula said as she put the kettle on. "I couldn't get Dawn out of my mind. I mean, seeing her, being there when she gave birth ... it was incredible. When she said she wanted us to be there I thought I'd pass out. And at first I nearly did. I mean, you know me with things like that. On TV and in films they never show how much blood and stuff there actually is."

"It's a bit like sex. It's never sticky and messy in films like it is in real life."

"Yeah, you're right." Paula paused. "Anyway. Being there was just indescribable, beyond words. It was a miracle."

"And Tony missed it."

A drum an' bass track was playing on the radio. Tony loved drum an' bass. Paula poured the contents of the teapot into the sink. "I wonder what's happening. Maybe we should ring the hospital."

"No news is good news."

"Guess so." Paula sighed as she rinsed out the teapot. She set it on the draining board.

"So, having seen it in full technicolour, d'you think you could go through with it?"

"Having a baby?" Paula pondered for a few seconds. "I didn't have any maternal urges — well, not strong ones. I reckoned maybe in my mid-to-late thirties, if at all ..."

"And now?"

"Well I still don't feel ready, but being there with Dawn, I don't know, let's just say that having a baby isn't such an off-the-wall thing for me. You know Germaine always wanted children. And sooner rather than later."

"Well he's got two now. Even if he ain't the father."

233

"Yeah." Paula popped two teabags into the pot. "How was it for you with Jhelisa? I seem to remember you were out raving when you went into labour."

"Yeah, and we had to get the club to call us a cab to the hospital."

The kettle clicked off. "Go on," Paula urged as she poured water into the teapot.

Ronnie had a faraway look in her eyes as she relived the experience. "You say you didn't have a maternal bone in your body. Well, honey, neither did I. I've never told anyone this, but during my pregnancy I felt like an alien had invaded my body and was using up my fluids, my energy. The one thing we didn't share was a spliff. Everybody told me how good I looked but I felt like a heifer. Sometimes I'd wake up and think I'd dreamt it all. Then I'd look down and see the bump. Paula, I got so scared — scared of being a mother, scared of giving birth, just plain scared. I couldn't say anything to anyone, because you're not supposed to be feeling like that, are you? I especially couldn't talk to Cameron about it. He was like Tony, excited as hell. He bought every book, every magazine and video to do with pregnancy and parenting. That's when we started to have rows about clubbing. He wanted us to cut down, change our lifestyle. I just wanted to stop feeling so trapped.

"As we were being taken to St Mary's I kept thinking, God, I'm going to be a mother. It still seemed so unreal, even though I was about to give birth. At the hospital Cameron didn't leave my side, not for a minute. He didn't want to miss a thing. He saw Jhelisa before I did. It was love at first sight for him. It took me a little longer. I was too scared even to hold her. You remember how, at christenings and kids parties and that, no one wanted me to hold their baby because they were scared I'd drop it? They reckon it's different with your own, that maternal instincts come naturally, but that ain't true. I felt a real failure when Jhelisa wouldn't breastfeed. That whole time was a nightmare for me."

Paula poured out two cups of tea. "But it's good now. I mean, you have a good relationship with Jhelisa ..."

"That's because she's a wonderful kid. I know everyone says that about their own, but she really is." Ronnie got up and went to stand by the window. She fiddled with the cord of the window blind. "She doesn't deserve to have parents who fight all the time."

Paula frowned at her as she added milk to her tea. "What's happened?"

"We've split up."

"I thought maybe something was up."

"How come?"

"I don't know, just a feeling I guess." She stirred her tea. "Is it serious this time?"

Ronnie nodded. "He's moved out."

"I don't mean to make it sound like nothing, but it's happened before, and you sorted it out then ..."

"Yeah, well, I don't know this time. I really don't. I don't want to lose him, P." Ronnie turned and looked out of the window. The sky was cloudy. It looked like it might rain.

Paula reached across and rubbed her sister's shoulder. "You said anything to Mum yet?"

"About what?"

They both turned round. Shirley had entered the kitchen. Ronnie let the cord slip from her hand.

The stitches made it difficult for Dawn to walk, but she had to get back to the maternity wing for her son's one-thirty feed. She knew she should have been using a wheelchair, but when a porter had gone off to find her one she'd begun the long walk back to her bed unaided.

Nurses, doctors, patients and visitors swarmed around her as they went about their business. It was funny how life went on during the best of times and the worst of times. As

235

she passed by a kiosk selling sandwiches and chocolate bars, Dawn realised she couldn't remember when she had last eaten. She knew she should have something, for her son's sake, but she couldn't face it right now.

When she reached the maternity ward she didn't recognise any of the nurses. There had been a shift change. The ward was busy and noisy, pregnant women mingling with new mothers. The screen had been removed from around Dawn's bed, and she could see her mother sitting down on a chair cradling the baby, who was awake and crying. Paula and Ronnie were standing nearby, talking to a male nurse.

As Dawn neared her bed the nurse pointed at her. She saw her sisters nod, then the nurse continued down the ward.

Paula looked at her. "Dawn?"

Dawn took a deep breath to compose herself. "Tony's suffered heart failure." She heard her mother gasp, but went on. "Delayed shock, they said."

"Is he … ?" Ronnie couldn't bring herself to say the words.

Dawn shook her head. This had her mother and sisters confused, so she added, "He's a tough bastard."

"Oh Dawn!" Paula cried and flung her arms around her.

"But you should have called us," Ronnie said, joining in the embrace.

"I know," Dawn admitted. Then she broke away. "Hey, my little boy needs me."

She gently took her son from Shirley. "Could you two get me something from the snack bar?"

Her sisters took the hint, and as they wandered off Dawn eased herself on to the bed, nestling the baby under her arm and starting to undo the buttons of her nightie.

Shirley spoke for the first time. "Dawn, I feel so bad that you went through all this alone, not even phoning when Tony—"

Dawn interrupted her. "Mum, when they were operating on him this morning, the one thing I concentrated on was that Tony had to pull through. Nothing else mattered — not even this little one ..." She glanced down at the baby fighting for food, and adjusted his position so he had better access to her breast. "Then, after, when they told me the operation was successful, I remember being on my own somewhere. I think it was the day room. I thought about how I'd treated Tony. He wanted to marry me, but I put him down. I should've been with him that night ..."

"Dawn, you would've been shot too," Shirley said, balking at the thought .

"Maybe, maybe not. But he was desperate for us to be together, and he didn't think staying at his brother's would be dangerous ..." Dawn's voice trailed off, and for a few moments the only sound around her bed came from her baby as it suckled her breast. "It's going to take time, but you and me both have the chance to make fresh starts, put the past behind us."

Shirley nodded and squeezed Dawn's hand.

Ronnie looked on as Jhelisa jumped on Cameron. He had barely had a chance to walk through the door.

Just before he'd arrived she had showered and changed into a short black jumper and cream hipster jeans, a look he had always liked on her.

"Have you eaten? Me and Jhel were about to have some chicken and rice." She took his denim jacket from him. It was wet from the rain.

Cameron rubbed his chin. He hadn't expected Ronnie to cook, and he had already eaten.

"Please, Daddy, please!" Jhelisa said, grabbing him by the hand.

Cameron let himself be dragged down the hall and into the kitchen while Ronnie slung his jacket on a chair in the living room. Then she changed her mind and neatly folded it.

Cameron surveyed the kitchen. The table had been set for three places. A steaming pot of rice had pride of place in the middle of it, and the aroma of roast chicken came from the oven. There was no smell of burning and the place was spotless. "You've gone to a lot of trouble," he said with a wry smile when Ronnie strolled in.

"None at all," Ronnie lied.

After her mother had overheard her and Paula talking that morning, Ronnie had reluctantly filled her in on her marital problems. She had expected a blast of "I told you so"s, but instead Shirley had been calm, helpful even. She'd suggested that Ronnie phone Cameron (which she had intended to do anyway, in order to update him on Tony and Dawn) and try to persuade him to come round — cook him a meal, make sure the place was clean, prove to him that she didn't want to lose him.

So she had, and he'd agreed. He'd told her he was missing Jhelisa, and although he hadn't said the same about her, Ronnie knew she had jumped the first hurdle cleanly.

Paula had driven them all back from the hospital. Ronnie hadn't even entered her mum's house, but had hopped straight into her car and driven home. She'd spent two hours tidying the place, hoovering, washing the floors, polishing — probably the most housework she'd done in their entire marriage. Then she'd dashed to the play centre to pick up Jhelisa. When they returned Ronnie had started the most difficult task: cooking. And she'd surprised herself by not burning anything.

That was the second hurdle. Good signs all the way.

"You look exhausted," Cameron said as she removed the chicken from the oven.

"I've not slept since, you know, all this …"

"I'm not surprised. What's the latest on them?" Cameron had assumed her lack of sleep was solely down to Dawn and Tony.

"Dawn and the baby are fine. It looks like Tony will be too," she said as she placed the tray on the table. Cameron whizzed a mat under it just in time.

"I'd like to see them and the baby."

"You can see them any time. She's being discharged from hospital tomorrow. But Tony's still in intensive care — only immediate family allowed."

"Why's Uncle Tony in hospital?" Jhelisa wanted to know.

"He got hurt."

"How?"

Ronnie and Cameron looked at each other. They didn't want to mention guns.

"He had an accident, that's all we know for now."

"Can I visit him?"

"When he's better."

"Can we visit him together? You, me and Daddy?"

Ronnie glanced at Cameron. He was pouring out a glass of apple juice for Jhelisa; his hand was steady, but his Adam's apple was not. "Of course," she said brightly. She placed a chicken thigh on Jhelisa's plate.

"Sabrina's mum says that you and Daddy are splitting up."

Ronnie's jaw dropped. "Why did she say that?"

"I told Sabrina that you and Daddy had a fight and he left. She told her mum, and her mum told me you were splitting up."

"Please, darling ... Sabrina and her mum have big mouths — and you shouldn't be telling people our business." Ronnie gave her daughter a reassuring smile. "Now eat up."

Jhelisa put a spoonful of rice in her mouth. "Well, anyway, I can tell Sabrina she's wrong, because Daddy's here now. Aren't you?"

Cameron smiled at her.

He couldn't think of anything to say.

Cameron padded out of Jhelisa's room and into the living room.

Ronnie was reclining on the sofa. She looked up at him. "What story did you read her?"

"*Pocahontas*."

Ronnie patted the sofa. "Why don't you sit down?"

"I can't stay, Ronnie."

She sat up. "But I thought, maybe—"

"I'm going to look at a flat tomorrow — just off Warwick Avenue."

"Is it for rent or for sale?" she asked in a small voice.

"Rent."

She sighed with relief. That didn't sound too permanent. "Cameron—"

But he didn't let her finish. "This is so hard for me, Ronnie. I don't think I could ever love another woman like I love you, and yet I know if I stay with you I'll go insane. For a long time I thought I could change you, but now I realise I was fooling myself. You'll never change. And it's not fair for me to expect you to." He picked up his jacket from the chair and put it on.

"There's nothing I can say to make you stay, is there?"

Cameron shook his head.

When he had gone, Ronnie hugged her knees and rocked herself gently back and forth, letting her tears stain her trousers.

Dawn sat beside Tony, stroking his hand and trying to ignore the tubes and wires sprouting out from all over his body. With her free arm she supported their baby.

"You've got a beautiful son, Tony. Evan. I hope you don't mind him having my dad's name.

"They let us stay a whole week. Normally they chuck

you out after three days, but we were a special case. But they really need the space now, so I have to take him home.

"Shirley wanted to give us her room because of the double bed. Yes — *us*, Tony: you, me and the baby. I don't know how you'll feel about that, but at least we'll be together. It's what we've always wanted."

She leaned forward and kissed him on the forehead, as he had a tube coming out of his mouth.

"I love you. *We* love you."

The departure lounge at Heathrow was crowded and bustling.

Jhelisa squealed with excitement as she watched yet another plane take off. She had especially chosen this table because it was near the window. "Will your plane be like that, Auntie?"

Paula laughed. "The company I work for wouldn't put me on Concorde!"

Evan stirred in her arms. She smiled at Dawn, who was sitting next to her. "I can't believe how big he's got in only three months."

Tony smiled as he eased his left leg. His thigh injury had left him with a permanent limp. "Yeah, he changes every day."

The day after Dawn had left hospital with the baby, he had regained consciousness. He'd spent another two weeks in intensive care and then a further three weeks on a normal ward. He still faced months of physiotherapy for his leg and shoulder, but thankfully the stomach wound had left no lingering after-effects.

"You'll have to keep me up to date with photos," Paula sighed.

"Hey, you make it sound like you're never coming back," Dawn said.

Paula smiled. "Of course I am ... Christmas, your

wedding ..."

Dawn and Tony squeezed hands. They had decided to wait until after the trial before they wed. Fortunately, Tony's attack and the subsequent arrests had merited only a few lines on the back pages of a couple of the national daily papers. Each had hinted at a yardie/drug connection, much to the local black community's disgust.

Tony's assailant, a thirty-year-old named Garrett Barnes, had been charged with attempted murder, possession of a firearm, and various road traffic offences. He would be pleading guilty, but with mitigating circumstances. After all, it was only natural that he would want to avenge the brutal, near-fatal beating of his younger brother Travis, a former bouncer at Freddie's. Only one of Tony's brothers was in custody awaiting trial for the attack on Travis Barnes. Duane had been arrested while visiting Tony in hospital ten days after the shooting. (Claude Marshall, the intended victim, would be arrested if and when he returned from Jamaica. If Travis Barnes had died, the police would have sought extradition.) Duane was likely to face a charge of attempted murder, but his solicitor believed he could get the charge reduced to grievous bodily harm. He would no doubt get a custodial sentence, having been in trouble before, but he would probably be out within two years.

Apart from Dawn and Tony's decision to get married, at least one other good thing had come out of the incident. The dailies may not have been interested in the story, but the local paper had. One of their journalists had interviewed Dawn while Tony was still in hospital. They'd run the story on the front page of their next edition, highlighting the problem the young couple had had in getting housed. They'd managed to convey much sympathy for the young family's plight, portraying Tony as a 'new man' because he intended to stay at home with the baby while Dawn worked full-time. The bad publicity for the council had prompted swift action. Early the following week, Dawn and Tony had found themselves housing association tenants of a ground-floor two-bedroomed flat on a newly built low-rise block in Willesden Green. Tony had later joked that it had taken a bullet to dash them to the top of the housing list.

"Mummy, Mummy! I saw a Concorde!" Jhelisa shouted, waving at her mother and grandmother as they made their way towards them.

Ronnie was carrying a tray of drinks. "That's nice, peaches," she said as she set it on the table. It was good to see Jhelisa happy. She had become withdrawn since Ronnie and Cameron had officially separated last month.

"You can buy a plane now, Mummy."

"Why's that, hon?"

"You're famous!" And Jhelisa began to sing "The One and Only" tunelessly.

Everyone around the table snorted.

"Don't mock. We're getting played to death on Choice and Kiss," Ronnie said tartly. "Watch it rise to number one!"

It had been a memorable Saturday afternoon in early September that she, Michael and Marvellous Lee had spent in the recording studios on Willesden High Road — mainly because Marvellous had insisted on take after take and they had run over studio time, but it had been worth it.

The pre-hype at the clubs, and especially at the carnival, where Ronnie had marked her most successful deejay spot to date, had aroused immediate interest from the two main London-based dance music stations. Now Radio One and Capital were starting to give it airplay. Several music magazines and papers had given it favourable reviews, one of them describing it as "funky, refreshing, and with a bass to be proud of".

Both Ronnie and Michael had been interviewed by the music press. But it was Marvellous who'd received the most exposure. His albums, once deleted, were being hurriedly pressed again. At least two notable labels were interested in signing him. But he'd decided to sign to Michael's new label

The Real Deal, which, although based in the States, would have a distribution arm in London.

Ronnie was now in a position to pick and choose her gigs, and she worked her timetable around Cameron's schedule, so that one of them was always there to look after their daughter.

"Paula, that's your flight boarding, isn't it?" Dawn pointed to the departures screen. A red light was flashing next to flight BA245 London–New York. Sure enough, a flight announcement came warbling over the tannoy.

Paula heaved a sigh and gave Evan a last cuddle before handing him back to Dawn. She could hardly believe that at the beginning of the year she had been engaged to be married. Now the flat she'd shared with Germaine was on the market, and he was living with her ex-best friend in Birmingham.

Paula had grown tired of the gossiping at work, which hadn't died down as she'd hoped. She had also grown tired of seeing Germaine's name popping up in the in-house magazine — "Germaine Valentine scores again for Stennard & Blake" — or in the internal mail. She'd needed to get the whole thing out of her system, and New York seemed to offer the best way of doing that without resigning her post. Roger Harcourt had hardly been able to suppress his relief.

She gathered her hand luggage together as her flight was announced a second time.

She hugged Tony first, a warm, tight embrace he hadn't been expecting. "You keep making my kid sister happy." she told him, feeling a lump rising in her throat.

Then she scooped up Jhelisa and whirled her around.

"Are you going to be near Disneyland?"

"No, honey, not very near," Paula replied.

"Oh, because Mummy says she's going to take me there and we can visit you too."

Paula laughed and shook her head at Ronnie. Then they hugged.

"I'm going to miss you, you uptight dry bup!" Ronnie slipped a card into Paula's jacket pocket. "Make sure you ring a certain person in New York — you know, if you ever get lonely or feel ready to start a relationship."

Paula pinched Ronnie's waist, making her squeal. "I'm already on that tip, babe. I had his number from time. You see if I don't ring the guy," she said, doing a fair impression of her big sister.

Then she looked at Dawn, who'd passed Evan to his father so she could hug Paula.

"I hope witnessing my labour hasn't put you off motherhood," Dawn sniffed, a tear rolling down her cheek.

"Just for a few years," Paula said, then found herself choking back a sob too.

Finally she hugged Shirley, and that was when she broke down.

Once Paula started, Shirley began sobbing, Dawn bit her lip, but couldn't stop the tears, and Ronnie tried to keep a handle on herself, though she was glad she was wearing waterproof mascara. Tony, with Evan asleep in his arms, exchanged bemused glances with Jhelisa.

Then Shirley stepped away. Her camera was lying on the table.

"I want a picture of my three girls together."

"You'd better let Jhelisa take it, then," Paula advised, remembering that the photos Shirley had taken at Evan's christening two weeks ago had been akin to abstract paintings. Nobody could work out who was in them; all they could see were arms, legs, eyes, even a close up of Pastor Duchess's nostril.

"D'you know how to take a picture?" Shirley asked the little girl.

Jhelisa nodded. She could use a computer and had taught Ronnie how to programme the video; using a compact camera was child's play. She picked it up and aimed at the three sisters and pressed the red button.

All three managed a smile.

"I hope she rings him," Ronnie said to Dawn as Paula headed off towards the departure gates.

"Who?" Shirley wanted to know as she wiped away a tear.

"You'll see," was all Ronnie would say.

Shirley looked to Dawn for a better explanation, but Dawn shrugged her shoulders innocently. Their mother ought to know: there are some things that sisters keep between themselves.

BESTSELLING FICTION

I wish to order the following X Press title(s)

❑ Single Black Female	Yvette Richards	£5.99
❑ When A Man Loves A Woman	Patrick Augustus	£5.99
❑ Wicked In Bed	Sheri Campbell	£5.99
❑ Rude Gal	Sheri Campbell	£5.99
❑ Yardie	Victor Headley	£4.99
❑ Excess	Victor Headley	£4.99
❑ Yush!	Victor Headley	£5.99
❑ Fetish	Victor Headley	£5.99
❑ Here Comes the Bride	Victor Headley	£5.99
❑ In Search of Satisfaction	J. California Cooper	£7.99
❑ Bursting The Cherry	Phyllis Blunt	£6.99
❑ Flex	Marcia Williams	£6.99
❑ Baby Mother	Andrea Taylor	£6.99
❑ Uptown Heads	R.K. Byers	£5.99
❑ Jamaica Inc.	Tony Sewell	£5.99
❑ Lick Shot	Peter Kalu	£5.99
❑ Professor X	Peter Kalu	£5.99
❑ Obeah	Colin Moone	£5.99
❑ Cop Killer	Donald Gorgon	£4.99
❑ The Harder They Come	Michael Thelwell	£7.99

I enclose a cheque/postal order (Made payable to '*The X Press*') for

£ _____

(add 50p P&P per book for orders under £10. All other orders P&P free.)

NAME _____

ADDRESS _____

_____

Cut out or photocopy and send to:

X PRESS, 6 Hoxton Square, London N1 6NU

Alternatively, call the X PRESS hotline: 0171 729 1199 and place your order.

Keep updated with the HOT
new novels from
The X Press.
Join our mailing list.
Simply send your name and
address to:

**Mailing List
The X Press
6 Hoxton Square
London N1 6NU**

X Press Black Classics

The masterpieces of black fiction writing waiting for you to discover

❏ The Blacker The Berry   Wallace Thurman   £6.99
*'Born **too** black, Emma Lou suffers her own community's intra-racial venom.'*

❏ The Autobiography of an Ex-Colored Man   James Weldon Johnson   £5.99
'One of the most thought-provoking novels ever published.'

❏ The Conjure Man Dies   Rudolph Fisher   £5.99
'The world's FIRST black detective thriller!'

❏ The Walls of Jericho   Rudolph Fisher   £5.99
*'When a buppie moves into a white neighbourhood, all hell breaks loose. **Hilarious!**'*

❏ Iola   Frances E.W. Harper   £6.99
'A woman's long search for her mother from whom she was separated on the slave block.'

❏ The House Behind The Cedars   Charles W. Chesnutt   £5.99
'Can true love transcend racial barriers?'

❏ A Love Supreme   Pauline E. Hopkins   £5.99
'One of the greatest love stories ever told.'

❏ One Blood   Pauline E. Hopkins   £6.99
'Raiders of lost African treasures discover their roots and culture.'

❏ The President's Daughter   William Wells Brown   £5.99
'The true story of the daughter of the United States president, sold into slavery.'

❏ Joy and Pain   Zora Neale Hurston, etc   £6.99
'Jazz age Harlem stories by a master of black humour writing.'

I enclose a cheque/postal order (Made payable to '*The X Press*') for

£ _____

(add 50p P&P per book for orders under £10. All other orders P&P free.)

NAME _____

ADDRESS _____

✂ **Cut out or photocopy and send to: X PRESS, 6 Hoxton Square, London N1 6NU**
Alternatively, call the X PRESS hotline: 0171 729 1199 and place your order.

'N'
LOUD PROUD ©

As seen in PRIDE MAGAZINE. London's most happening club night, **Loud 'N' Proud.**©

Every month a host of celebs shake it down with London's nicest club crowd. Hip hop, Garage, Ragga and Rare Groove sounds. Live performances and give-aways.

Not to be missed...
For more information on the next **Loud 'N' Proud**© clubnight contact 0171 460 0684.

As a special promotion X Press readers can pay for one ticket and get another one absolutely free. Just cut out the coupon below and bring it along to the next clubnight.

Loud 'N' Proud ©

'TWO FOR THE PRICE OF ONE' COUPON.
THIS COUPON ENTITLES THE BEARER TO ONE FREE TICKET TO ANY **Loud 'N' Proud** CLUBNIGHT. THIS OFFER ONLY APPLIES IF ANOTHER TICKET IS BOUGHT AT THE SAME TIME

**The Dotun Adebayo Show
Every Tuesday evening
10.30pm - 1.00am
on BBC GLR 94.9FM (London)**

Time to hear what you've been missing.